CULTURE CREEP

ALSO BY ALICE BOLIN

Dead Girls: Essays on Surviving an American Obsession

CULTURE CREEP

NOTES ON THE
POP
APOCALYPSE

ALICE BOLIN

MARINER BOOKS

New York   Boston

HarperCollins books may be purchased for educational, business, or sales promotional use. For information, please email the Special Markets Department at SPsales@harpercollins.com.

The Mariner flag design is a registered trademark of HarperCollins Publishers LLC.

FIRST EDITION

Designed by Chloe Foster

Library of Congress Cataloging-in-Publication Data has been applied for.

ISBN 978-0-06-344052-4

25 26 27 28 29 LBC 5 4 3 2 1

CONTENTS

INTRODUCTION

TRUE CRIME WATCHERS WILL HAVE NOTICED A THE-
matic creep in the genre's subject matter in recent years. Dead
girls are out. Cults are in. Trust me, I've seen all the documentaries. I can tell you about Heaven's Gate, Scientology,
NXIVM, Love Has Won, Children of God, Peoples Temple
(of Jonestown infamy), the Branch Davidians, the Fundamentalist Church of Jesus Christ of Latter-Day Saints. You have to
pay me good money to watch a serial killer show these days,
but I can't get enough of cults.

When I was a kid, cults seemed like nothing more than
groups of wacked-out weirdos providing novel, horrifying news
stories that took over headlines once or twice every decade. I
never thought that the Christian church slowly annexing my
Idaho hometown might not be so different. With this new glut
of programming, it's clear that cults are subtler and more pervasive than I ever imagined. During all the true crime documentaries I watched to procrastinate while writing this book, the
stories about cults started to speak to me as an essential part of

American life going back to the Puritans, those Christian radicals who colonized Massachusetts in the seventeenth century. They sublimated their fears of the unfamiliar land's wildlife, weather, and indigenous inhabitants to stories about Satan, demons, and witches, seeing everything through a lens of spiritual warfare that Fundamentalist Christians of today have hardly built on in four hundred years.

Conservative Christian sects are the sources of some of the most powerful strains of cult thinking in the U.S. today, especially since the invention of social media and American politics' descent into chaos, but it would be a mistake to think this phenomenon exists only on the political and religious fringe. Psychologists generalize cults as regimes of thought control, often switching out the loaded term "cult" for "high-control group" or "high-demand religion." These are authoritarian organizations that subordinate everything in members' lives to a single leader or idea. They use jargon, shibboleths, and dog whistles to redefine the boundaries of reality and re-create the world in the group's image. They seek to replace members' identities with ones that exclusively reflect membership in the group. Experts make distinctions between the destructive cults we are most familiar with and ones that are more loosely affiliated or benign, but they do not sidestep the fact that workplaces, mainstream religions, corporate brands, and subcultures can behave like cults. Instead, they encourage us to examine how our lives are shaped by groupthink and indoctrination.

I see some cultiness in the pop culture fandoms I have taken part in even casually, which are communities obsessed with layers of insider knowledge, rules of comportment, demands for loyalty that often cause feuds and schisms, and a sense that

whatever drama is gripping the subculture is the most important issue to the world at large. When you log on to a fan discus-
sion board, whether for *Star Trek*, *Animal Crossing*, or Britney
Spears, your fan self is cordoned off from your normal self, so
that even if you think about the community all the time, you
might be embarrassed to talk about it in your everyday life—
outsiders just don't get it. The internet has provided us with
tools for this compartmentalization, especially in its anonymity,
so that you might start to see the actions of your fan self as
being performed by some separate entity, a hive mind you sub-
mit to within the bounds of the community. This can allow you
to do things while acting as your fan self that you would never
do otherwise, like the abusive brigades and pile-ons fandoms
sometimes mount on perceived enemies.

There are other reasons the internet has formed such a fertile
field for spreading cult thinking, beyond providing a potential
charismatic leader with a virtually unlimited supply of marks.
The fracture into siloed communities is a reaction to the overwhelming hugeness of the internet itself. This is an appeal of all
cults, that they shrink down reality to a manageable size, especially when feats of infrastructure and information have made
our world more accessible, populated, complicated, and bewil-
dering than ever before. Cults do this by limiting members'
choices, something modern humans supposedly enamored of
their personal freedom strangely crave. The internet is the ultimate venue for the tyranny of choice: there are nearly unlimited videos to watch and pictures to look at, topics to learn
about, people to talk to, products to buy. It has fulfilled the
dream of the ideal consumer who has total agency to consume
as they please, an unencumbered individual perfectly expressing

their monumental human will. As attractive as this dream is, we should know by now that it is not what we want. All the decisions are exhausting. Some part of us longs to cede control and have someone else tell us what to do.

I am realizing now that this is a classic corporate bait and switch, where the powers that be provide a distressing array of choices and then generously decide for you. If we look closer, we might notice that business interests, despite their avowed belief in consumer freedom, have been engaged in aggressive methods of thought control since the 1960s. In the postwar era, advertising executives teamed up with social psychologists to devise ways to manipulate basic human drives for acceptance, purpose, sex, and status to precisely implant desires for consumer goods in the brains of the public. This horrifying application of social science research formed the origin of the modern field of marketing—and the marketers have only gotten more brazen since. With the smartphone and the social internet came the golden age of "persuasive design," which encompasses features that make applications as addictive as possible, like the infamous "infinite scroll" that is now a part of nearly every social media experience, where a user never gets to the end of a page or a logical stopping point but is instead encouraged to browse forever.

This convergence of religious, technological, and business thought is not some coincidence. We can think of "cult" as a business model that corporations have adopted from spiritual leaders and metaphysical scammers—Scientology founder L. Ron Hubbard is supposed to have said the only way to make a million dollars is to start your own religion. Cult capitalism approached its zenith with the transition to the branding economy in the early 1990s, when the most successful companies on earth transformed from organizations that made and sold products to symbols that marketed products. Naomi Klein wrote in 1999 in *No Logo*, still the definitive dissection of the branding economy, about the spiritual quintessence that corporations attempt to project with their brands, an über-personality larger than any product or service. One can see the branding revolution expressing a pseudo-religious devotion to the tenets of capitalism, a belief that technological revolution will not cause the system to break down, as haters like Karl Marx predicted, but instead make the exchange of capital more lofty and sacred, ascending from speculating on physical products to ineffable ideals. There were material as well as philosophical reasons for the abstract turn in the economics of the 1990s, namely the globalization of trade and the newfound supremacy of finance, which allowed companies to take advantage of cheap labor in the global south to sell products they were no longer responsible for creating. And high finance's conquest of the world was facilitated by a breakthrough in communication technology that would allow virtually every computer on earth to be connected in a "world wide web."

Social media is now so completely soaked in the principles of the branding economy that we are encouraged to see even our small social media pages as constructing a "personal brand." The Italian feminist Silvia Federici writes about women who "remake" their bodies through plastic surgery and other cosmetic enhancements as engaging in a process of "self-valorization," a means to celebrate themselves and bolster their egos "in a world where at every turn we face competition and constantly undergo an experience of devaluation." Our social media narcissism fulfills a similar need, asserting our value and propping us up amid the assault that late capitalist work and the disintegration of the social safety net have mounted on our humanity. Decisions about aesthetics, voice, and audience on social media come so naturally to us that we instinctively filter our personalities into something recognizable, memorable, and appealing for our followers. Crafting a personal brand is like founding a mini cult of personality, as we become authoritarian leaders commanding a domain where our taste and sensibility reign supreme, attracting followers who listen to us, praise us, and, ideally, give us money.

The intricate structure of the social web takes the form of concentric ripples of influence, with each of us attracting our own followers but also joining the followings of celebrities, subcultures, and franchises, which are in turn subordinate to the platforms that sell them to us. The huge ideological cults swallowing the rest are the values of late capitalism—competition, branding, deregulation, rent seeking—and our faith in the miraculous power of computers themselves. I typed "capitalism is a death cult" into Etsy and was served up pages and pages of coffee mugs, stickers, and t-shirts with the phrase on it. Amazon wouldn't let me search the phrase at all. Both results feel indicative of something: how our resistance is either proscribed or assimilated in cult capitalism, always dead-ending in a corner of the maze, where even our rage against the machine becomes just another way to feed the machine.

It also shows how the corporate grip is tightening around our actions online, with the blandness and propriety demanded by advertisers enforcing a system of self-censorship more prudish than the authoritarian film and TV codes of the middle of the last century—TikTok users, fearing their videos will be repressed at the first indication of controversy, commonly speak in an arcane and childish kind of code, referring to sex as "seggs" and murder as "unaliving." Capitalism appears to be undergoing an escalation common to the cult life cycle, where leaders must continually up the stakes to maintain control. We should take caution from the Puritans, who were so convinced of the righteousness of their spiritual project that they eventually executed nineteen people for witchcraft. Cults comfort their followers with delusions of their own importance, but they also control them through paranoia and terror, which is why their leaders almost always start to talk about the end of the world.

When I was a kid in the '90s, there was a craze for stories of the Christian apocalypse, spurred on by the popular Evangelical book series *Left Behind*, which described the struggle of nonbelievers left on earth during Armageddon. Americans have a dissonant relationship with changes to the old order. The founding of this country is treated like a happy and even sacred break with the past, ringing in the modern era of governance and the flowering of democracy and free enterprise. But Americans are also conservative and terrified of the future, dogged by an unspoken feeling that our ride on the hegemonic gravy train cannot last forever. It is easy to see why doomsday religion reached a fever pitch in the first years of this century, when our Evangelical president launched a new holy war against Muslims in the Middle East, euphemistically casting his mission as spreading a mystical substance known as "freedom." You know another word for "apocalypse"? "Millennium."

Apocalyptic thinking has continued to dominate the first two chaotic decades of this century even in the secular world, where we are haunted by visions of a catastrophe where nuclear weapons or climate change destroy all life on Earth. A popular school of wishful thinking encourages us to envision an apocalypse resulting from global consumer culture and technological hubris averted by the invention of some miraculous tech breakthrough, re-creating on a catastrophic scale the familiar scenario where marketing creates a problem for its product to solve. And computers have provided us with new ways of talking about the end of the world, too, inviting us to choose either the doomsday of the singularity, when superintelligent robots seize power, or the rapture of human consciousness being uploaded to the data cloud.

In these twin visions, technocapitalism serves as the heir to the old-time religion of Puritans. The grandiosity of their idealism reveals a ruling class who has gotten too comfortable with catastrophe. Disaster capitalism has been one of the most profitable modes of business in the new millennium, with corporations following the apocryphal Churchill dictum to "never let a crisis go to waste." They do this by providing services consumers are forced to use to ameliorate the conditions of disaster, like the billions Amazon and the videoconferencing software Zoom made during the COVID quarantines. Corporations also use crises to extend their control, having cover for their corruption—like with price gouging under the guise of inflation—and an opportunity to create a new world order where they are even more firmly insinuated into our lives. Considering how enthusiastically corporate interests have benefited from the worst crises of our time, I have no doubt they will continue to profit from ushering in the apocalypse if we allow them to. Doomsday cults may imagine a Judgment Day of disaster, plague, monsters, and rivers of blood, but this does not mean that they want to prevent it. In fact, their organizing belief is an eager anticipation of the day when the Messiah comes to destroy this wicked world.

In 2021, the most perennially online doomsday cult, QAnon, staged an alarming rupture of the boundary between the internet and real life. QAnon is a loosely organized fascist internet conspiracy group who believe that President Donald Trump was sent to rid the American government and then the world of the cabal of corrupt child molesters who control global wealth and power. QAnon followers believe in a coming day of reckoning, the Storm, when Trump would be reinstated as president and arrest the corrupt actors in the deep state, the Democratic Party, and liberal Hollywood. These beliefs led directly to the storming of the U.S. Capitol on January 6, 2021, when angry Trump supporters tried to overthrow the results of the presidential election. You see, it can be hard to distinguish a passive belief in a coming sea change from an instruction that you form the wave. This is the dual power of the apocalypse when charismatic leaders invoke it: it paralyzes most people in their tracks, but it motivates others to extreme, irrational action, usually conforming to Yeats's construction that "the best lack all conviction, while the worst / Are full of passionate intensity." Maybe that's what I'm worried about, that all the ink I've spilled here is just hemming and hawing. I've been dragging my feet while those inoculated with cultish certainty and purpose are leaping unafraid into the future.

This is the first of this book's three central subjects: cults, corporate thought control, and the end of the world as we know it, although I see it less as the apocalypse and more as the old world dying while the new one struggles to be born. The basic appeal of cults and prophets is that they provide us with answers about what will happen next. All humans fear the future as a container for our own deaths, a vision so distressing that many of us would rather imagine the end of the world than one that will go on without us. I, too, have been grasping for certainty about the future the entire time I have been writing this book, between the years of 2019 and 2024. It has been a maddening challenge to write a book of cultural criticism during this volatile time, and I have revised these essays over and over to accommodate the daily current of news about elections, disease, war, tech, climate disaster, and corporate scandal.

I turned in this draft the day before the 2024 election, and I am reluctantly revising it now, the day after, having learned that Trump was elected to serve another term as president. It was the third consecutive presidential race with Trump as the Republican candidate, and once again swing state polls had been too close to call. Trump's candidacy this time around has been marked both by an increasingly bizarre public presence and an escalation of openly fascist rhetoric, with the former president frequently threatening to deport millions of people on his first day in office. He ran against Vice President Kamala Harris, who was thrust into the race when President Joe Biden dropped out in August, forcing a clash between the notorious sexism and racism of this wing of the Republican party and a woman who is the child of Indian and Jamaican immigrants.

The Harris candidacy reflected a best of times, worst of times situation for American women. Late polls seemed to indicate that she was being buoyed by support from women outpacing that of men by double digits, particularly older, rural, white women. It seemed like there were the rumblings of a renewed feminist movement centered on outrage at the reversal of Roe v. Wade, with women uniting not just around abstract notions of equality but an actual political demand, the right to safe and legal abortion. At the same time, though, this was only possible because the country's right wing became so emboldened that they played their ace in overturning Roe. And Democrats retreated rightward on immigration, trans rights, and fracking this election, in (as it turns out) futile efforts to appeal to those same older, rural, white women. America-first feminism has been an unspoken strain in the Democratic party for years, but it seemed especially stark this year, when many treated regaining abortion rights for American women as contingent on immediately shutting down discussions about, for instance, the women and children being killed by American bombs overseas. Now that Trump has won, the narrative of the election is the exact opposite of that feminist fairytale: a rejection of feminism and identity politics, a new swell of backlash from resentful men.

The Harris campaign was a fascinating case study in the strange byways feminism has been down in this millennium. We went from a nationwide regression in the early 2000s centered on ogling teenage pinups to massive stars like Beyoncé openly calling themselves feminists ten years later. After that came the first humiliating defeat when Donald Trump beat Hillary Clinton in the 2016 presidential election and, only a year later, a reckoning about sexual abuse in Hollywood with #MeToo that would become the most consequential American feminist movement so far this millennium. Even with #MeToo, though, the movement suffered from a resistance to stating any political demands beyond "stop rape." Feminism grew increasingly indefinable from the advent of the Second Wave in the mid-1960s, culminating with pop stars reclaiming the word in the 2010s. Theirs was the feminism of glib t-shirt slogans like "Feminism Is the Radical Notion That Women Are People." The word functions as an identity—a brand—a collection of individual feminists rather than a collective movement. At this point it is difficult to distinguish it from a celebration of womanhood, something we may see as harmless until we remember all the ideological baggage that concept is weighted with, such that Christian nationalist troll Matt Walsh made an entire transphobic "documentary" called *What is a Woman?*

I wish that I could say that with the overturn of Roe, pop culture feminism has given way to a movement with real electoral strength and concrete demands. Instead, women are revealed once again as less a united political class than an occasional coalition—indeed, the antifeminists have proven themselves more organized, passionate, and politically effective currently. The idea that privileged women are coming to the rescue is a pipe dream; a feminism that does nothing but prop up privileged women's choices is bankrupt. Where we go from here, and the fate of feminism in this century, is the second subject of this book.

✳

The final subject is more submerged: a hidden narrative of the five hardest years of my life. You know what happened in 2020: COVID, work went online, didn't see my family in a year and a half. In the first few days of 2021, I suffered second and third degree burns on my legs when I slipped while holding a pan of hot water. It was the worst pain I've ever experienced, and I would experience it day after day, in the cold showers they made me take to wash my wounds and the twice-a-day bandage changes. I was in bed for a month and off work for six weeks. "Burns are very traumatic," my doctor told me impassively in the days after my injury. She was right, and I would have daily flashbacks to my burn in the kitchen or the shower that lasted for a year.

At the end of 2022, my mom suffered a stroke during heart surgery and had to be in intensive care for a month, where she got pneumonia and was intubated. She spent the first three months of 2023 in a rehabilitation hospital, regaining use of her left side and learning how to walk again. I was terrified, but it was a strange privilege to watch her brilliant brain unscrambling itself. In her early days in the hospital, she would speak to us and the staff in the many languages she knows, including Russian, German, Swedish, and French, in addition to imitating Cartman singing "O Holy Night" on *South Park* and ominously quoting long passages from the Bible. Her linguistic skill came in handy when she was on the ventilator, because she would finger spell to us in American sign language, the alphabet to which the rest of my family and I had to frantically cram on YouTube.

Then, in March of 2024, after my mom had made a full recovery, my godfather and favorite uncle was found dead at the age of sixty-five. He was an eccentric lawyer with a gentle, hilarious charm who I had always adored, from when I was five and he would show my brothers and I *The Simpsons* episodes he had taped from the TV. We waited over two months for the results of the autopsy, which revealed that he had died from the effects of alcohol abuse, a problem he had kept all but hidden from us. Maybe his drinking got worse during the pandemic. Maybe it was just his bachelor lifestyle, drinking and smoking too much and going to the doctor too little. In my eulogy, I talked about his generosity, all the gifts he had given me in the three and a half decades I knew him, from a photograph of a solar eclipse when I was seven years old to a Martin guitar when I was thirty-four. People told me at the funeral how proud he was of me and how much he loved me, but it didn't make me feel better. He loved me, and then he died, and the amount of love for me on this earth diminished dramatically all at once. Otherwise, where did the love go?

When I list this all out, these years seem eventful. In my memories from the COVID era, though, I mostly remember the negative space, the depression that swallowed up time between emergencies. I picture myself in bed, zoning out to YouTube or playing video games or scrolling endlessly on my phone. In the past five years, I have spent more time staring at a screen than ever before in my life, a life whose chief activity has been staring at screens. One of the most difficult aspects of the plague years has been the reluctance to count our own losses or seek sympathy from others around us, since our friends and neighbors are going through the same hardships as us, if not worse. Streaming entertainment and smartphone distractions became a way to turn away from a pain that would be unseemly to indulge in. We tell ourselves we should be grateful—after all, it could always be worse.

I have sought escape everywhere, and this book was often what I was trying to get away from, but the regimens of self-improvement, the nostalgia fuel, the endless streams of entertainment, and the immersive worlds of video games have thwarted me, becoming the very subjects of its essays. Writing has helped me to get some of this out of my system, as I try to understand what happened to me in this strange string of years. I harbor hope that finishing this book will mark a new season in my life, forcing the end of an era that has been so isolating and difficult.

But I am also wishing for the end of an era for all of us, and not just the end of the COVID era. It's time to end the long twentieth century, a period of stagnation exemplified by how many of us would rather treat nostalgic entertainments as a sensory deprivation tank than face a future currently staring us down. People will realize before long that these diversions are not a fair exchange for the radical transformation an unrestrained capitalist class is making to our communities, lifestyles, work, and climate—the drastic change in weather patterns that we have already experienced is one of the losses we haven't been able to count yet. If I take hope from anything in my experience of writing this book, it's that the distractions don't work, at least not forever. No matter what, I am eventually shunted back to the inescapable nature of reality, which exists as a single moment spinning like a gyroscope between distorted dreams of the past and future.

1

THE ENUMERATED WOMAN

WHEN I THINK ABOUT IT NOW, IT'S AMAZING THAT I allowed my body to remain mysterious for as long as I did. I didn't know what calories were until I was twenty-two, when I did most of my grocery shopping at the gas station. I consumed Honey Nut Cheerios, spaghetti and soy sauce, instant mashed potatoes, Top Ramen (with the flavor packet), and the worst cheapest beer there is: Steel Reserve. I won't deny that my body felt terrible or that I was somewhat spitefully neglecting myself, and still this attitude toward food seems healthier, at least emotionally, than what came next. I remember my roommate marveling at how uncompulsive my diet was. "You never come home from the bar and eat a huge bowl of pasta," she said. Indeed, since I ate only gross, plain meals to fulfill biological necessity, I hardly ever thought about food at all.

I reached a breaking point when I felt so icky and exhausted that I finally reflected that I had not eaten a vegetable in several days. I started cooking stir-fries and beans and rice at home and eating fruit for snacks, but I also imposed an 1,800-calorie restriction on myself for reasons I still can't pin down. I've never dieted to lose weight, except for when I have; I am, after all, a woman raised in America. But this was less a weight-loss plan than an exciting new form of masochism, and I enjoyed forcing myself to wait an hour to eat another clementine, my body rumbling scarily with hunger. Like most experiments, my first diet was over quickly, and I am thankful that I learned to cook and discovered the joy of consuming micronutrients other than sodium. It is clear to me now, though, that like all energy, the self-loathing inherent in eating only junk food was only converted, not destroyed.

It was all over for me, though, when I discovered every disordered eater's best frenemy, the nutrition tracker MyFitnessPal. This app is little more than a database of foods and their nutrition information, so that the user can track the calories and nutrients they're consuming. Nothing in its design—it is extremely ugly and has few bells and whistles—can explain the sinister, beguiling hold it has over its users, other than that it so completely satisfies, streamlines, and elevates the compulsions dieters have always indulged in, the foremost being to write down all the food you eat. I began tracking my food during one of the loneliest times in my life, when I had quit my job in Los Angeles and spent the day either writing or taking long walks to Denny's, Ralphs, or Daiso. I tracked my walks, too, with other, complementary apps. I lost weight, but I have never deluded myself that ten pounds would make much difference in how I looked or felt, and I took more satisfaction in seeing all the details I had stored about my life than in changing my body. Tracking was an answer to my boredom and a way to leave some record of days that felt empty, like a holding pattern.

During this time my body seemed increasingly insubstantial. There was no one else to see it, much less touch it, like I was a ghost haunting my own life. Tracking made my body real, until I didn't feel real without it. I had completed my transformation into the Enumerated Woman.

Later that year, I started dating someone who gave me his old Fitbit, a device that is the Enumerated Woman's dream. With this motion-sensing bracelet, I could track not only my daily steps but my food, sleep, and menstrual cycle with the Fitbit's accompanying app. I wore it 24/7, so tracking never had to begin or end. My then-boyfriend and his incredibly competitive family would compete in weekly step challenges and took huge pride in demolishing one another's records. (They are still the only "friends" I have on the Fitbit app, were I ever to log on to it again.) But I was never in it for competition, only for love—mostly self-love, a narcissistic pleasure in knowing new, arbitrary facts about myself, like how many thousands of steps I took during one podcast episode. As the Objectivist poet George Oppen wrote in the opening lines of his great poem "Of Being Numerous," "There are things / We live among 'and to see them / Is to know ourselves.'"

I remember sitting in my dirty apartment reading Oppen's books *Discrete Series* and *Of Being Numerous* in my first fog of hunger in my early twenties, his poems' austerity suiting my neurotic whims. These twin opuses, published in 1934 and 1968, respectively, contemplate the noisy symbols of modern life, shorn from their contexts by institutions including the military, advertising, and the faceless urban landscape. I would put excerpts from Oppen up on my Tumblr, further fracturing poems that are known for their jagged or jumbled fragmentation, posting lines like these from *Discrete Series*:

> Thus
> Hides the
>
> Parts—the prudery
> Of Frigidaire, of
> Soda-jerking—

It is uniquely fitting to showcase already fragmented lines that are *about* fragmentation on social media, services famous for overwhelming their users with information while simultaneously stripping context, authorship, or grounds for understanding. One can tell from the titles in *Discrete Series* and *Of Being Numerous* that Oppen was preoccupied with numbers and mathematics, anticipating the supermachines that would use algorithmic languages and the exchange of fragments of information—bits of bytes, those vaunted zeros and ones—to reshape our world and our sense of ourselves. Oppen wrote in 1968,

> Obsessed, bewildered
>
> By the shipwreck
> Of the singular
>
> We have chosen the meaning
> Of being numerous.

He didn't know the half of it.

Of Being Numerous spurred this essay's title and my rumination on the numbers (steps, calories) that for a time came to define my experience. (It arose independently, weirdly enough, of Natasha Lennard's 2019 book, *Being Numerous*, about big data, surveillance, and fascism, though those topics will become important here, too.) Admittedly Oppen's "numerousness" is not only about modern materialist alienation but also about Robinson Crusoe, the loneliness of poetry, and the palimpsest of New York City, where the physical world is encoded with history, memory, social myths, and fictional narratives. He was not writing about my Fitbit. Nevertheless, I hear echoes of the ironic first lines of his poem, in which we human beings come to know ourselves through the "things we live among," in the (not at all ironic) rallying call of what is known as the quantified self movement: "know thyself."

Wired magazine coined the phrase "quantified self" in 2014, defining a collection of tech nerds who monitored not only their steps but athletic performance, moods, heart rates, and other vital signs in an effort to optimize their bodies and (taken to its logical extreme) defeat death in its current form. *Wired* characterizes the niche community that claimed the "quantified self" name during the 2010s as optimistic and resourceful, hoping the data it crowdsourced would have wide applications to improve public health and happiness. (*Wired* writes that, in quant spirit, it measured the narcissism of self-trackers and discovered that they were no more self-obsessed than average, adding that "self-tracking culture is not particularly individualistic. In fact, there is a strong tendency among self-trackers to share data and collaborate on new ways of using it.") But there is a mistake in focusing on the niche QS community, which elides more "everyday" tracking in *Wired* and other coverage of this phenomenon. These articles do not address the fact that most people who track their calories or movement are doing so not out of enthusiasm for healthy living but because of an optimization culture that they cannot choose to opt out of.

Jia Tolentino writes in her essay "Always Be Optimizing," from her 2019 collection, *Trick Mirror*, about how women in the twentieth century have been fooled into ever more efficient pursuit of the feminine ideal, which is now, as it has been for centuries, to be beautiful, young, and obedient. According to Tolentino, the futuristic iteration of the perfect woman is exemplified by the space-age technology of the athleisure she wears to do her barre workout, both clothing and exercise engineered to manipulate a woman's body to a tight and gravity-defying industry standard, acting as something like a femininity assembly line. What Tolentino describes is the ideology of the "body project," a term coined by Joan Jacobs Brumberg in 1997 for the never-ending series of diets and exercise regimens that American women are expected to undertake, implicitly understanding a woman's body as unruly and untrustworthy, in need of constant vigilance and control. The key feature of the body project is that it is never complete, and even young girls are taught to see self-improvement as the basic point of their lives. This is a convenient paradigm for industries selling, among a basically endless list of diet and health products, ninety-eight-dollar leggings and forty-dollar barre classes.

Tolentino is critical in her essay of what she calls "mainstream feminism," which "has had to conform to patriarchy and capitalism to become mainstream in the first place." This is a common way of referring to a feminism that emphasizes individual women's pursuit of happiness and career success and approves of any choice that will aid in those goals, including body projects undertaken to conform to the sexist ideals of beauty. A more precise term for this phenomenon is "postfeminism," a philosophy co-opting certain elements of more radical feminist politics, like freedom of choice, but using them to reinforce traditional gender roles and other oppressive hierarchies. Postfeminism is the discourse of women's magazines; beauty, fitness, and "wellness" influencers; and Oprah Winfrey, Beyoncé, Gwyneth Paltrow, Taylor Swift, and anyone else selling women's empowerment as either the indulgence in expensive consumer goods or the punishing self-discipline necessary for women to succeed in a man's world.

The Fitbit, Apple Watch, and other trackers are the perfect technology of the postfeminist body project. (Even the old-school diet company WeightWatchers is now essentially just a calorie-tracking app.) As the political scientist Rachel Sanders writes in her wonderful article "Self-Tracking in the Digital Era: Biopower, Patriarchy, and the New Biometric Body Projects," a postfeminist paradigm controls women by transmitting gender expectations through experts, media, and celebrities, reigning through "glamorized norms rather than through gender-based prohibitions." Today those norms are most potent on social media, where an imperative to share and consume becomes an imperative to conform, and good health and beauty are ever more thoroughly conflated. Many tracking apps have a social element, allowing you to either add "friends" on the app or post your stats directly to social media. It is easy to scoff, "Who cares?" at Facebook friends who post their runs, weigh-ins, or calories burned during a lunchtime workout, laughing it off as a symptom of millennial oversharing syndrome. But these apps wouldn't have these features if people didn't use them and, more to the point, if they didn't serve a purpose, in this case to encourage obeisance to the app's demands, which are simple: all apps, no matter their purpose, want only to be used.

It is a critique that is common to all "social" tech that in framing personal information as public property, we become not only tolerant of the surveillance these apps perform on us but enthusiastic participants in it. Sanders writes that self-tracking apps and devices "produce a 'spectacular body' whose movements, habits, and internal workings are rendered more visible, knowable, and thereby potentially more manageable." This phenomenon is intimately connected to the spectacle the female body has always been and to the spectacle modern women are expected to make of themselves on apps like Instagram and TikTok. It is easier to "know thyself" when thyself is diminished not only to what others can perceive of you but to a field of data—not very accurate data, as it turns out, but manageable at least, at last.

I tracked intermittently during the years after I got my first Fitbit, having months where I logged my food obsessively but also long stretches where I lost my Fitbit or was too busy to worry about every morsel of food that went in my mouth. (Among self-tracking's other problems: it is an unsustainable habit.) But for a little over a year, during the editing and release of my first book, I was caught in an infernal MyFitnessPal and Fitbit feedback loop. This was a strange, two-pronged obsession, where

I was terrified of gaining weight and minutely controlled my food and exercise but also enthralled with the workings of the app itself and its rewards and metrics, spending hours playing with it daily to manipulate my results. People talk about how fitness apps have "gamified" exercise, but they don't talk about how easy it is to game the apps, adjusting the calories burned during exercise or falsifying steps to get the number you want on the screen—which isn't to say that I hadn't developed a real exercise addiction. Eventually I was biking four miles to the gym, then squatting nearly two hundred pounds, followed by high-intensity interval training on the elliptical machine (with my Fitbit clipped to my underwear to be sure it would record my steps), and finally biking home, feeling hollowed out and foggy. I can see now how the Fitbit fed into my desire to feel productive, to have evidence that I was getting something done, even if it was only four hours of exercise a day. I was also teaching, freelancing, and frantically promoting my book on social media, feeling that I could be marshaled to work by an email at any hour of the day—it makes sense that I stayed alert, tracking my progress to ten thousand steps a day, often marching in my slippers in front of the TV.

Social science literature theorizing self-tracking emphasizes how tracking apps reflect the philosophies of neoliberalism, that magical political system that extends state and corporate control of everyday people while abdicating their duty to provide in material ways for their well-being. The neoliberal public health apparatus maintains a moralistic emphasis on prevention, particularly of obesity, casting health as something individuals owe to society—that they should, if necessary, spend all their time and money on. It also frames health as purely a result of individual choices rather than social circumstances. There is a growing understanding of the abundance of food deserts in the United States, areas where there is no grocery store for miles, so that the poor rely on fast-food chains and convenience stores for food. For people living in food deserts, the advice to "eat a healthy diet rich in fruits and vegetables" is moot. Similarly, it is logical that if we want people to walk more, we should give them sidewalks and public transportation, not pedometers. Of course, this switch in emphasis from social to individual responsibility—from public transportation to pedometers—is of huge advantage to the neoliberal austerity state in its efforts to cut funding for the kinds of infrastructure that would actually improve public health, particularly in the only developed nation on earth without socialized healthcare.

While the neoliberal approach to healthcare may appear as the state declining to intervene in its citizens' lives, it is anything but. It relies on social programming—marketing, an emphasis on abstract moral values, and an atmosphere of competition in both personal and professional spheres—to control behavior and demand obedience, in a system of ideological indoctrination that is not unlike a cult whose brainwashed followers insist that they are not being coerced or manipulated. That's not to say that there isn't any overt coercion involved in the spread of step trackers: one hallmark of the tech era is that everything is voluntary until one refuses to participate, in which case it becomes mandatory, a case in point being the pedometers that now exist on every iPhone. If we hear about the Fitbit less often now, that is only because it has been replaced by the ubiquitous Apple Watch, a device that tracks the wearer's steps and move-

ment minutely, in addition to compiling data on other bio-
metrics like sleep and heart rate, even for users who may have
gotten the device primarily for its non-health related features.
We are all Enumerated now.

Many employers also implement self-tracking programs to
promote employee health and keep insurance costs down, with
incentives for workers who get a certain number of steps. While
these programs might seem benign, all of us should be leery
of allowing employers to perform this kind of surveillance. In
2018, Amazon patented tracking bracelets that would direct
warehouse workers' movements and detect if there was any
lag in their productivity. Many once believed the technological revolution beginning in the mid-twentieth century would
ring in the end of work, but instead of creating robot factories,
corporations like Amazon have discovered that it's more profitable to turn low-paid workers into what *The Guardian* called
"human robots." You might wonder how we've gotten here. It's
an image out of a ham-fisted techno-dystopia, a woman wearing her boyfriend's hand-me-down Fitbit juxtaposed with her
gothic double, a worker in a stifling warehouse being puppe-
teered by dystopian wearable tech. Maybe I'm being dramatic,
but consider that the pro bono labor you unwittingly put into
Enumerating yourself, collaborating on a massive data aggregation project with millions of other users, has perfected the
technology corporations needed to further subjugate their most
vulnerable workers.

While everyone is subject to the pressures of the neoliberal lens on health, there is a reason I emphasize its effects on
women, not least that it turns exercise into another entry in the

practically endless catalog of labor that women are not compensated for. Postfeminism and neoliberalism are not only compatible philosophies but twins of a sort, mutually reinforcing systems to enlist women to collaborate in their own oppression. As neoliberalism has the discourses of public health and prevention, postfeminism has traditional standards of beauty, the two of which dovetail neatly in the concept of "fitness": the (incorrect) idea that health can be visually manifest in a thin, muscular body, and therefore the pursuit of this body is a public good. Influencers post videos from their six a.m. gym sessions, tacitly assuring their followers that in a sexist world, in economic and healthcare systems marked more than anything by precarity and injustice, all a girl needs is to hustle harder.

I began to truly burn out on self-tracking at the end of 2018. I ate whatever I wanted while on a Christmas trip to Florida with my partner and his family, and I left my Fitbit at home. The last workout I have recorded from this time was a punishing lower-body dumbbell circuit I did on January 3, right after we returned home. I remember thinking the entire time that it was too intense, I wasn't up for it, I was too tired. At that point, I couldn't imagine not finishing a workout. The next day my parents came to visit, and I spent their entire stay feeling anxious, uptight, and miserable; after dropping them off at the airport, a micro-movement I made as I drove somehow strained what seemed like every muscle in my torso.

I know that was the moment I decided to stop going through life feeling like shit just to suit the impositions of my iPhone.

What strikes me now, though, is that despite all the evidence I have from that time of what I ate and how much I moved, there's still so much I want to know: how I felt, why I made the decisions I did, the day-to-day doubts and difficulties I had as I removed the organizing apparatus of my life. I didn't keep a journal then, like I do now, and my Fitbit was not interested in my feelings. Despite the fiction I collaborated on with my apps, my true self was never an algorithm, never a space-age cyborg. I was not the Enumerated Woman.

It is obvious by now that social media companies are essentially massive ad agencies that make money primarily from the advertisers who pay to parade their products in front of demographically appropriate eyeballs. As basically every critique of Web 2.0 has pointed out, regular people are not Google's and Facebook's customers. Their customers are advertisers, and their product is us. What interests me is why we are content to sell ourselves for so cheap, happily donating labor to monopolies that hardly need our charity. The artificial intelligence programs Silicon Valley has been aggressively foisting on us the past two years and supersecret algorithms that supposedly make social media apps so addictive are the product of millions of hours of labor on the part of regular people, doing simple tasks like clicking on links or taking steps as well as much more complex and analytical ones, like correcting translation programs. Computers are no more intelligent than they have ever been. The impressive feats they can accomplish are the product of all of us accidentally volunteering hours and hours and hours teaching them, not to mention the ingenuity of the human engineers who program them.

One reason these algorithms are kept so secret is because they may be less precise than they pretend, with their recommendation engines operating on what may at times be no more than random chance. We as the users imbue these programs with power, motivated by an ideological investment in the mystical promise of computer technology. We obey algorithms that dictate our tastes, telling us what to watch on Netflix or listen to on Spotify, whether they actually reflect our interests. We navigate "personalized" Instagram, Facebook, and YouTube feeds, which often seem to base their recommendations on broad (and frequently wrong) guesses about our demographics. If we really look at it, we are doing all the work, both in providing the computers with our data and acting as if they know us better than we know ourselves, despite all evidence. This was obvious when I would manipulate my data on the Fitbit app: I noticed all the inconsistencies, like the times steps would show up after I had driven for four hours. Still, the numbers, as fake as they were, were enough to motivate me to exercise too much and eat too little, to keep using the app, which was what Fitbit was counting on.

The technologist and philosopher Jaron Lanier writes in his famous polemic *You Are Not a Gadget* about how people seem determined to believe computers are smarter than they are. In the Turing test, robot intelligence is judged by how successfully the machine can simulate conversation; the intelligent robot could convince its human interlocutor that it is also human. But as Lanier points out, "The Turing test cuts both ways. You can't tell if a machine has gotten smarter or if you've just lowered your own standards of intelligence to such a degree that the machine seems smart." This is a creepy thought for those who fear the singularity, the scenario in which robot intelligence surpasses that of humans, leading to their takeover of planet Earth. I am not sure any sci-fi writer could have come up with this present scenario, where humans voluntarily allow robot intelligence to surpass ours because we love computers so much. Many more of us than would admit it are adherents of the cult of tech, believing that advances in computing represent not only technological breakthroughs but the apex of human accomplishment. There is a mainstream belief that computers will one day become so smart that they will not only achieve sentience but will constitute all we know of the world, when our consciousnesses are uploaded to the cloud to exist in immortal peace or torment, depending on whom you believe: Google's Sergey Brin (an eternity spent inside the boundless possibility of the internet) or the TV show *Black Mirror* (capitalism literally owning your soul).

To see how badly we want to believe in the promise of computer intelligence, one need look only at the recent breathless reception of artificial intelligence technology, programs that, after reading millions of words of fan fiction and Reddit posts, can help you write an email. The computing power these programs require is resource intensive, using approximately sixteen ounces of water per prompt, and they have not proven to have much practical value—why would we want a procedurally generated stock photograph of a bicycle when it is just an uncanny aggregation of the limitless other stock photographs of bicycles on the internet? This is only speaking of its value for consumers, since corporations are already using the chum AI programs are spewing all over the internet to devalue human work—but the aggressive corporate embrace of AI was made possible because users were taken in by the party trick, the novelty of a computer creating something sophisticated seemingly independently.

There are obvious ideological upsides for those in power to cast human beings as inferior to computers, when this notion leads directly to the further consolidation of their wealth, and it has become such a pervasive ontological discourse that it is practically the water we swim in. The idea of uploading a human consciousness to the cloud, now often spoken about as the height of the potential of networked computers, casts the mind as a complicated computer, instead of speaking of computers as shitty facsimiles of the human brain. There must be some drive in the human psyche that takes comfort in shrinking ourselves, simplifying ourselves, surrendering ourselves.

I guess this is the crux of the thing, returning finally to that ancient credo appropriated for the tech age: "know thyself." In some ways it is not mysterious why ordinary people would consent to a scheme where they exchanged economic opportunity for a free Facebook account. The social internet provides an emotional service to its users in reinforcing the myth of the consistent self. The rise of social media co-occurred with the emergence of the "personal brand," where taste, voice, subcultural signaling, and consistent visual style came to stand in for an identity. Even regular people feel the pressure to be a streamlined version of themselves online, not least because it's satisfying, getting to see ourselves as other people might. If this is possible only when we ignore the uncomfortable, confusing, and inconstant nature of personality, so much the better.

Women are better and more invested than men, by and large, at projecting a coherent personality on social media, maybe because we hear what goes unsaid: that you are what you appear to be, a "profile" of recognizable traits, and you will be judged and categorized accordingly. Women are expert at this game, instinctively seeking their roles from a limited number of female archetypes. I think of the scores of personality quizzes I took in teen magazines as a youth, finding out which *Dawson's Creek* star I was or which lipstick to buy based on my astrological sign. It was comforting to allow an outside source to tell me who I was, to be handed a persona that wrote over the thoughts, emotions, and cravings that seemed overwhelming and uncontrollable because they were. They were real.

I see now that this was social training, not just a canny anticipation of the social media age, but an education in how women must control and contort ourselves to succeed. The body project, for which teen magazines were once another training ground, has taken on new legitimacy in this precarious time, in spite of a pervasive "body positive" rhetoric. There is at least some evidence that a socially acceptable body is directly associated with higher earnings for women, with a 2010 study finding that "very thin" women make approximately $22,000 more than their average weight counterparts, whereas "very heavy" women make $19,000 less. (Researchers also found that any weight gain tends to decrease women's earnings. For men, increases in weight have a *positive* effect on pay.) Add to this the outsized effects that the eroding safety nets of neoliberal regimes have on women: with no childcare or paid family leave, women are often stuck with part-time, freelance, under-the-table, or direct sales work. It is no wonder, then, that the Fitbit or the Apple Watch becomes a welcome productivity tool, a way to do more with less time and support, to hustle both literally and figuratively.

The deck is stacked against women, and no number of steps

will set it right. This is reason enough to resist the siren call of self-tracking. But there is a deeper injustice churning beneath even that, one that came before the internet and has shaped our idea of its uses and limits. It arose with the twentieth century, a time enraptured with its own numerousness, when everything became "mass": mass production, mass marketing, mass communication, mass incarceration, and mass violence. Both soldiers and their prisoners are given ID numbers, with the mechanized warfare of the twentieth century making this process of dehumanization all the more efficient. Oppen wrote often of history as the offspring of numerousness, human lives reduced to crowds, demographics, statistics, serial numbers, and dossiers of data—and history is always about violence.

With this warning in mind, those who worry about their place in history will consider how they have allowed themselves to be Enumerated by tech. Of course, we cannot opt out of having our lives appropriated by history, but we may pause to think which causes we agree to be subsumed by and whether we have consented to all our data has been used for. This is not the only time human beings have enthusiastically allowed themselves to be diminished in this way, and it is not always a bad thing—in fact, many gurus will tell you that it is necessary to obliterate the singular self to attain enlightenment. The internet often manipulates a necessary, even beautiful part of human nature: the desire to be part of something bigger than us, submitting ourselves to a stream of knowledge that is larger than any single person could fathom. But the internet is One Big Self not in a transcendental sense but more like *Star Trek*'s the Borg, a terrifying alien empire assimilating entire peoples to create the most deadly and sophisticated army in the universe, connected through a giant computer so that the entire population shares one mind. Our current paradigm of network computing excels at copying and anonymizing any original work that is posted to it, so quantity is paramount and quality is nothing at all, and any individual user is just contributing to the big project, the internet itself. When we efface ourselves so easily, and for ends we neither agree to nor can fully comprehend, how much more will we be willing to do the same to other people, to let numbers stand in for their humanity?

Even with all that said—much more than I ever intended when I set out to write an essay "about my Fitbit"—I have hope! I believe that human beings are not only smarter and more complex than computers but also that, as susceptible as we are to strongmen, indoctrination, and regimes of control, we have another urge toward self-assertion, exuberance, and random disobedience. I don't doubt that human beings will outsmart or outstupid every attempt by tech companies to control them. This innate rebellion often creates novel innovations in tech, when people employ online tools not for the ends for which they were designed but in every possible useful and perverse way. I remember seeing this firsthand, when Facebook introduced status updates in 2008, a stroke of lucky genius that would change social networking forever. At first, status updates all began with the user's name and the word "is," and they were designed to let people know your location, as in "Alice is at the library." The first person I saw who flouted this convention was my college friend Alex, who, a few days after status updates were introduced, posted: "Alex is the cruelest month." Cut to: the mini op-ed that is the modern Facebook post.

I found a 2019 study of self-tracking attrition that reinforced this hunch, from the German psychologists Christiane Attig and Thomas Franke. In the results from their survey, they listed common reasons people abandoned their Fitbits or Apple Watches: subjects reported that their devices were not accurate and that they felt addicted or obsessed with them, unable to do the kinds of exercise they wanted to do because the tracker couldn't record them. But they also reported spontaneous experiences of freedom from the tracker—going on vacation, having a dead battery, or forgetting about it for a day—that seemed to break the spell. "Some users stated that they did not miss the tracker," Attig and Franke write, "or even felt relief when their routinized use was disrupted and thus consciously decided to stop tracking." Even more encouraging are the people who were not dissatisfied with their devices but no longer needed them. They used them for a time to train themselves to exercise more, and with the new habits and information the tracker was able to provide, they could go on to live a more active life without them.

I find this fascinating, because despite this being evidence that the tracker "worked," it is the opposite of what it wants: as I have said before, apps want to be *used*, which means they want to use us. But we are still capable, despite persuasive design, of assessing our needs and placing them above the hungry algorithms that seek to eat up every second of our lives. I'll admit that I sometimes still check my steps on my iPhone's pedometer. But most of the day my phone stays in a room where I am not, sitting quietly or dinging and buzzing to itself, as I wander around my house, vacuum the carpet, jump around with my husband, or just lie still, letting my life go on inside me, known but not recorded.

2

FOUNDERING

ONE SATURDAY IN THE SPRING OF 2021, A LITTLE achy after receiving our first doses of the COVID-19 vaccine, my husband and I decided to stay in bed and click on the first thing suggested to us by our TV. It was *WeWork: Or the Making and Breaking of a $47 Billion Unicorn*, a documentary produced by Hulu about the New York start-up WeWork's spectacular fall from grace. The film mostly chronicles the misdeeds of WeWork founder Adam Neumann, the surfer-dude dolt who turned a good idea—coworking spaces that would lease small offices to tech start-ups—into a surreally overvalued conglomerate, before he made a mortifying attempt to take the company public that eventually ended in his forced resignation. As a consolation prize, Neumann infamously received a $1.7 billion golden parachute.

The WeWork cautionary tale is partly about slick marketing, which is what seems to have convinced its investors that it was a tech start-up. WeWork's business was mostly real estate flipping, and their advantage over other office space brokers was a laid-back interior design and a clubhouse atmosphere, with good snacks and beer on tap. But Neumann tried to position WeWork as something much more than a real estate company: he borrowed the tech industry's idealistic language about changing the world but upped the ante, insisting that the company's sole mission was "elevat[ing] the world's consciousness."

This is a smart idea when trying to keep billionaire investors' money spigots flowing. A real estate company has a finite worth, based on markets, profits, and expenses, but a company that "elevates the world's consciousness," well, who knew where they might go with it? There is evidence, though, that WeWork executives were starting to buy into their own marketing—to get high, so to speak, on their own supply. (This is not a reference to Neumann's heavy marijuana use, one of the reasons given for the WeWork board asking him to step down as CEO, or to the cannabis company WeWork bought and for some reason did not rename WeEd.) As Gabriel Sherman writes in *Vanity Fair*, Neumann was known to make insane pronouncements about "wanting to be elected president of the world, live forever, and become humanity's first trillionaire." WeWork was so convinced of the nobility of its mission that it created its own fanciful accounting metrics to make it appear as though it were turning a profit, I guess to compensate for the ineffable measure of consciousness evolved. In reality, it had billions of dollars of debt and a long, murky path toward breaking even. It lost money every year and still made claims to profitability that were only not "lies" if you subordinate reality to fantasy.

Luckily for Neumann, there are many powerful people who do just that. He was massively enabled by SoftBank CEO Masayoshi Son, whose Vision Fund is the largest venture capital

firm on earth and who, as Sherman writes, did more than anyone to create the tech bubble that birthed so many multibillion-
dollar "unicorns." When Son met Neumann, he asked him, "In
a fight, who wins—the smart guy or the crazy guy?" "Crazy
guy," Neumann answered. Son told Neumann that he wasn't
crazy enough yet; he needed to think bigger. This was exactly
what Neumann did, spending profligately not just to grow the
company, but on himself. Neumann was living in Oprah-level
lavishness, with Maybachs, private planes, and a $90 million
collection of five mansions, including two in the Hamptons.
This makes no sense—the astronomical investment, the extrav-
agant spending to attract more investment—except in the world
of venture capital, where unfathomable amounts are pledged
on hunches. The implosion of WeWork was so satisfying in part
because it felt like a repudiation of the hubristic wastefulness of
the venture capital system, a triumph of reality over ego.

Not that anyone seems to have learned their lesson, least of
all Neumann or Son, who came out of this debacle with either comfortable (Neumann) or unimaginable (Son) fortunes.
WeWork pushed its romantic origin story, which involved
Neumann and cofounder Miguel McKelvey's idyllic childhoods
thousands of miles apart: Neumann on a kibbutz in Israel,
McKelvey on a hippie commune in Oregon. From this forma-
tive experience of communal living, so the story went, they
created WeWork, what Neumann described with the impossible concept of the "capitalist kibbutz." Neumann used skepti-
cism about the role of the tech industry in our lives even as he
tried to position himself within it, hilariously calling WeWork
"the world's first physical social network," like every cult leader
who acts like they've invented religion.

These canned origin stories are what passes for good story-telling in an age when we are eager to swallow anything tech jams down our throats. The Hulu documentary ends sentimen-tally, with Neumann's assistant describing how he made her believe in the company's mission, before it depicts the loneli-ness of the COVID-19 pandemic, making a poetic point about Neumann taking advantage of the human need for community. It probably would have been better to end with the fallout for the company's investors and the bursting of the broader uni-corn bubble, which went on to presage the collapse of crypto. The movie wants to show that the emperor's new clothes are no clothes at all, but in the end, it buys what Neumann's selling, too.

Neumann fashioned himself after the spiritual tech-guy arche-type, like the shadow side of Jack Dorsey from Twitter, whose Buddhist renunciation act contrasted dissonantly with the fa-mously toxic website he founded. But Neumann has his own shadow in Billy McFarland, the con artist laughingstock who took entrepreneurial speculative fiction to Icarian heights with his Fyre Festival. The twenty-six-year-old McFarland and the rapper Ja Rule went all in on a pipe dream to hold a luxury mu-sic festival on what was once Pablo Escobar's private island in the Bahamas. Marketing the festival on social media was their sole concern—they reportedly paid Kendall Jenner $250,000 for an Instagram post—when it might have been food, bathrooms, and housing for their five thousand ticket holders. When their guests arrived, instead of luxury villas on a deserted private is-land, they found hurricane tents and inflatable mattresses on a residential construction site. The privileged would-be concertgoers spent a terrifying night of *Lord of the Flies*–style chaos in the tents before the festival was canceled, prompting schadenfreude the likes of which Twitter had rarely seen.

McFarland is a scammer to his core, and he was released in 2022 after serving four years in prison for fraud. Despite the spectacle he made of himself, his con artistry was small ball in our current financial paradigm. When comparing McFarland's case with Neumann's, one could interpret McFarland's mistake as not going crazy enough—why be satisfied with scamming a party in the Bahamas when you could have five houses, a Maybach, and a private jet? Neumann would have kept coasting on his good marketing and made-up numbers if SoftBank hadn't backed out of what was going to be a $20 billion deal with WeWork, forcing it to go public and submit its finances to investors' scrutiny. I'm not saying that McFarland is the same as any other tech entrepreneur, but it's easy to see how the tech market draws con artists like roaches to grease. For one thing, McFarland was punished not for defrauding his customers—whom he put in serious danger, in addition to stealing their money—but his billionaire investors. Once again, the flows and reversals of capital float above real life, with all our ant-like obsession with cause and effect and human suffering.

There is an eerie echo of McFarland's folly in the story of the fraudulent crypto exchange FTX. Sam Bankman-Fried, the company's spectacularly corrupt founder, was arrested in the Bahamas, where he had set up both his company's and his polycule's home base because of the country's "friendly regulatory environment." Bankman-Fried, before he almost single-handedly set off the crash of the crypto market, was once the face of Nice Capitalism™, a millennial who lived modestly so that he could give his money away in the name of "effective altruism" and who was allegedly planning to use his billions to sway American elections toward progressives. As with McFarland, his attitude toward the citizens and governments of poor Caribbean nations should have been an early tip-off as to his true character.

One of Silicon Valley's most dearly held and deleterious myths is of its boy geniuses, an image Neumann, McFarland, and Bankman-Fried all exploited to varying degrees. McFarland reportedly idolized Facebook's Mark Zuckerberg, cultivating his personal brand as a tech prodigy who dropped out of college his freshman year to start a short-lived social media platform called Spling. I would be willing to bet that he styled himself not only on the real Zuckerberg but on Zuckerberg as he was fictionalized by the screenwriter Aaron Sorkin in 2010's *The Social Network*, one of the most influential documents in shaping the narrative of Web 2.0. My husband and I also watched *The Social Network* when laid up from the vaccine, finally giving in to the constant pressure from the Mechanical Turks inside our streaming services' recommendation algorithms. I had never seen it before, and more than ten years after it was made and amid a tech backlash with its target squarely on Zuckerberg and Facebook, I found the movie's tone strange, as it portrayed Zuckerberg as a manipulative misogynist who is nevertheless one of the visionary geniuses of our times. As Zadie Smith pointed out in her 2010 essay on the film, "Generation Why?," this does not really conform with what we know of Zuckerberg, who is so bland that his only explanation for why he invented Facebook, beyond a mystical fixation on the word "connection," is that he liked "building things."

The unwitting assault on democracy, community, and the human sense of self by a bunch of college sophomores who liked building things is not a bad story, but it's clear why it is not the one that Sorkin chose. As Mark Harris wrote in *New York* magazine in 2010, the film's central narrative question could be stated as "What exactly does it mean to be an asshole?" Women in the film's first and last beats tell Zuckerberg that he either is or isn't an asshole, and in the intervening two hours, he confidently fucks people over like an oblivious poster in the "Am I the Asshole?" subreddit. But this does not make him a villain; it is more of his tragic flaw. One must imagine that Elon Musk has done some of this same rationalizing as he has gone from being hailed as the real-life Iron Man to his new role as Twitter's head troll. Moving fast and breaking things means some people will think you're an asshole. Or maybe you *have* to be an asshole to be effective—assholes are the real good guys! Harris innocently reports in *New York* that Sorkin and the film's director, David Fincher, relate to Zuckerberg, having "been at some point in their professional lives on the receiving end of the word *asshole*." (The film was produced by famous abusers Kevin Spacey and Scott Rudin, for whom this theme must be particularly poignant.) *The Social Network*'s alternate title could be *Sympathy for the Asshole*, having been created by a team of men who have internalized the myth of their own temperamental genius and are intoxicated by stories of others who have done the same.

This is a favorite theme of Sorkin, who has become the go-to screenwriter for contemporary Great Man stories. His Steve Jobs, from the biopic *Steve Jobs*, is a total dick, questioning his daughter's paternity in the national press and screwing over his collaborators and mentors. And still his genius is assured, if ineffable: in one scene Apple cofounder Steve Wozniak blows up at Jobs, telling him, "You can't write code. You're not an engineer. You're not a designer . . . So how come ten times in a day, I read Steve Jobs is a genius? What do you do?" Jobs's response is that, like a conductor, he "play[s] the orchestra," co-ordinating technicians under his sweeping business vision. Tech founders' self belief is broadcast by the geniuses they name their businesses after—Tesla is a conspicuous example, and Apple is, of course, a nod to Isaac Newton. *Steve Jobs* and *The Social Network* are full of mini-monologues about the future of computing and the lives of historical Great Men like Alan Turing, creating little biopics within biopics. (When Sean Parker tells Zuckerberg the tale of the ill-fated founder of Victoria's Secret, Zuckerberg replies, "Is this a parable?" Yes. It is.)

Intelligence is signified in Sorkin's work by simply knowing a lot of facts, and his nerd heroes are often being asked difficult trivia questions so that they can answer them correctly, like the sixth grade brownnosers they once were. As Joan Didion said of Woody Allen's characters in 1979, "They reflect exactly the false and desperate knowingness of the smartest kid in the class," but at least Allen's characters are dilettante writers with teenage girlfriends, not the supposed incarnations of the spirit of American innovation. Furthermore, this juvenile intelligence and ruthlessness seem to go hand in hand. One of the leitmotifs of Sorkin's tech biopics is, as I am sure he read on BrainyQuote .com, "Great artists steal." Zuckerberg and Jobs in his movies are defiant about their practice of plundering other people's hard work. This Sorkin does not exactly share with them, since his biopics are ahistorical fantasias, telling stories that are, for better or worse (read as: worse), mostly Sorkin's own invention. "What is the big deal about accuracy purely for accuracy's sake," Sorkin told *New York*, "and can we not have the true be the enemy of the good?" Here he sets up a curious opposition, though he claims to be knocking it down. Is he saying that a movie does not necessarily have to be true to be good? Or that it is harder to make a true story good, meaning interesting, even when audiences are expecting one?

Well, to begin with, Sorkin seems to see his movies as opportunities to write as many quips, factoids, and little condescending lectures as possible, in a style that bears no resemblance to how any human talks. "I'm really weak when it comes to plot," he told *New York*. "With nothing to stop me, I'll write pages and pages of snappy dialogue that don't add up to anything." With this, Sorkin has offered up a more cogent critique of himself than fawning critics of his films are able to muster, despite the weakness of his plots being plain to see. (I thought *The Social Network*'s structure was sloppy, with its exposition provided by flashing forward to deposition hearings, until I saw *Steve Jobs*, which dramatizes the hours surrounding three of Jobs's famous product launches and has the narrative momentum of three YouTube videos.) This might be why he is drawn to biopics, whose stories are already inscribed like a treasure map to destiny. By seizing on poetic license, he can push those popular narratives even further, plating up the Zuckerberg and Jobs of our dreams, our very own assholes to rival the assholes of history like Henry Ford, Thomas Edison, and Walt Disney. Sorkin's appeal is not to artistic ingenuity but national pride, creating corporate propaganda so satisfying that his lines from *The Social Network* have become tech truisms ("We lived on farms, then we lived in cities, now we're going to live on the internet"), reshaping reality around itself.

I can admit that this version of the Facebook story is easier to face than the truth. As Smith writes in "Generation Why?," Facebook was a haphazard invention, with little thought given to its look or function, reducing all of us in the end to the nineteen-year-old who invented it. There is a strange resonance with Smith's unanswerable questions—"Why? Why Facebook? . . . Why do it like that?" she asks—and the granddaddy of all tech scams, Enron, the energy provider turned online trading marketplace whose unironic motto was "Ask Why." In addition to wreaking havoc on Texas and California energy sectors (damage that, in our climate change–addled present, we are still suffering from), Enron's executives were maestros of fake accounting, hiding billions of dollars in debt to keep the firm's stock price high before its epic collapse in 2001. The definitive book on the Enron scandal, adapted into a documentary with the same name, is called *Enron: The Smartest Guys in the Room*, and its executives loved to congratulate themselves for their intelligence, casting it as the means to justify any sordid ends.

In a Sorkinist reading of history, American progress is safeguarded because the assholes we endow with great power are inoculated with visionary genius. But intelligence, popularly taken to mean devious cleverness or maybe just privilege, has never been synonymous with moral goodness, and we should no longer blindly celebrate people for so low and ambiguous a bar as "changing the world." Why? Why Facebook? Why Enron? Why is our economy an unregulated wasteland of self-dealing, where theft is not an aberration but the very foundation of the world's greatest fortunes? Whether avarice or accident, no reason at all. Elon Musk has become the archetypal tech founder not only for his passion for self-beatification—he revived the dream of space travel! and he makes *electric* cars!—but for a kleptomaniac streak greater even than Zuckerberg's, maneuvering from Tesla investor to cofounder and eventually booting both of the original founders from the company.

Tech is only the latest sector to take cover in the American mania for founder myths, with the virtual requirement that they be mostly made up. Elizabeth Holmes, the sociopath founder of the fraudulent medical start-up Theranos and one of Silicon Valley's few girl geniuses, would often speak in her origin story about her beloved uncle dying of skin cancer igniting her passion for medicine. In *Bad Blood*, John Carreyrou found that her uncle died eleven years after Theranos was founded, and they were never close to begin with.

This narrative impulse comes from our own epic origin story, our misplaced pride in the genius of the Founding Fathers that has become one of the main stagnating forces of American government. Our stubborn American status quo, where wealth and political power are so ludicrously concentrated, was seemingly incarnated in the founders, some of the smartest guys of the eighteenth century, whose inspiring opening salvo, a poetic ode to all men being created equal, was maybe more marketing than actual game plan. With this they got the foreign policy apparatus of France to buy into what might be the most ambitious and visionary start-up venture of all time, the United States of America. The figures of the founders are narcotizing antidotes to the reformer spirit: depictions of them as revolutionaries foreclose any further revolution as redundant. It is no wonder they are foisted on us by the entire spectrum of cultural gatekeepers, including politicians, publishing, Disney, the Tonys, the Grammys, and the Pulitzer Prize. Why else would we be so taken in by the romanticized story of our most corrupt and problematic Founding Father? Yes, you know the one.

Lin-Manuel Miranda got the idea for his musical *Hamilton* when he bought a copy of Ron Chernow's biography of the Founding Father at the airport. "When I encountered Alexander Hamilton I was immediately captivated," Miranda said. "He's an inspirational figure to me. And an aspirational one." Miranda has popularized the fantasy that Hamilton's was a New York immigrant story, like those of Miranda's parents, who moved to New York from Puerto Rico. But Hamilton was not an immigrant as we now think of them: he did move to New York from the Caribbean, but it was as an English citizen moving between two of England's colonies. (Despite American citizenship, Puerto Ricans living in the United States are seen as more "foreign" than Hamilton would have been.) And disregarding rumors kicked up by *Hamilton*'s popularity, he was white.

Miranda's casting of the Founding Fathers with Black and Hispanic actors was a stroke of genius, since it clouded Hamilton's politics in a confusion so profound that few people felt like questioning them. One might even forget to notice that the musical portrays no actual people of color. As the historian Lyra D. Monteiro wrote in *The Public Historian*, *Hamilton* repackages the same myths of the founders that we have received from time immemorial, particularly the myth that white men were the only people of any importance living in America during this time. One marketing campaign for the musical, Monteiro points out, promised "the story of America then, told by America now," thus implying that the United States was a white nation at its inception, with American diversity as some Obama-era innovation.

Despite his overtures to the subjectivity of history, with the final song in *Hamilton* repeating the question "Who lives, who dies, who tells your story?" Miranda misses the irony: that he has perpetuated a narrative by white men about white men, because the founder biography is an essentially white genre, especially the ones you can buy at the airport. With a different historian as his guide, Miranda might have been able to tell a more nuanced story about New York in this era. But, as Monteiro writes, "there are few historians of color who work on the founding fathers, let alone on Alexander Hamilton specifically—most are driven instead by projects that chip away at the exclusive past typified by the cult of the founders."

The surface-level connection to Black culture is in the same tradition as the Hollywood cliché of getting poor Black kids interested in Shakespeare by rapping the sonnets. As Monteiro writes, people describe *Hamilton* condescendingly as making history "accessible," presumably to contemporary people of color who might otherwise have found the story of the founders alienating, and with good reason. Maybe I'm crazy, but as I sat down to watch the live version made available on Disney+, I assumed that a hip-hop musical about the Founding Fathers would be at least somewhat tongue-in-cheek, poking holes in our pieties about the founders. Instead, I watched a very long, self-serious, and detailed biography of Hamilton, a true *School-house Rock!* situation, with a sentimentality about its subject worthy of the Disney Company. This combination—a performance of diversity crossed with the familiar sanding down of the sharper edges of American history—makes *Hamilton* "one of the most brilliant propaganda pieces in theatrical history," as Matt Stoller writes, and one, if Disney has anything to say about it, that will be shown to schoolchildren annually for the rest of forever.

Stoller's essay "The Hamilton Hustle" from *The Baffler* is an exhaustive and illuminating rundown of all of Alexander Hamilton's faults and misdeeds. Hamilton not only was in favor of centralized government but was vehemently anti-democracy, calling the American people "a great beast." Instead, he envisioned a United States run by an elite coalition of wealthy financiers and military officers, and much of his career was dedicated to fucking over the small farmers who formed the majority of the American population. As the secretary of the treasury, Hamilton imposed a tax on whiskey, which was used as an alternate form of currency by western farmers, with the hopes that it would foment an uprising (the famed "Whiskey Rebellion") that he could crush with military force. He got his wish, using "indefinite detention, mass arrests, and round-ups; [seizing] property (including food stores for the winter); and [having] soldiers administer loyalty oaths."

Hamilton's authoritarianism had long-lasting effects, eviscerating the economic power of the middle classes and creating stratification and inequality that we still recognize today. It is baffling that educated, progressive people so willingly accepted

Miranda's fairy tale about the father of modern finance so soon after the 2008 financial crisis, where the craven stupidity of Wall Street bankers nearly caused global economic collapse. But this may be exactly why *Hamilton* was such a phenomenon. As Stoller writes, Hamilton is so resilient a figure in the American popular consciousness that "the shifting popular image of Hamilton is itself a gauge of the relative strength of democratic institutions at any given moment"—that is, the more popular Hamilton is, the less healthy American democracy is. Hamilton-mania has had many iterations, with one acute case in the Wall Street–dominated 1920s, when the millionaire secretary of the treasury Andrew Mellon put him on the ten-dollar bill. Our new wave perfectly coincides with another moment of human dignity being hijacked by high finance. Chernow claims falsely that Hamilton was an abolitionist (he married into a family of slaveholders and sold enslaved people), doing the same work to obscure Hamilton's repugnant politics that the appearance of diversity does in the musical, but even in this new liberal guise it's still the same story. According to Stoller, the mission of glorifying Hamilton has always been "to subvert democracy by helping the professional class to associate the rise of finance with the greatness of America, instead of seeing in that financial infrastructure the seeds of a dangerous authoritarian tradition."

This is a familiar leftist critique of contemporary liberalism: that the appearance of progress, particularly involving narratives about "strong women" and "breaking down historic barriers," stands in for the real thing. With this frame, *Hamilton* is the quintessential Obama-era document, with Obama's secretary of the treasury, Timothy Geithner, calling Hamilton the "original

Mr. Bailout." Geithner's blanket bailout of the big banks, with the architects of the financial crisis going totally unpunished, was a travesty we are only beginning to reckon with, but one thing it did for certain is pass the baton of bank-friendly economic policies between the Bush and Obama administrations, with Obama's innovation being an even closer relationship with tech founders, the titans of our new Gilded Age. The early 2020s were an extension of the Obama era, with Obama's former vice president, President Joe Biden, overseeing the bailout of Silicon Valley Bank in the wake of the crypto collapse, continuing the federal government's function of shielding the architects of our destruction from punishment.

Barack and Michelle Obama have said of their greatest strength, "One way of looking at what we've both been doing for the last 20 years, maybe most of our careers, was to tell stories." This is true, and they are maybe a little too good at it, allowing the eloquence of Obama's own immigrant narrative in the most well-written and moving presidential campaign books since John F. Kennedy's to deflect from deep flaws in his record. Maybe this is why I am a bit grumpy about the Obamas' choice to start a film and TV production company with their post–White House popularity, moving decisively into the realm where they have always most excelled: celebrity. Their company is called Higher Ground Productions, which they claim is an ode to Stevie Wonder, but this phrase inevitably evokes Michelle Obama's catchphrase on the 2016 campaign trail: "When they go low, we go high." This policy of tight-lipped civility was no match for the emergency of the Trump moment—it's embarrassing when one thinks of how low we have sunk from there—but it was a savvy act of image preservation, one that ensured that the Obamas would weather the Trump era un-scathed, no matter if the rest of us will.

There are many points of irony in the Obamas' new me-dia ventures, including Barack Obama's podcast with the other most popular man in America, Bruce Springsteen, hilariously called *Renegades*. Despite the cringe, their activities are at least less ethically questionable than the Clinton Foundation, the charitable venture Bill Clinton started post-presidency to re-habilitate his image and accrue hundreds of millions of dollars in personal wealth. For me, where it gets murkier is with the connections Obama fostered while in office, including with the Netflix founders who hosted a fundraising dinner for Obama's campaign in 2012 that brought in $700,000. Because of this, according to *Vanity Fair*, "it was already more or less a given that the first couple were Netflix bound" when they decided to start their company, signing a multiyear deal with Netflix that is said to rival their $65 million deal with Penguin Random House. Just as it is for Silicon Valley founders, for the Obamas, "good storytelling" is synonymous with good branding. And, of course, big streaming companies like Netflix do not see their "content" as separate from the demands of marketing. To them, good stories are the ones people want to hear because they've heard them before, thus the knockoffs they produce of all their most popular shows: iterating, iterating, iterating. Who lives, who dies, who tells your story?

One of the stranger episodes in the current documentary film boom was the appearance, in January 2019, of competing doc-umentaries exploring the Fyre Festival debacle on Netflix and

Hulu. They were only slightly different. Hulu's features an interview with Billy McFarland and focuses more on what this event can tell us about the millennial generation, where Netflix's relies on interviews with McFarland's staff to provide a play-by-play; in the end, it was mostly the same story told by mostly the same people. Despite the hype these rival documentaries produced, this was less a case of competition than more iteration: like many people, I ended up happily watching both.

There is more to be learned from the case of the twin documentaries than meets the eye, though. McFarland famously procured the services of the hipster marketing company FuckJerry to create the devilishly effective social media marketing campaign that architected the illusion of Fyre Festival's legitimacy. As Jo Livingstone wrote in *The New Republic*, FuckJerry, through its affiliation with Vice Media, ended up with a heavy hand in producing Netflix's documentary. "By the time of Netflix's announcement, the producer list had become dominated by personnel from companies contracted directly by Fyre Festival," Livingstone wrote, with FuckJerry's CEO at one point having final cut over the film. This explains the defensive stance that FuckJerry staffers take in their talking-head interviews, claiming that they had nothing to do with the actual festival planning and that they were left in the dark about the issues that were arising with the event.

This supposed exposé being used to launder the image of one of the parties responsible for the Fyre Festival scandal should alarm us. Livingstone points out that FuckJerry is running the same hustle with the documentary that it did with the Fyre Festival, using social media savvy to subvert the truth. This is what happens when all entertainment, politics, and public performance are reduced to marketing, everything flattened through the libertarian determination of what people want to see. Big tech companies allow documentaries critiquing tech on their platforms because people like them, perhaps because they make us feel less like the dupes we are for the tech industry. Since I wrote the first draft of this piece in 2021, there have been so many tech scandals and meltdowns that I have been able to shoehorn in only a few of them here, and it is interesting how we seem to have as healthy an appetite for stories of tech villains as tech founders. Sam Bankman-Fried makes a great headline whether he's the barefoot CEO giving all his money away or the incompetent crook gambling with his investors' savings. We love Elon Musk whether he's exploring space or destroying Twitter (now X). It's the ultimate postmodern nightmare, where truth and taste are not only contested but irrelevant. Verisimilitude is an aesthetic stance, not only for biopic hockers like Aaron Sorkin but for documentarians, whose work is often less about argument than access.

One simple reason that documentaries have abounded in the past five years is because of the amount of video footage that now exists of basically everyone since the rise of reality television and the iPhone. This is the remarkable thing about Netflix's pandemic sensation *Tiger King*, whose subject, the disgraced zookeeper Joe Exotic, seems to have filmed himself more than any person since L. Ron Hubbard. In this way, streaming TV services have been influenced by the social media feeds that have become the main source of American entertainment, with YouTube as a crucial link between the two. These feeds exemplify the total victory of spectacle over argument, a stream of unlimited, barely distinguishable content, narrativeless and authored by everyone. Tech founder myths have been used to distract from how debased our entertainment has become and the power normal people hold in creating and transforming it. We look at the dominance of social media apps and start seeking the Great Men behind them, completely ignoring the billions of users who have donated their time, confessions, and creativity to make them compelling.

One sees this startlingly with HBO's documentary series *Q: Into the Storm*, which seeks out the men behind the mega-conspiracy theory QAnon. The documentary filmmaker Cullen Hoback had remarkable access to Jim and Ron Watkins, the father-son duo in the Philippines who ran the anonymous message board 8chan, where Q, a supposed "deep-state" operative, posted warnings of a cabal of powerful pedophiles who can only be stopped by a heroic President Trump. Hoback comes to the same conclusion that many other journalists already have, that Ron Watkins has been writing Q's posts since 2017, and that both Jim and Ron had heavy interests in promoting QAnon, both for the success of their websites and for the influence they could wield over American politics.

Hoback's work focuses probably too much on the sideshow, giving a platform to the loony tunes who make up the QAnon media universe and the bizarre and unappealing Watkinses. Not only is ridicule ineffective in fighting conspiracies but Hoback makes the assumption that if he can only unmask the real Q, the entire theory will unravel. But Q was never one person: Ron Watkins did not originate the persona, and the anonymous message board that was QAnon's birthplace was crucial for its development, as a kind of collaborative fiction written by a web of different authors. Several years on, it was less a conspiracy theory than a terrifying augmented reality, one which turned the world into a matrix of clues, in which owls, Wayfair, and the Rothschilds all take on sinister meaning. Its spread has been truly viral, "insinuat[ing] itself into Christian churches, anti–sex trafficking campaigns, wellness communities, and New Age spirituality," as Adi Robertson wrote in the Verge, leaving lives in its wake, and not only in the deadly Capitol riot, where a shirtless man in a horned headdress held a sign reading "Q Sent Me."

QAnon is a case study in the power of emergence, though of course it was all in service to perhaps the least deserving Great Man on the planet, Donald Trump. In terms of sheer people power, it acted like a microcosm of social media or even the United States itself, this concentration of human ingenuity misdirected to benefit people who are already rich and powerful. This is another way of saying, as my Marxist brother tells me, that workers create value. But I am not just preaching that "the people have the power," since regular people have very little power in this time of inequality, price increases, stagnant wages, environmental injustice, and war.

The current billionaire class has more power than any human beings have ever had, and they wield it with remarkably little responsibility. (We might remember Amazon's Jeff Bezos's trip to outer space, an indulgent boondoggle made possible through the funds he made exploiting a global pandemic.) Billionaires must be cut down to size through every means possible, from breaking up monopolies to tax reform to financial regulation to union drives. But we also need to stop swallowing these Great Man stories whole and recognize them for what they are: an ideology of dominance. I do not exaggerate when I say that this ideology is not only impoverishing the narratives available to us but endangering human lives and the future of civilization. Just as it did after the Hamilton-soaked 1920s, though, the wheel is beginning to turn. Tech billionaires' public image is in the toilet, with these former "visionaries" seeming ever more embarrassing, monomaniacal, shortsighted, and pathetic. The fickle winds of marketing are finally blowing against them, though it will take more than that to stop them all from failing up like Neumann, who was so incompetent that he got paid over a billion dollars to quit his job. Who wins, the smart guy or the crazy guy? The crazy guy, and he's getting crazier every day.

3

LEAN IN/BEND OVER

OF THE NEWS STORIES OF SCAMMERS AND CHARLA-
tans that have abounded in recent years, none has consumed
me like that of NXIVM, the self-improvement cult/pyramid
scheme/sex trafficking ring that wreaked havoc on C-list TV
stars, billionaire heiresses, and the city of Albany, New York,
for the first decade and a half of this century. I watched HBO's
2020 docuseries about it, *The Vow*, and then the Starz docuseries about it, and then, once I decided I may as well write
something about it, I read practically every article about it in
The New York Times, *New York Post*, *Vice*, *Forbes*, *The Hollywood
Reporter*, even the *Albany Times Union*.

By the time the story reached the popular consciousness, it
was more or less over—the organization's leader, Keith Raniere,
was found guilty on seven counts of racketeering and sex trafficking in 2019 and sentenced to 120 years in prison. The most
sensational headlines of the case were about the former teen
actress Allison Mack's involvement in a secret sadomasochistic
group within NXIVM known as DOS ("Dominus Obsequious

Sororium," a phrase in bastard Latin that supposedly meant "lord over the obedient female companions"; the initials were also interpreted, more simply, as "Dominant Over Submissive") in which she and her fellow "masters," women in Raniere's inner circle, recruited other women as "slaves," some of whom were groomed for sex with Raniere. Grotesque details abound in this story, the most infamous being that slaves were branded with a soldering iron near their crotches with a symbol containing both Mack's and Raniere's initials. But this was only the end of Raniere's prodigious organized crime career, the moment when, drunk with power and having gotten increasingly horny and twisted, he went too far and was caught. Raniere left thirty years of scams and thousands of victims in his wake, a serpentine trail of exploitation he was enabled in by his followers, billionaire investors, celebrities, the police, and, on one occasion, the Dalai Lama himself.

The Vow closely follows former high-ranking members within NXIVM as they leave the group, and it contains remarkable footage of them trying to convince others to leave and to use the media to pressure the FBI and the New York attorney general to press charges. It also attempts to answer why anyone would be caught up in something so heinous, what the filmmakers call the love affair before the betrayal. I suppose that's why the first episode appears oddly positive in its depiction of Executive Success Programs (ESP), the personal growth seminars that were most members' introduction to NXIVM.

Former members talk about being amazed by the "technology" that Raniere invented to help them overcome their fears and limiting beliefs. This technology, in reality, is nothing more than a proprietary blend of therapeutic methods cribbed from cognitive behavioral therapy, Scientology, Ayn Rand's theory of objectivism, direct-selling techniques, and, most notably, neurolinguistic programming (NLP), which NXIVM cofounder Nancy Salzman was practicing when she met Raniere in 1998. NLP, a kind of hypnotherapy, has been derided as pseudoscience, and of course none of Raniere's methods were, as he often bragged, "mathematically reproducible." What is more telling is his reliance on Salzman's area of expertise to form the basis of his teachings. Members spoke of Salzman as "downloading" information from Raniere in order to create ESP's educational modules. If this is true, she must have extrapolated liberally from Raniere's ideas in her creation of a practical curriculum. Unlike L. Ron Hubbard, the founder of Scientology, Raniere has never written a NXIVM scripture or treatise or even workbook; he didn't teach or manage money or answer emails. There were women for that.

In *The Vow*, Raniere appears to be the laziest and least charismatic cult leader of all time. "What this show teaches me," I told my husband midway through the first episode, "is that anyone can start a cult." Raniere slept all day and spent all night either going on long walks or playing in the midnight NXIVM volleyball games he insisted on. He exercised control through the myth he created of himself, based on lies or half-truths: that he was the smartest man alive, with a 240 IQ; that he had taught himself calculus at the age of twelve; that he was a judo champion and a concert pianist. He had his acolytes disseminate this information about him to every recruit, so in person he could appear humble. Salzman herself appears in the second season of *The Vow*, after having pled guilty to conspiracy racketeering, and she says she would cook Raniere breakfast every morning, after which he would talk on the phone for hours. "People probably thought he was working," Nancy said, "but he would just be lying on my couch."

To the naked eye he seems remarkably stupid, having never read a book other than *The Fountainhead* and *How to Win at Gambling*, which he's seen reading in a widely published and very weird picture, lying on a bed in his underwear. For years members of NXIVM videotaped, recorded, and transcribed everything he said, writing their own Gospel of Keith, but the philosophy we hear him drone on about in *The Vow* is full of anodyne platitudes, some of which seem to literally be taken from Hallmark cards.

What Raniere knew was mostly how to sell, having learned techniques of persuasion as an Amway salesman in the '80s. People often remark that the supposed "charismatic leaders" of cult movements seem to be anything but charismatic to those viewing the movement from the outside. Raniere, like David Koresh, Marshall Applewhite, L. Ron Hubbard, or Charles Manson, is unattractive, creepy, and inarticulate, with an off-putting, restless energy. But this emphasis on personal magnetism is a misunderstanding of the essential skill of the cult leader, which, like with any con artist, is the ability to spot a mark. Their eccentric personas serve as a test to weed out people who are too discerning, skeptical, judgmental, or willful in favor of people who are vulnerable, gullible, nonjudgmental, idealistic, and naive. I am not trying to imply that people who get involved with cults are weak, since authoritarian leaders prey on their victims' strengths just as they do their weaknesses. In fact, they often surround themselves with attractive, dynamic people who draw others to the group, so leaders can parasitically appropriate their followers' charisma as their own.

Raniere knew how to pitch his contradictory, Randian idea of ethics to the right people. (N.B. It is hard not to put scare quotes around "ethics," as it is hard not to put them around basically every word that Raniere twisted for his own purposes.) Since it was devised as an executive coaching program, riding a trend for such services in the late 1990s, the ESP curriculum taught that its members' personal business success was the only thing that could create a happier, more peaceful world. "I pledge to ethically control as much of the money, wealth, and resources of the world as possible within my success plan," read part of its twelve-point mission statement, which members were required to recite. This was appealing for the organization's entertainment industry recruits, who were often desperate for a formula for professional success, even as they said they came looking for personal fulfillment and a way to change the world. "I had some idea that I would become a famous actor and use my celebrity to help people," says Sarah Edmondson, one of the former NXIVM executives featured in *The Vow*, echoing the wishful thinking of many people who were drawn to NXIVM. Theirs was a well-meaning selfishness that was validated by Raniere's "me first" humanitarianism.

This was even truer for the one-percenters who went through ESP. Sara and Clare Bronfman, the heiresses to the Seagram's liquor fortune, bankrolled NXIVM for twenty years to a comically lavish degree: buying the organization a private jet, funding its litigation against ex-members, covering $65 million Raniere lost in the commodities market, buying an island in Fiji to use for retreats, and pulling strings with massive donations to convince the Dalai Lama to visit Albany in 2009. It seems that the most profound teaching Clare Bronfman gained from ESP was that her masses of wealth were not something to be ashamed of. "I thought that money made people bad," Clare told Vanessa Grigoriadis in *The New York Times Magazine* in 2018. But through Raniere's teachings, she learned that "money's money. And people are people. So rich people can do good and bad, poor people can do good and bad."

Raniere and NXIVM exercised a hold on their superwealthy members by offering them teachings that were a mix of what they wanted to believe and what they most feared. Your money is a good thing, they were told, but you are blowing your chance to use it to help people. The only way they could do that, of course, was to give as much of it as possible to NXIVM. If you look closely, these ideas about privilege and complacency lace through all of NXIVM's teachings, including the way women were recruited for DOS. As time went on, Raniere's teachings became more misogynist, particularly at NXIVM's women's retreat, Jness, which started in 2006. There Raniere taught that women were naturally emotional, where men were rational; this difference made women dishonest, disloyal, unreliable, and lazy. (Echoing sexists since Aristotle and before, Raniere continued to have zero original ideas.) The other fundamental difference was that women were protected their whole lives, never facing humiliation or discomfort, thus making them rely on men instead of themselves. In this way, as Raniere and his lieutenants sought to break their female students with a form of tough love, they could claim they were doing it for the women's own empowerment.

This reasoning is obviously faulty: humiliation is arguably a fact of life for women more than it is for men, not least because our bodies are considered public property for anyone to ogle, touch, or comment on. But this story of a sheltered upbringing rings true for some women, and I can imagine that for the child actors and heiresses in NXIVM, when Raniere derided women as "spoiled princesses," it felt personal. "Coming from a family where I've never had to earn anything before in my life, [it] was a very, very moving experience . . . It was the first thing that I had earned on just my merits," Sara Bronfman said of being promoted in NXIVM in *Forbes* in 2003.

This is one answer to the question that plagues conversations around DOS and NXIVM: How were more than a hundred women convinced to join a secret organization where from the beginning they were called "slaves," forced to collateralize their commitment with naked photos and secret confessions, and vowed loyalty to their masters for life? One answer is that many of these women had already internalized the belief that they were weak and spoiled, with no ability to work for anything, helped along by Jness indoctrination. DOS was described as a "badass bitch boot camp" that would steel their commitments and help them achieve their goals. And even more than that, it was the only way they could help the cause of women, preventing nightmares like the election of Donald Trump as president from ever happening again. Yes, that's right. This brutal sex cult, where young women were dogged by their masters to stay on starvation diets so they'd be more attractive to Raniere, was pitched as a sort of Pantsuit Nation, a secret group advancing the cause of feminism.

Raniere's most persuasive evidence that his goal with NXIVM was to empower women, despite the misogynist sentiments that came out of his mouth, were the women who ran every aspect of his business, from cofounder Nancy Salzman on down. These women helped to sanitize his message and explain away misgivings students might have had while also acting as his enforcers, like when the Bronfmans pursued legal vendettas against ex-members. It is significant that women recruited other women for DOS, since it would probably have been a less appealing prospect had Raniere pitched it himself. The women high up in NXIVM could make legitimate claims on empowerment, although they paid a high price for it: Raniere's five codefendants, all of whom pled guilty rather than stand trial with him, were women.

Raniere's female deputies were caught in the same bind as his hero, the author Ayn Rand. In her view, in order for women to be totally free, they had to devalue traditionally feminine work, communication, and ways of knowing, subjecting themselves to the punishing dominion of logic and ambition. As Sam Anderson wrote of Rand in *New York* magazine in 2009, Rand saw herself as "a machine of pure reason, a free-market Spock," who claimed "that she could rationally explain every emotion she'd ever had." This triumph of stereotypically masculine values is linked directly with the emphasis both NXIVM and Rand placed on the righteousness of achieving success within the capitalist system. If you believe that time is money and that money is necessary for doing good in the world, then it follows that emotions, instincts, and physical needs would be subordinated to a numb efficiency and all-consuming self-discipline and self-denial. Rand is only one of the people who has examined the capitalist system and come to the conclusion that to succeed in a mechanized society, humans must become like the machines they rule over. This message is particularly pointed for women, who are seen as inherently emotionally fragile and erratic. In Cheryl Sandburg's 2013 corporate feminist manifesto *Lean In*, these female emotions are shown as a serious obstacle to women in business, albeit one that is easier to deal with than systemic inequality. (As the first chapter asks, "What would you do if you weren't afraid?") Sandburg does call out changes needed to remedy a sexist corporate culture, but her book also encourages women to disillusion themselves—to quit thinking they can "have it all" and expecting to advance professionally as quickly or smoothly as men in their same positions. "Having it all" is an obsession of corporate feminist literature, a euphemism for having a job and raising kids too, which is a financial choice that most women have no choice but to make. In fact, corporate feminism exists exclusively to reconcile a political paradox in the status of privileged women. If the thesis is Rand, the "free-market Spock," and the antithesis is the tradwife who quits a high powered job to raise eight children on a homestead, then the synthesis is Sandburg, the woman who acknowledges the difficulty in balancing traditional feminine roles with climbing the corporate ladder, and responds to these challenges with creativity that enhances her success in business. Sandburg refers to the corporate ladder as "the corporate jungle gym" in *Lean In,* offering a visual image of her essential advice, which is for women to blaze their own trail within strictly contained boundaries.

Lean In ordained Sandburg as the high priestess of corporate feminism, encapsulating as it did the philosophy's essential teaching: through ingenuity and self development, privileged women can achieve business success on par with that of men.

This should serve as evidence that women's equality has been achieved, so we need not question the systemic barriers to women's economic advancement and the unchecked nature of corporate power. This individualistic approach replaces the class solidarity of the women's movement with a trickle-down feminism, where elite women think wishfully that their success will intrinsically benefit marginalized women, all the while ensuring that the opposite is true. Not that leaning in is that sweet of a deal for most privileged women either. The corporate feminist glorification of career striving keeps women distracted and overwhelmed, too busy to hazard much of the introspection, compassion, or alarm that might motivate them to engage politically, if they weren't too exhausted for activism anyway.

As with so many things, NXIVM was a distillation of this effect. Members were trained to focus so monomaniacally on their goals that they had little time to question the ethical pitfalls of pyramid selling, the organization's regressive views of gender, and the exploitation of women Raniere was committing before their eyes. Raniere structured NXIVM as a consortium of interlocking businesses, charities, and projects, including a preschool, acting seminars, and an a cappella ensemble. This structure was for legal reasons, to ensure Raniere would be able to continue his work even if authorities shut down one of the organization's branches. But it was also his way of hiding his worst abuses and beta testing fringier ideas. He took a more overtly apocalyptic tone with his outreach in Mexico, where students were taught, according to *The New York Times*, "that Mr. Raniere had developed a sophisticated mathematical formula to predict that the world would end within 15 years."

In addition to the secrecy and confusion built into its arcane corporate structure, the self-interest the group preached must have kept members from asking questions about the organization. Salzman, Raniere's closest deputy and collaborator, reportedly had no idea about DOS, even though her daughter was in the organization's inner circle. This blindness predictably covered Raniere's worst offenses. Some of his trial's most horrifying details came from the testimony of a Mexican member the courts called Daniela, who moved to Albany when she was sixteen to work with NXIVM. She started having sex with Raniere when she was eighteen and soon learned of Raniere's sexual relationship with her underage sister, whom he called "Virgin Camila." At one point, Raniere convinced Daniela and her older sister, who was also sleeping with Raniere, to go to bed with him at the same time. Later, Raniere had Daniela's parents confine her to her room for two years for what he called an "ethical breach": her admission that she was attracted to a man other than him. All this abuse was compounded by the fact that Raniere had helped Daniela enter the country illegally. "I was without a doubt a captive from [the] moment I was illegal in the country," she said at trial.

One of the women featured in *The Vow* talks about being drawn into DOS by her desire to lose weight, with much of the "goal setting" and "accountability" the group promised revolving around the starvation diets the group pushed on her. Cult experts identify the restriction of food and sleep as common methods of thought control, since hungry, tired people are unlikely to see their situation clearly or have the strength to leave. But what are we to make of it when people join a cult seeking help to restrict the food they eat? NXIVM was not the first cult to emphasize personal responsibility and the limitlessness of human potential while simultaneously tightening its hold on every aspect of its members' lives. It could do this because the control the group exercised was primarily mental, creating, as Lawrence Wright said of Scientology, a "prison of belief." In a postfeminist paradigm, a thin body is the outward expression of self-control, a woman rising above human urges and taming her unruly body, showing she is capable of the self-denial that capitalist success requires. But if this is the motive, then could it really be said that the "self" is exercising control? This makes DOS a useful illustration of the dovetailing of two thought prisons, each masquerading as a kind of freedom: the intersection of cult indoctrination and capitalist ideology.

This is how I've come to see the NXIVM story: as one of the harbingers of the broader Postfeminist Apocalypse, a sign of how degraded feminist rhetoric has become. DOS was, for one thing, the horror movie version of a multilevel marketing (MLM) company. MLMs, which have received more attention in recent years on social media and podcasts and in YouTube videos as fraudulent get-rich-quick schemes specifically targeting women, use individual salespeople to sell makeup, leggings, essential oils, and a million other consumer products directly to their friends and family for a small commission. The real money is not in selling but in recruiting other salespeople who stand below you on the pyramid and will attract other recruits, all of whom owe you commission. Raniere ran his first illegal pyramid scheme in the early 1990s and signed a consent order with the attorney general of New York to never run another multilevel marketing company. He broke this order almost immediately, starting another MLM called Innovative Network whose members received discounts on "top-grade health products." Shortly after, in 1998, he started Executive Success Programs, where to move up the ranks, members had to aggressively recruit other students to take the ESP intensives, which were by invitation only. All of NXIVM's programs were extortionately expensive, with five-day intensives costing between $2,000 and $10,000, and students were pressured constantly to re-up, often going deep into debt. The only exception to this was DOS, which was, at least on the face of it, free: members could join for the low, low cost of naked pictures and a lifetime vow of submission. But they were still expected to recruit their own slaves, preferably women who were young, thin, and single.

It is extremely telling that Raniere used the MLM model for every venture he ever undertook, even enlisting a harem of sex slaves. He was drawn to an industry that targeted women's vulnerabilities and subordinated them to him, the imperial apex of the pyramid scheme. At least 99 percent of MLM sellers lose money, but these companies still recruit with the promise that prospective salespeople can grow their own business in their spare time. This sales pitch is targeted at women who have trouble working otherwise, often because they are caring for children, and takes advantage of the kinship networks women build among friends, neighbors, and relatives. Just as Raniere did with DOS, these companies are sure to couch their predation in the language of feminism, marketing themselves as empowering a new class of #girlbosses, even as they prey on women's economic precarity.

In the fall of 2020, at the same time everyone on Twitter was rapt by *The Vow*, Amy Coney Barrett entered the news cycle on a black stallion, one of the horsemen of the Postfeminist Apocalypse. (Who would be the other three horsemen? Camille Paglia, Hillary Clinton, and Margot Robbie as Barbie?) Barrett is the right-wing judge Donald Trump appointed to replace Ruth Bader Ginsburg on the Supreme Court, an obedient judicial foot soldier handpicked by the Federalist Society to advance its great conservative judicial fantasy: total adherence to the original intent of the framers of the Constitution. Strict constructionism has become one of the tenets of the Christian nationalism Barrett springs from, in seeming parallel to the Fundamentalist Christian belief that the Bible should be read literally. Constitutional originalism and biblical literalism are overtly connected in the minds of many on the far right, who, in a stance that would horrify many of the document's writers, hold that the Constitution is a divinely inspired work of pseudo-scripture.

Since the outset, when her law professor at Notre Dame secured her a clerkship with Justice Antonin Scalia, Barrett's career has been paved by men who saw her as a useful political tool. In a profile in *The New York Times*, Elizabeth Dias writes how Barrett benefited from a Republican initiative "to cultivate female and minority candidates for the courts to help counter the perception that the party was interested mainly in promoting white men." Trump had planned for years to nominate Barrett in the event of Ginsburg's death, setting up an obvious, if cheap, comparison between the two female judges. Opposition to her nomination was of course met with Republican whining about women supporting women, with the Republican senator Martha McSally saying, "You would normally have the feminists on the left lining up to defend her. So we're asking, where are those women?"

As Ellen Willis wrote in 1979 about the pro-life movement, "Its need to wrap misogyny in the rhetoric of social conscience and even feminism is actually a perverse tribute to the women's movement." The same is true now: as Barrett sealed the deal on the American Right's fifty-year quest to overturn *Roe v. Wade*, we were told that feminists were being hypocritical in our opposition to her. In truth, conservatives' clumsy use of rhetoric is an instinctive appeal to something more basic than the formalized women's movement. They are calling on women's powerful loyalty to one another, thus recognizing it as feminists' most potent tool. When the pro-life movement became ascendant in the late '70s, it was because of its brilliant methods of undermining that loyalty, most often by reframing abortion not "as a political issue affecting the condition of women," as Willis writes, but "as an abstract moral issue having solely to do with the rights of fetuses." Right-wingers may have learned caution from the feminist axiom that "the personal is political," since depersonalization is their tactic of choice in responding to feminist demands, encrypting their hatred of sex workers and trans people, for instance, in campaigns against pornography and "gender ideology."

Barrett belongs to a fringe Catholic sect called the People of Praise who famously used to call its women leaders "handmaids," though it stopped after Hulu started airing its series *The Handmaid's Tale*, possibly seeing it as a little on the nose. All members are assigned a male "head" who counsels them spiritually and practically; married women are "headed" by their husbands. If Barrett managed to pursue a career that is mostly foreclosed to women in her religious group, especially those who have seven children, there is no reason to believe she sees this as a right worth fighting for, her solidarity with other women having been thoroughly eroded by both her conservative indoctrination and adventures in leaning in. According to *The New York Times*, "[The People of Praise] is almost entirely run by men in part because it 'communicates to all men their shared responsibility for the life of the community,' ensuring men do not leave family and community matters to women." This statement also nods toward feminism, with its emphasis on men pitching in with domestic duties. But it can be interpreted as a radical rejection of the high status of women in even many conservative church communities, where they can gain positions of authority and influence through teaching, volunteering, and music ministry. As MLMs exploit close-knit networks of women for their buying power, conservative Christianity has been seeking to cut those networks off at the root, making women ever more directly beholden to men.

But when you look at all this manipulation up close, something startling becomes clear: they are afraid of us.

There was an unsettling symmetry to the Amy Coney Barrett hearings, an echoing dread many women felt even if they didn't examine it. Brett Kavanaugh's confirmation hearings were a notably ugly moment in the Trump presidency, in what was a daily stream of ugly moments. Kavanaugh had been credibly accused by multiple women of sexual misconduct and seemed likely to be blocked from the court by the country's newfound intolerance (albeit belated and uneven) for gendered violence and discrimination. At his hearings, Dr. Christine Blasey Ford testified before the Senate Judiciary Committee for four hours, calmly describing how Kavanaugh had sexually assaulted her when he was seventeen and she was fifteen. When it was Kavanaugh's turn to testify, he threw a disturbing tantrum where he cried, yelled that he liked beer, and whined that he may never be able to coach children's sports again. And still he was confirmed by a 52–48 vote in the Senate, with the moderate, pro-choice Republican Susan Collins giving a mealymouthed speech on the floor of the Senate defending her yes vote by saying that Kavanaugh had assured her that he would not vote to overturn *Roe v. Wade*. I can't be the only one who felt this like a blow to the chest. It was not only that Kavanaugh's outburst had gotten him what he wanted. It was the feeling that Kavanaugh's confirmation was the end of #MeToo as we knew it.

#MeToo was a wave of global feminist activism that began as a social media campaign encouraging victims of sexual assault and harassment to stand in solidarity. What the movement revealed was the power of victims when they spoke in concert, giving one another strength to divulge experiences they had been shamed or intimidated into silence about, and it ended the reigns of terror of many famous abusers, like Harvey Weinstein, Bill Cosby, and R. Kelly. It was a heady time, a sea change, when an avenue opened up for the wronged and disenfranchised to challenge people whose power had once been unassailable. The failure represented by Kavanaugh's confirmation was like a sudden shaft of fluorescent light illuminating the failures of the movement. Now, along with Barrett, he had been handed the power to make life harder for millions of women, and Chief Justice John Roberts's activist court has been working manically since Trump appointed them, with the conservative justices' shameful decision to overturn *Roe v. Wade* as only the most infamous item on their agenda.

It is easy to recognize now that the #MeToo message was muddled and undermined. Despite all the conversation it generated, feminists failed to emphasize that there is a larger system keeping women on the margins of American life, of which sexual violence is only one tactic of enforcement and for which justice against individual abusers serves as a salve and not a cure. Conservatives acted like the sexual assault accusations against Kavanaugh were a way of getting him thrown out on a technicality, and in some way, maybe they were right. Sexual abuse has been reduced to a way of classifying bad people, aberrations who needed to be punished, rather than an overwhelming pattern that reflects the values of the culture we all subscribe to. And despite how it may have seemed when #MeToo was toppling giants of the entertainment industry, its power would be more difficult to extend to those in political office. In retrospect, Anita Hill's testimony at Clarence Thomas's confirmation hearings in 1991 was a precedent for how little anything revealed at these hearings would affect senators' votes. He had been confirmed as a Supreme Court justice after allegations of sexual harassment that were more serious, systematic, and documented than those against Kavanaugh, who after all was only a teenager at the time of the alleged assault. Despite anger at the abuses of Donald Trump being one of the catalysts of the #MeToo movement, he, along with Bill Clinton, is one of the obvious examples of how unpersuasive sexual misconduct allegations are to voters. Democrats were convinced, delusionally as it turns out, that Trump's comments about grabbing women by the pussy would prevent his election in the first place, and none of the half dozen other allegations that have come out since then stopped him from receiving the 2024 Republican nomination for president.

A person could be forgiven for falling for the political theater of Supreme Court confirmation hearings, in which senators are supposedly trying to ensure that only those who are paragons of erudition and moral judgment receive a lifetime appointment. Collins claimed to have been persuaded by Kavanaugh's stated position on *Roe v. Wade*, not allowing either the testimony of his accuser or his behavior at his hearing to throw his credibility on that issue into doubt. He lied to her about this, as we could have predicted, and he probably lied about other things during his testimony. But I doubt Collins has lost much sleep over her decision—it was never about Kavanaugh anyway, never about one man, one lie, or one case, but a vast system of connections and concessions that have kept her in power, maintaining her tenuous place in the Republican Party. Those who are hung up on the impact one man can have on the lives of others are playing small ball. Yes, the decisions of one Supreme Court justice would seem to upend the lives of normal people all the time, but that just shows how little power most of us are really playing with.

Since the height of its cultural power, #MeToo has devolved into a circular conversation about celebrity "cancel culture," abandoning exactly the women who most need defending, those at the intersection of race, class, and gender oppressions who are not only the most likely to be sexually harassed and assaulted on the job but the most likely to suffer from abortion bans, the lack of childcare and paid parental leave, and the assault on affordable healthcare. In other words, when there was a national conversation around gendered violence, there was a failure to overtly integrate it with the other issues at the heart of the feminist cause. There were barriers to this, of course, one of which was that the movement's power was in its ad hoc coalition united by the barest of feminist demands: Stop harassing us. Stop raping us. Anonymous hotel workers and Fox News anchorwomen were gathered, uncomfortably and temporarily, under the same banner. If some of us saw the inconsistency in fighting for women to be able to safely spew hatred at the favored TV station of a right-wing presidential administration, it still seemed like a net good, not to mention a source of delectable schadenfreude, to see the consummate creep who had run the network, Roger Ailes, go down in flames.

NXIVM is a #MeToo story, too, with high-profile cases of serial abusers like Harvey Weinstein causing authorities to take Raniere's crimes more seriously. There had been newspaper articles as early as 2012 detailing NXIVM corruption and accusing Raniere of violence, notably including the statutory rape of a twelve-year-old and two fifteen-year-olds when he was still running Consumers' Byline. But when former DOS slaves took their story to *The New York Times* in 2017, they were told that it wasn't necessarily newsworthy, at the same time police told them that the branding of their flesh was consensual. After #MeToo, the tide turned quickly against Raniere, with an exposé in the *Times*, the exodus of dozens of members from NXIVM, and, soon enough, federal charges.

This was the kind of ambiguous happy ending that those of us who have consumed enough crime stories are familiar with. Judging by his track record, it seems like locking up Raniere will prevent him from preying on more victims. But the recourse the justice system offers for the victims he already has pretty much ends there. Not to mention that a common tactic of cult leaders is to make sure everyone is complicit in their crimes, so that members must reckon not only with their own trauma but the overwhelming guilt of inflicting trauma on others when they leave the organization, an MLM model of psychic injury.

Maybe this is why the end of the NXIVM story is less satisfying to me now than when I first watched *The Vow*. The show's second season follows Nancy Salzman, who is initially defiant, defending the teachings she devised and the company that she ran as a force for good that Raniere twisted to evil ends. She seems to slowly begin to see the manipulation built into the curriculum and to confront the fact that she herself was brainwashed, controlled, and manipulated by Raniere. At first, I resisted the show's attempts to humanize her, showing her taking care of her aging parents and the deep devotion of daughters, despite the fact she got them involved with NXIVM. But when she was handed her three-and-a-half-year sentence, it was nothing like the jubilant scenes of Raniere's sentencing coming down. It was heartbreaking to hear her talk about having to move her ninety-two-year-old mother into assisted living, since she couldn't live independently without Salzman's care. This isn't to say that Salzman wasn't guilty of crimes and abuses, and she may never take accountability for many of them. But the roles we see her play on *The Vow* are uncomfortably familiar: the perfect deputy, the fixer, the cheerleader, the team player, the apologist. How many of us, in the organizations we are a part of, have traded status for complicity; have remained loyal to tradition over trusting our intuition; have chosen feeling useful over questioning what ends we're working toward?

Clearly there is more ambiguity between victim and perpetrator than our culture would like to allow for. NXIVM students would vow, "There are no ultimate victims; therefore, I will not choose to be a victim." This is an excellent way of convincing the people you are victimizing not to see it that way, but it is also a common refrain of contemporary American self-help, where daytime TV shows and inspirational speakers encourage people to forgive even the worst injuries and move on, not to be victims but survivors. #MeToo did important work to break this stigma, although at times it encouraged another kind of black-and-white thinking, making the same mistake of Second Wave feminists when they cast women as the perennial victims of men, with some in the 1970s women's liberation movement categorically describing penises as weapons. This is done for an understandable reason: in a puritanical society invested in the sexual purity of women, more outrage and attention can be drummed up for gendered abuses with a sexual tinge. This single focus on sexual violence ignores the other patterns of violence that undergird American society and limits the reparation possible to the realm of singular perpetrators and victims. The ultimate moral inconsistency of cancel culture is that a person can be canceled for rape but not for dropping a bomb.

This small-minded morality also makes feminists the uncomfortable bedfellows of the American justice system, which is just about the worst possible arena for the reconciliation of feminist demands that one can imagine. One of the weaknesses of #MeToo was its true crime dynamic, where stories were framed as whodunits, cases that could be closed when the perpetrators were put to justice. There developed an unfortunate focus on throwing abusers in prison, an effort that rang with dissonance as a reckoning with the racist police state and incarceration system was happening at the exact same time. The carceral direction of the movement also degraded the concept of rape culture, which became a topic of conversation in the early 2010s as a way to understand the passive voice surrounding victimization. If three out of five women are sexually assaulted, and most of those assaults are committed by people the women know, that means that a huge number of men—our friends, brothers, fathers, colleagues, boyfriends, and husbands; people we know to be kind, reliable, smart, and honest—are rapists. The idea of rape culture attempts to explain our rituals of dating and sex as an alienating mess we all inherited but none of us consented to, a process that frequently robs people of all genders of their humanity, derived from an ideology of power that can cause otherwise good people to commit horrible violence. That was the initial message of the #MeToo hashtag when it overtook social media: this is ordinary, it is happening all the time, right under your nose.

I return to the image of the women of NXIVM working frantically for their own empowerment, unaware of the abuse that was going on under their noses, even when it was happening to *them*. They represent all the women on the postfeminist treadmill, where liberation can be seen but never reached, no matter how fast you run. People often criticize so-called choice feminism because it benefits privileged women for whom more choices are available. We don't talk enough about how an emphasis on supporting individual women's choices means that some women will choose to hurt other women, whether directly, as the only conservative woman on the Supreme Court has done, or indirectly, through our complacency in propping up abusive systems. In an individualist paradigm, the only aims we can unite around are the things we don't want, the violence that all women are terrified of.

Real solidarity will require a renewed focus on the things we do want, and we must dream bigger than the consumer goods and status symbols that are the contemporary markers of a successful life. Aims like socialized medicine, free childcare, government income for stay-at-home parents, prison abolition, and an end to the military-industrial complex were there at the radical origins of the women's movement of the 1960s, and we're still waiting for them after six decades of lucky women achieving their own empowerment and never looking back. But #MeToo may have taken us further in that direction than it appears at the moment. In revealing that the executives and icons held up as the paragons of capitalist success had engaged in the systematic exploitation of women, the movement raised the question of the other kinds of exploitation they may have engaged in to get there. (It appears to me that #MeToo was a precursor to the successful writers' and actors' union strikes of 2023. Hollywood executives were in a weakened position after decades where they were used to carte blanche, finally being made to answer for how they treated their employees.) #MeToo also showed that the old Second Wave adage still holds true: sisterhood is powerful. This is the irony of NXIVM, too, that as much as members allowed the cult to efface their identities, the groupthink isolated them from one another. The most poignant subject of *The Vow* is the unity victims showed after they escaped Raniere's control and their drive to help other people get out of the group. They prove that we cannot save ourselves. We can only save one another.

4

STARDATE

1. YESTERDAY'S ENTERPRISE

I remember when I learned that my generation would be called the millennials.

As a teenager, I scoffed at the thought that this term would ever be widely used. Yes, my childhood was marked by the turning of the millennium. I listened to the album *Millennium* by the Backstreet Boys thousands of times and watched the "slime drop" on Nickelodeon on December 31, 1999, with millions of other children I was not yet thinking of as sharing my demographic. "Millennial" has an apocalyptic ring, invoking the wacky fundamentalist Christians who invaded Massachusetts four hundred years ago and in some ways started this whole unhinged American project. Yes, my adolescence was marked by apocalyptic thinking, since right after this hyped-up milestone for the Gregorian calendar, we descended into a decade of militarism, patriotic paranoia, Evangelical fervor, and cultural barrenness. That was also the decade the winters started getting shorter. I saw it with my own eyes. No snow until January.

Then I was young. The things I liked were the things young people liked. It had not yet occurred to me that there would be people even younger, who would have their own icons and crazes, and then people my age would be just another generalizable slice on the pie chart. When millennials became the villains of every trend piece, I felt an itchy despair that has only broadened as we transform from pesky kids to underachieving thirtysomethings. There is something humiliating about being a product of history. Generational thinking means not even your trauma is your own, and what you love is not a product of personal taste but ever more sophisticated and invasive kinds of marketing.

I rarely feel more like a millennial than when I am streaming TV, particularly on a laptop, in the prone position in bed. "Streaming" is an apt dystopian metaphor, indicating a passive flow of consumption with no beginning and no end. Between 2017 and 2020, I moved from Boston to Memphis, got married, got a full-time job, and published a book. My material circumstances were changed, but my physical attitude was the same: you could find me flat in the prone position, with my laptop resting on my hip or even my chest, zapping '90s TV shows directly into my brain.

I watched the six seasons of *Sex and the City*, a show I had never seen even a second of. I was nine when it started airing, and my parents didn't have HBO anyway, and neither did anyone else I knew in my entire home state of Idaho. For some reason I had always assumed it was vapid, crass, and problematic, which at this point sounds like another way of saying "fun." When I finally watched it, I found that it was all of these, and enjoyably so, in addition to being one of the most comforting TV comedies ever created, at least for a white American woman in her early thirties. The show was based on the bestselling essay collection of the same name by Candace Bushnell, a book of dishy New York vignettes drawn from her sex and relationships column in *The New York Observer*. Following four single women in turn-of-the-millennium New York, *Sex and the City* is a picaresque of set pieces: brunch spots, nightclubs, fancy parties, yoga classes, galleries, artist lofts, the ballet.

The show is singular in how it emphasizes fun as the point of life. Work is important to all four main characters, yet we rarely see them there. We never see their families of origin, and (other than the uptight and conventional Charlotte) they don't worry much about marrying and starting families of their own. The show's plots give primacy to what we have been trained to consider secondary: sex, friendship, adventure, and expressions of style. Despite the creator and head writer both being men, the show had a groundbreaking writers' room of primarily women, and they wrote by a rule that if a storyline strained credulity it had to have happened to one of them or someone they knew. In this way they somehow created a show that was both a campy farce and a mirror on women's lives.

My other virtual happy place was 350 years in the future aboard the exploratory starship USS *Enterprise* on *Star Trek: The Next Generation*. *Next Generation* played nearly constantly on syndicated TV in my childhood. My dad is a Trekker from way back, and as a six-year-old I was mostly fascinated by the range of father figures in the *Next Generation* cast—from Data, the android sweetie pie, to the impossibly wise Captain Jean-Luc

Picard, a sexy surrogate grandpa with a gleaming bald head—a small Elektra could choose from. I have never been into sci-fi (when it comes to genre fiction, I'll choose the crime thriller every time) and am always amazed at how easily my husband and dad follow the show's byzantine plots, many of which involve warp coils. It doesn't help that the entire premise is generally explained in the first three minutes of the episode, the time when I am paying absolutely no attention. Despite the show's action, which includes strange alien races and starship battles most episodes, I found it wonderfully vibey and somnolent. The crew members of the *Enterprise*, no longer only representing potential daddies for me, were like soothing and often boring friends who let me zone out while they talked about Jefferies tubes again.

Despite forming the template for contemporary science fiction and essentially inventing fan culture, *Star Trek* began in 1966 as a low-rated curiosity that was green-lit only because Lucille Ball wanted a science fiction pilot to film on the Desilu Productions lot. It was conceived as a space western, where the roving crew came into contact with strange new cultures each episode, led by the hunky and swaggering captain James Kirk. The show was influenced by the Cold War space race, in which the United States and the USSR both took their imperial ambitions to the skies, dreaming of spheres of influence that could be measured in light-years. The show felt more futuristic than science fiction ever had, in part because of its diverse cast, which included a Black woman as communications officer. *Star Trek* creator Gene Roddenberry wanted the show to be political from the beginning, using the *Enterprise* as his Trojan horse to sneak in anti-war, anti-racist, and pro-woman messages on to prime-time TV. The original series never had high ratings and eked out three seasons only because of letter-writing campaigns from rabid fans. In the decades that followed, though, it became one of TV's first cult hits, developing a devout following in syndication. Only after the success of the *Star Trek* feature films, in 1987, did Roddenberry agree to try for a reboot, a new version of the *Enterprise* with a whole new cast, reflecting the social quandaries of a new age.

As *Star Trek* and *Sex and the City* intermingled in my Trump-addled brain, I quickly realized that they had similarities that went beyond how well they paired with marijuana (read as: extremely well). I first noticed that each episode is figured as a sort of "entry": In *Next Generation*, episodes usually begin with a voice-over from Picard's captain's log, narrating the crew's mission. In *Sex and the City*, episodes are interspersed with voice-over from Carrie Bradshaw's eponymous relationships column in the fictional newspaper *The New York Star*. In this way, both shows are framed around ethical questions, like fables probing the complexities of modern social and technological problems.

Furthermore, the two shows are not mere morality tales but products of progressive political agendas: an anti-capitalist, pro-science humanism for *Star Trek* and Third Wave feminism for *Sex and the City*. *Next Generation*'s peaceful, productive future where space explorers opt to spend their leisure time reading hardback books instead of gorging themselves on the infinite exotic pleasures that could be synthesized on the Holodeck was comforting to me when the distraction machines in all our pockets conspired to create one of the most unjust, reactionary, and anti-intellectual ages this country had ever known, as exemplified by our social media addict president, whose favorite book was his own ghostwritten memoir. Unfortunately, *Sex and the City* was radical for simply putting four women on TV at the same time. But it also enthusiastically, if sometimes clunkily, depicted its characters experimenting with sexual taboos including sex toys, anal sex, group sex, and bisexuality in a way that had never been seen before on mainstream TV, particularly when centering on women's experience.

It is not lost on me that I was using advanced computer technology to re-create the experience of watching syndicated TV during listless afternoon hours when I was home sick from school. This feeling is these video services' main draw, the dream of entering the stream and becoming one with the television, allowing it to massage the baser parts of your brain. Corporate entertainment in the sequel century has more to do with who mediates its distribution than who produces it, with an ever more crowded field of streaming platforms fighting over art that is sometimes debased even by its creators as "content" or "intellectual property." There have been many original hits for these streaming platforms, but their closely guarded properties are nostalgia vehicles: the most painful shots fired in the so-called streaming wars were the exodus of *Friends*, Netflix's most popular show, to HBO Max (now Max), and the announcement that every season of *The Simpsons* would be available to stream on Disney+.

People have long complained about a movie landscape crowded with sequels, but streaming has created an atmosphere of infinite reruns, with random reboots of shows like *Full House*, *Arrested Development*, and *Gilmore Girls* seeming less to move the story along than to point backward at the original, an encouragement to, as Netflix always urges me, "Watch It Again."

I know many people who are living in an eternal rewatch of *The Office* (the pop star Billie Eilish said in 2019 that she had watched every episode of the show twelve times), taking some comfort I don't understand in simulating the purgatorial feeling of spending every day at an actual office.

This boundless buffet of TV hits has been an interesting experiment in what "holds up," judged mostly by three criteria: (1) what still looks good; (2) what is still funny; (3) whose political faux pas are easiest to ignore. *Friends*, with its remarkable cast of six very cute, very funny actors, ticks the first two boxes so well that the fact that there was only one Black guest star in ten seasons can be forgiven by its generation Z devotees. *Sex and the City* is a streaming-era treasure because, despite political content that ranged from arguably progressive to plainly offensive, it cultivated the feel of a classic. The first episode was directed by the great New York filmmaker Susan Seidelman, whose films *Smithereens* and *Desperately Seeking Susan* defined the city's downtown post-punk scene. *Sex and the City* layered the aesthetics of problematic faves *Annie Hall* and *Breakfast at Tiffany's* on an '80s club kid dream, uptown and downtown locked in a permanent embrace.

Much of this has to do with the show's fashion, which is its most important legacy. The writer Anna König notes that there is seemingly no expiration date to the fashion press's references to *Sex and the City*: magazines have slavered over the show's clothing continually since it aired. This enduring interest seems paradoxical, König writes, since the fashion system by definition thrives on novelty—otherwise, none of us would ever buy new clothes. But the clothing on *Sex and the City* is not fashion—it is costume. Carrie Bradshaw's clothes in particular are a prime example of the show privileging fun over practicality. It's less getting dressed than playing dress-up.

Carrie is an always delightful mélange of irresistible *Vogue* girl and fashion victim. She is often daringly simple and undone, wearing only a body-hugging dress with bra straps showing and $2,000 heels instead of jewelry. Some of the show's immortal outfits are the fugliest, though, like when Carrie wore hot pants with a velour tube top with a black trench coat and a grandpa's flat-brimmed hat. The actor who played Carrie, Sarah Jessica Parker, and the show's legendary costume designer, Patricia Field, drew inspiration from the classic British spoof *Absolutely Fabulous* and the capital-F fashion the show's hot mess main characters wore. "Straight types just don't get the irony," Field said of the show's clothes.

But "irony" would imply that the audience sees something that Carrie doesn't, that the show is laughing at her sacrificing herself on the altar of fashion. I see the opposite in *Sex and the City*'s most daring costumes: a challenge to the watcher's eye that subtly estranges the show from contemporary New York and the mundane world as we know it. Carrie is living in a fairy tale of her own writing, or maybe on her own planet.

2. TIME'S ARROW

This feeling of timelessness plays out literally on *Next Generation*, despite the strong early '90s vibe of the cast's feathered haircuts and the ship's DOS-prompt computer interface. The show is set in the year 2370, but its plots rarely concern themselves with future versions of Earth. Instead, the future is more associated with the black vacuum of space. This is the constant view through the ship's many windows, one that I cannot imagine promoted good mental health among the crew. The *Enterprise* exists not in but *on* time, with its impossibly fast warp drive obliterating the relationship between time and space as we know it, literally warping space to travel faster than light.

This innovation opens *Next Generation* writers to other surreal engagements with the laws of time and space, with plots revolving around wormholes, temporal loops, an interdimensional trickster god, and super-realistic, time-compressing holograms, like the one that convinces Picard he has lived fifty years as an iron weaver on a distant planet. This must have reflected some of the postmodern exhaustion of the '90s, when advances in physics and computing more than ever revealed the slippery and subjective nature of reality. These time-bending episodes also seem to intentionally undermine *Star Trek*'s utopian vision, concerning itself not only with a peaceful future but all its possible alternatives. There are plots where the *Enterprise* encounters alternate universe versions of itself where Starfleet is still at war with the Klingons or Captain Picard is a professional failure. Progress is on a razor's edge with ruin, always tenuous and reversible.

While engaging in my favorite pastime, trawling EBSCOhost for academic articles about *Star Trek*, I found a wonderful piece published in 1994 by a mysterious and possibly pseudonymous scholar named F. S. Braine. (His terse bio identifies him only as "an environmental planner with E.E.A. Inc. in New York," and online he is basically nowhere to be found, except as the author of this article. I am making an uneducated guess by assigning him masculine pronouns.) Braine connects *Star Trek* to the American tradition of technological utopianism that dates to the turn of the last century. In the utopian novels that were published in the 1880s and '90s, a technologically advanced society was convenient, clean, and orderly. This optimistic vision betrayed underlying anxiety about the changes that accompanied rapid industrialization, urbanization, and technological breakthroughs like the use of electric power. These works reflected a certain "*fin de siecle* melancholy," as Braine writes, one that is all too familiar now, when innovations like the smartphone, the social internet, and cloud computing have transformed our experience of entertainment, work, and privacy, and climate change and environmental devastation loom as the direct consequence of industrial "progress."

There was a social use in a vision of the scientific, rational future as a fait accompli, illustrating the end toward which all these painful societal changes were aiming. *Star Trek*, as Braine writes, serves the same function, sparing us "the dreaded transition" into the future, to create the ideal "entertainment for a nervous age." Something seems to have changed in science fiction's relationship to the future from one century to the next, however. As David Graeber writes in his essay "Of Flying Cars and the Declining Rate of Profit," those reading speculative fiction at the turn of the twentieth century would have been taking in a vision of the future that more or less came true, a world of "flying machines, rocket ships, submarines, radio, and television." Graeber's essay is about the peculiar disappointment that plagued the children of the decades after World War II that the high-tech future they were promised was never realized. This future included not only flying cars but hoverboards, intergalactic space exploration, robot maids, body modification implants, and food replicators.

Graeber writes how people scoff at his complaints that these technologies never materialized, casting him as either childish or ungrateful, a spoilsport refusing to acknowledge that we live in an age of technological marvels. But with the discontinuing of the American space program, we abandoned the project that most exemplified American futurism. Graeber writes that despite popular narratives attempting to convince us that we have arrived in the future, the most consequential innovations since World War II are "technologies of simulation," allowing us to stream impossibly real representations of space battles onto the tiny screens that live inside our pockets. These entertainments are so well devised that we have all but accepted that dreamworlds are there for us to consume, but we should not actually expect to live in one.

Despite the staying power that the *Star Trek* franchise has enjoyed for the past sixty years, I am beginning to see why it is the only notable utopia American popular culture has produced in that time. Just like the dystopian fiction that has gained more purchase in American media, utopia always contains a social message, and it is risky to explicitly create a fictional world to be idealized and worked toward. Conceptions of the future and where society is headed are collective, contested, and crucial to our ideas about the present. *Star Trek*'s creators bore the responsibility of writing a prescription for what in contemporary society should stay and go, and it is often the elements in *Star Trek* that feel familiar to the way we live now, rather than its fanciful sci-fi departures, that are the most suspect. Why does Starfleet still use a rigid military hierarchy in this peaceful future? Why are the highest-ranking women officers on *Next Generation* in stereotypically feminine nurturer roles, as doctor and counselor? And why did that counselor wear a sexy skintight body suit instead of a uniform, despite holding the rank of lieutenant commander?

As Graeber writes, our concept of the future is "like an alternative dimension, a dream-time, a technological Elsewhere." Any undertaking that imagines it is freighted with our hopes, fears, fantasies, and expectations. But in writing this piece, it has come into focus for me just how much nostalgia creates a kind of sacred time, too, another arena where our dissatisfaction with the present can give way to fanciful dreams and unnamed longings. This is another way of thinking about what "holds up": the most seductive mental images of the future and past, like those found in old TV shows, are the ones that speak to our wishes and beliefs about our own time. Carrie Bradshaw's outfits are a frantic collage of referents: French and Italian fashion, vintage flea market finds, nameplate necklace and gold hoop earrings appropriated from Black New Yorkers, visible underwear. It speaks to our current idealized life on the internet, where eclecticism indicates cultural capital. But Carrie, in her resistance to quit smoking and "get on email," in her romantic daydreams of dressing like Audrey Hepburn and going to the ballet, knows she is a dying breed, a vestige of an old New York where a girl could mix business with pleasure over long martini lunches. The show's reluctance to move into the twenty-first century validates our own weariness of it, like a vision of Pandora's box, unopened.

It is strange to remember that *Next Generation* is also a nostalgia vehicle, one of the first of nearly endless reboots appealing to the most sentimental of all generations, the baby boomers. Set a hundred years later than the original series, its new vision of the future—influenced by Carl Sagan, quantum physics, and the early tech industry—directly revised the 1960s popular imagination. That future was out of date, without its advancements actually being achieved. This is a loop it seems we're stuck in as a culture, like one of the temporal disturbances from an episode of *Next Generation*. We continually revise our ideas about the future and the past so that we can stay stubbornly in any time but now. It was inevitable that CBS would pick up the *Next Generation* story with *Star Trek: Picard* in 2019, and *Sex and the City* made its return with 2021's reboot *And Just Like That . . .* Unfortunately, all this cultural recycling is delaying the inevitable: a reckoning with the ideologies of the twentieth century and our long-running refusal to admit that the future has arrived to claim us.

3. GREAT SEXPECTATIONS

I grew up three hundred miles from the nearest city with a million people, so I never grew up calling anywhere "the city," but this phrase often indicates the suburbs' focal point, those on the edges longing for the epicenter. Maybe this is why *Sex and the City*'s lessons often feel a bit remedial. Season one has a hilarious episode about the brave new world of rabbit vibrators, and the next week "The Baby Shower" aired, a similarly ballsy condemnation of suburban motherhood as a lobotomizing cult. But the next episode shows Carrie fretting over whether her accidentally farting in front of her boyfriend has made him lose all desire for her. I have trouble believing that any woman who has reached the age of thirty—one whose *job* is writing about sex and relationships—believes she has successfully created the illusion that she never farts.

Used to these madcap storylines, the *Sex and the City* fan might find the book it is based on a bitter pill to swallow. Compiled from Candace Bushnell's column of the same name from *The New York Observer*, the book is a dark and bizarre look at dating in 1990s New York, where men are pathologically childish, cruel, and self-centered, and women are domineering, striving, and manipulative. "Relationships in New York are about detachment," one interviewee tells Bushnell, and they would have to be, when she is writing case studies of men who are fixated on dating models and women who, when they get the family they've schemed for, are incestuously obsessed with their own infants. Bret Easton Ellis is said to be the basis for one of the book's pseudonymous characters (bad-boy novelist "River Wilde," LOL), and Bushnell's subjects are all American psychos, people who have been made monstrous by an atmosphere of ambition, competition, and insecurity, both in social and economic spheres.

The dark edge in Bushnell's writing reflects less a brave new world than a world that is the hideous extension of the old one. She references Edith Wharton's novels of New York often, marveling at the excesses of a new Gilded Age like the one Wharton chronicled, where New York "high society" is a fickle system of hierarchies and arcane codes of conduct. As far as I could tell, *The Age of Innocence* is about two people who spend a lifetime not fucking, out of a deep sense of propriety, duty to family, and a paradoxical devotion to each other. ("I wanted *Madame Bovary*," I told my husband after finishing it, "and I got *Madame*

Very Boring.") *Sex and the City*, on the other hand, is about a world where love, the most abundant substance in the universe, is profoundly scarce, and people feel no sense of duty except to their own images, bank accounts, and addictions.

The other reference Bushnell gets the most mileage out of is to the legendary *Cosmopolitan* editor Helen Gurley Brown's *Sex and the Single Girl*, from which the title *Sex and the City* is drawn. Brown's 1962 how-to guide for modern single women to dominate both in relationships and at the office was radical in one way, advising women to cherish being single rather than seeing it as a sign of their deficiency. The book also foresaw (or maybe wrote the script for) a generation of girlbosses, casting women's femininity and sexiness as their greatest tools for achieving liberation, since they allow them to manipulate men. Brown's archetypes of the men one meets on the dating scene like the "Don Juan," the "divorcing man," and the "homosexual" become Bushnell's (and Carrie Bradshaw's) humorous shorthands like "modelizers" and "Bicycle Boys." By the time *Sex and the City* was published in 1996, Brown's midcentury ideas of gender—with men cast as insensitive, impatient, and oafish and women as sexy, silly, and scheming—had calcified, constraining the childish, unfeeling fuckboys and desperate gold diggers and frigid career women of Bushnell's New York.

This jokey pessimism about heterosexual relationships is the subject of much "chick lit," an essentially 1990s genre of popular literature (of which *Sex and the City* is one notable example), concerning itself with the impossible situation of single, straight women who wanted to achieve some sacred nexus of social freedom, professional success, and romantic bliss. Standing in the way of this dream were the rules of feminine behavior they had been taught to live by, the punishing standards of beauty they were held to, and men's wholesale refusal to acquiesce to even the most minor of feminist demands.

These books are comedies of manners, commenting through satire on the contradictory status of women in modern culture. Meghan Daum wrote that *Bridget Jones's Diary* "concerns itself almost entirely with the neurotic fallout of popular women's culture," but of course that is the point of the book, that Helen Gurley Brown's archetypal swinging single girl was an oppressive fiction, and her perfect job, apartment, body, and emotional equanimity were not achievable for almost anyone. But chick lit did not provide solutions for this feminist impasse even as it lampooned it, just as Jane Austen was not engaged in dismantling the British class system. In *Bridget Jones's Diary*, her Mr. Darcy acts almost as deus ex machina: a nice guy comes along not to question why women have settled for so little but to signal that the story is over.

Chick lit both reflects and critiques essentialist ideas about gender and relationships that were so widespread in the '90s that *Men Are from Mars, Women Are from Venus* was the highest-selling self-help book of the decade. The situation was ripe for comedy of the laugh-or-you'll-cry variety: despite rounding on the second millennium CE, despite 60 percent of women working outside the home, despite powerful feminist and gay liberation movements in preceding decades, there was still a belief that heterosexual marriage and family were the apex of fulfillment in American life. Emily Witt writes in her book *Future Sex*, a collection of essays on how tech has shaped sexuality in the twenty-first century, about how free love is a common trope of early science fiction, representing as it did an innovative and complete break from current social norms. "Like outer space, the prospect of free love was always there," Witt writes, "humans just had to figure out how to make it hospitable to our needs." This attitude is present in *Star Trek*, though it does not seem to be an integral part of the series' philosophy. On *Next Generation*, the crew members of the *Enterprise* are all heterosexual and most primly single. (The swashbuckling Commander Riker is a refreshing exception. He seems to be the only one who takes advantage of his travels around the galaxy to have affairs with sexy aliens.) The woman in the one married couple on board spends what feels like entire seasons heavily pregnant and then has a messy birth in the ship's bar during a system failure. Like many people these days, Starfleet officers seem chill about the prospect of nonmonogamy but not up to trying it for themselves.

My friend told me that whenever she watches *Star Trek*, she rants to her husband about how ridiculous it is that women on the *Enterprise* still experience nine-month pregnancies exactly like we do now. With their super-advanced medical tech, why wouldn't they have remote incubation or a shortened gestation period, at least for those working on spaceships? For the same reason, I suppose, that there is still controversy over IVF and other forms of fertility treatments, nearly fifty years after the first test tube baby. Despite how human industry has eliminated or degraded the world's wild spaces, liberally meddling in the life cycles of animal and plant life, technologies that intervene on human sexuality and reproduction are still considered "playing God." Sex is deeply if cynically intertwined in current ideas of what is natural and sacred, which is probably also why the only kind of plastic surgery politicians are interested in legislating on is the kind that changes the look and function of a person's genitals. This appeal to nature baldly reflects patriarchal fears about the status of women if they were unburdened of the threat of pregnancy and the obligations of child-rearing. Witt writes in *Future Sex* how the men who created the first birth control pill designed it so the patient would still have a completely unnecessary monthly period, simply because it seemed unnatural to eliminate it—and this is still a common feature of contraceptives today. It is exactly decisions like this that have kept women bound to the cult of motherhood when technology could have expanded our ideas of parenthood, family, and female identity. As usual, in the struggle between modernity and tradition, women's roles and bodies are the concession we make to the past.

The issues that *Star Trek* broaches allegorically and *Sex and the City* explores through satire were real, and painful enough to keep *Men Are from Mars, Women Are from Venus* on the bestseller list. But they are also self-reinforcing. It takes no more gender theory than intuition to notice that we all contain masculine and feminine attributes, and "man" and "woman" are not always useful categories for unique human beings, particularly in our idiosyncratic intimate relationships. How many people did not realize they lived in a world where men and women were so different that they might as well come from planets seventy-five million miles apart until they were told?

As Susan Faludi illustrated exhaustively in *Backlash*, ideological forces in the 1980s and '90s, as incarnated not only in governments but by academia, journalism, and popular entertainment, were highly invested in promoting the questions of sexuality and gender as a dangerous and unsolvable mess, making cleaving to traditional family structures and gender roles a can't-live-with-them, can't-live-without-them situation. There exists underneath this message a reproach of twentieth-century radical movements in general, although the women's movement was a popular punching bag: life was absurd, liberation was impossible, and compromise was the only way forward, even when we were compromising our deepest desires. The anguish lacing through the satire-obsessed '90s burns like a hangover, at the same time mocking and cherishing the inert residue of hope that history might keep moving forward, rather than oscillating stupidly between revolution and revanchism.

4. FUTURE IMPERFECT

In fact, many governments at that time were attempting a political stance that combined revolution and revanchism as if they were never opposed. The 1990s in the United States and western Europe were marked by the politics of the Third Way, a (supposedly) center-left movement seeking to inject the welfare state with neoliberal ideals of free trade and entrepreneurship, thus creating not a compromise between right and left but a wholesale rejection of the paradigm of a political spectrum in favor of a new politics of pragmatism. In practice, this meant global free trade, the gutting of welfare programs, and the growing political and cultural status of multinational corporations. These reforms were by no means irrelevant to women, and on balance they were negative, particularly for the poor women who were the predominant beneficiaries of these decimated welfare programs and staffed the world's factories with their debasingly cheap labor. But there was a small group of women who fared better, finding in the Third Way an ideology that encouraged them to seek empowerment at work and traditional stability at home.

The media theorist Stéphanie Genz has identified postfeminism, the form of feminism that dominated popular culture in the 1990s and 2000s, as feminism's "Third Way/ve." American women stood uneasily on ground Second Wave feminists had seized for them but found that identifying with a leftist political movement felt increasingly uncool and irrelevant. Feminism, with all its group manifestos and platitudes about solidarity and sisterhood, had not seemed to allow for all the vagaries of women's actual experience. This was most true for poor, queer, non-white, trans, and disabled women, but those in dominant classes also found they were still not totally represented, particularly when their life choices were considered traditional or self-demeaning. Third Wave feminism as a revolutionary movement was founded to answer these questions in the 1990s, and it was pluralistic from the beginning, with various communities under its umbrella advocating women's sexual liberation, interrogation of the racial hierarchies within feminism, and the importance of paying witness to the vast multiplicity of women's real lives. Postfeminism was the co-opting of those ideas to serve the interests of corporate culture and the neoliberal state, and it unsurprisingly gained more purchase in mass culture than the more nuanced and hardcore agenda of the Third Wave. The postfeminist solution for '90s feminism was to interpose consumer choice as the preeminent principle of feminist empowerment, where "choice" was expanded to indicate not only the linchpin of the abortion debate but a woman following her own bliss—assuming, of course, that she could afford it.

Sarah Jessica Parker, who along with playing Carrie Bradshaw was one of *Sex and the City*'s producers, once said that "these characters, and the actresses playing them, reap enormous benefits from the women's movement . . . If you grow up with the right to choose, vote, dress how you want, sleep with who you want, and have the kind of friendships you want, those things are the fabric of who you are." But the show is more about enjoying those benefits than fighting for them. This is a literal illustration of postfeminism, the idea that feminism has already "happened" and society can take its gains for granted. If the characters on *Sex and the City* are still constrained by essentially sexist expectations of gender relations—"Women don't fart" being one trivial example—they are choosing to look on the bright side. For its sometimes radical subject matter, *Sex and the City* is remarkably anti-political, particularly when watched in a time of post-Trump trauma. Carrie admits that she has never voted, and Samantha tells a horrified woman at a political fundraiser, "I don't believe in the Republican Party or the Democratic Party. I just believe in parties!" When Charlotte says (accurately) that Miranda's partner, Steve, is working class, Carrie chides her: "It's the millennium, sweetie. We don't say things like 'working class.'"

Neoliberal policies transformed New York City over the course of *Sex and the City*'s six-season run, with the city turning to corporate partnerships and ruthless policing to boost its economy, redefine its public spaces, and reduce (without actually solving) the problems of crime and homelessness. The show tracks these changes subtly and ultimately celebrates them. When Samantha moves to the once industrial Meatpacking District in season three, downtown's metamorphosis from bohemian slum to corporate playground is complete. The infamous episode in which Samantha battles with women she refers to as "tranny hookers," offended that they were hanging out on the street in the neighborhood she was attempting to gentrify, provides a shockingly concrete example of the limits of the kind of feminism the show promoted. The cast of *Sex and the City* were the winners in a Third Way New York: professionally powerful, wealthy, beautiful, independent, and white. But being reminded of the working-class people they had replaced was so painful as to be taboo. To Genz, this discomfort around politics is inevitable in life under the Third Way, "an inherently contradictory path that cannot be walked without anxiety and uncertainty."

Sex and the City's interrogative episode structure—with each new erotic quandary phrased in Carrie's column as something she "couldn't help but wonder . . ."—could be seen as an effort to navigate the dissonance of the postfeminist lifestyle. In the third-season episode "Boy, Girl, Boy, Girl," Carrie starts hooking up with a twentysomething whom she learns is bisexual. Carrie argues that bisexuality is only a trend and is, furthermore, "just a layover on the way to Gaytown." This episode is filled with biphobic chestnuts that have aged like milk, but characters don't take issue with homosexuality, just with bisexuals' refusal to "pick a side."

Sex and the City's redeeming strength and get-out-of-jail-free card is that it was interrogating the messy ways that women navigated the impossible standards they were held to and the places their lives intersected with politics whether they liked it or not. Characters are wrong, offensive, and hypocritical, which can be just as instructive as when they are virtuous and also happens to adhere to the truth of human life. The show also has the advantage of humor. It is a New York fairy tale about the absurdity of life in late capitalism, where the characters strain to make authentic choices against a backdrop of social and political constraints that thwart them constantly.

These constraints pressed down upon me unexpectedly when I was thirty. Since the University of Memphis, where I taught, did not allow intimate partner benefits, getting married was the only way that my husband, who was working full-time in food service, could get health insurance. Within a few days we had arranged to be secretly married by a judge with two friends as our witnesses. We had a big wedding with friends and family a year later, but our wedding at the courthouse felt appropriate, surrounded by a monument to the state's power in a city where its application was notoriously unjust. I had a glimpse of how people are forced into social arrangements because of economic convenience: getting married is cheap (which is not to say that weddings are cheap) and is subsidized by the federal tax code, while getting divorced is expensive, stigmatizing, and potentially dangerous, especially for women. Thus ideology shapes—and often consumes—our lives.

5. TO MARKET, TO MARKET

Just because it was set in the twenty-fourth century does not mean that *Next Generation* did not have to reckon with the Third Way. The show allegorizes Western optimism at the end of the Cold War as the end of the Klingon Wars and the inception of a new age of interplanetary governance, vast coalitions, and peaceful space exploration. *Next Generation* remained dedicated to the racial and gender diversity that was so groundbreaking in its original series, not only with women and non-white actors in main roles but with the characters of Worf, the first Klingon in Starfleet, and the android Data exploring the complex dimensions of difference that a futuristic spaceship might have to negotiate.

One might notice strange aspects to *Next Generation*'s diversity, however, which point more to assimilation than a true celebration of difference. Homogeneity on the planet level can be seen as a prerequisite to joining Starfleet, with the requirement that it has achieved planet-wide governance and social unification. Both the inevitable and best possible course toward the future in *Star Trek* runs right through empire, an idea that was undergoing a vast shift at the time of *Next Generation*'s first airing. During the years it aired, 1987 to 1994, the two hegemonic entities that had defined the world order for fifty years, the United States and the USSR, were exchanged for the global power of multinational corporations, which, in practice, often acted as an extension of American power.

It was a revolution of computer technologies that made global unification possible in the world of *Star Trek*, including replicators that could create any food or object the user imagined, thus rendering commerce ridiculous. This empire of tech is represented by the show's warp engine technology that enables superfast space travel: the development of that specific technology is another requirement for entrance into Starfleet and is the subject of the famous Prime Directive, that Starfleet crews must not make contact with a society until it has advanced enough to have developed it. Gene Roddenberry's pitch for the show was that it would be a space western, a "wagon train to the stars." This was truer than he knew, considering its vision of a vast galaxy united by the warp drive, a sort of Space Manifest Destiny.

We still live with the fantasy that American imperialism is not like those old, icky empires that conquered with military violence. We, as benevolent invaders, conquered with Facebook and Coca-Cola (and also military—and paramilitary—violence). The impossible dream of nonviolent empire is one way that late capitalism has sought to eliminate alternatives to itself: with a government that is simultaneously progressive and conservative, so the thinking seems to go, there is something for everybody! In the post–Cold War world, it became a tenet of common sense that we had tried alternatives to capitalism, both in the revolutionary movements of the 1960s and '70s and the vast failed experiment of the Soviet Union. They didn't work. This, as David Graeber points out in "On Flying Cars and the Declining Rate of Profit," makes neoliberalism a uniquely pessimistic ideology, one that discourages idealism or hope for a better future in favor of solutions that are realistic or doable. The best we can hope for is what we already have.

Star Trek, in spite of its bouncy optimism, broadcast a corollary kind of common sense: that technology, not political reform, would lead humanity into the future. This theory always had its holes, despite the obvious upsides of the green revolution and indoor plumbing. But we are now living in a supposed empire of tech, and it has left us with both infinite choice and no way to run. There is yet another third wave we haven't discussed, that of the third technological revolution, which, according to the Marxist economist Ernest Mandel, began with

the greatly increased productivity of the post–World War II
boom years. Mandel believed that this productivity could potentially lead to the end of work and the collapse of capitalism but theorized that under current regimes it would likely to
lead to parasitism and waste. This is exactly what we see in the
high-tech twentieth century, especially with the proliferation of
endless rent-seeking middlemen attempting to profit from the
technologies we are forced to use to do the business of our daily
lives. Late capitalist incentives are such that before this iteration
of the internet has even had the chance to turn forty, it feels like
a wasteland, full of procedurally generated slop for bot accounts
to comment on.

Far from being an age of rapid technological advances, this
wave of capitalism has been marked by consolidation and stagnation. Neoliberal regimes use the supposed political virtues of
centrism and compromise as a way to rebrand the weak-state
totalitarianism they have reigned in, with seemingly opposed
political parties all representing the interests of industry and
finance. And all the while, corporations have been seeking to
eliminate alternatives to themselves. Tech companies in particular have been gobbling up competition and creating monopolies that the U.S. government is either reluctant or powerless to
challenge. Most of the tech we use every day is owned by four
mega corporations, Apple, Google, Meta, and Microsoft, and
the choice not to use it—to call a friend instead of texting or
to disavow the smartphone altogether—is seen as eccentric and
potentially antisocial. And the way we use these technologies
is prescribed. Unlike in the early days of the internet, our options for how we present ourselves and move through online
spaces are limited, like a rat running through a maze. Indeed,

much of what I watch on my laptop is my taste reified by the lazy algorithms inside Hulu or Netflix. Instead of the curated recommendations we used to get from critics, with the algorithm system it's more like I'm getting recommendations from myself, most of which are shows I already know I like. Why start something new when I can just "Watch It Again"?

I don't know why it bothers me so much, how the internet has enabled twentieth-century culture to collapse on itself. For the record, I still think *Sex and the City* and *Star Trek: The Next Generation* are good shows. What depresses me as I scroll through the piles and piles of "content" that are now available to me to consume is the strange lack I feel of having an alternative. Tech enthusiastically engineers our free time, so that most people's main hobbies are looking at and posting on social media (and thus performing free labor for billionaires like Mark Zuckerberg) or streaming the shows they once enjoyed, perhaps watching them on repeat, in a solemn loop like the liturgical year. These enfeebled forms of both friendship and entertainment were ascendant during the jobless recovery following the 2008 financial crisis, when people were working more for less pay in an atmosphere of anxiety and inequality. I'm not the first one to note that the tech we have is excellent at providing distractions for burned-out workers but hopeless at addressing those workers' actual problems.

I'm interested in the concept of "lock-in" in computer technology, as Jaron Lanier describes in his book *You Are Not a Gadget*. In practical terms, one can see software as a tower of turtles, each built with software and designed to run on still other software. Certain elements of software design are "locked in" when too many other programs are designed to be compatible with these features. This means that arbitrary decisions become monumentalized and inevitably influence our concepts about computing and life. Lanier's examples range from human memories being analogized as computer files to tones from the ubiquitous music software MIDI coming to rigidly define the (ultimately ineffable) idea of the musical note. Aspects of tech are also locked in to our everyday lives, whether we rely on a GPS app to navigate our cities or social media to keep up with our friends or corporate streaming services for entertainment. Since lock-in always has ontological implications, I worry about what social concepts are being locked in alongside our technologies, particularly since I have no faith in the people running the tech industry to have ever thought much about it.

Emily Witt's *Future Sex* is something of a millennial follow-up to *Sex and the City*, with its essays taking place in early 2010s San Francisco, a boomtown if there ever was one. She documents the city's inhabitants seeking alternative and sometimes eccentric sexual arrangements, but ultimately, she finds that sex has become another site of lock-in. *Future Sex* has an entire chapter on how internet dating sites, conceived as places socially awkward men could thrive, were immediately encumbered with real-life gender roles, as women's inhibitions ran up against men's expectations and aggression. In the chapter about polyamory, Witt follows two millennials in their exploration of what a relationship might mean without monogamy. The polyamorists in question, twentysomethings named Wes and Elizabeth, live in a world made for them, working sixty-hour weeks at Google and then taking lovers at sex parties, EDM concerts, and their many trips around the globe. They are earnest in their quest for an ethical open relationship, but, as Witt writes, their interest in free love swells not from radical ideology but from a notion that "an action was right if it promoted individual happiness, regardless of its effect on others," undergirded by "a libertarian idea that if the right dynamics were set up every problem would work itself out." This, of course, is the mantra of Silicon Valley itself, where every problem tech creates is also a problem for tech to solve.

Wes and Elizabeth were supported in their nonnormative choices by every privilege, most notably their hoards of Google money. I knew people when I went to college in Nebraska who read *The Ethical Slut* and experimented with polyamory, but all of them were driven by ideas rooted in queer liberation, feminism, and other movements for radical change, not just their individual pleasure. I can't help but roll my eyes when I read about Wes and Elizabeth's jejune little wedding, where the bride wore Burning Man face paint and their private vows were obscured by the sound of the didgeridoo. "You can kiss each other," their officiant said to end the ceremony, "and other people." I am not criticizing their romantic arrangement, but it does piss me off that they see their unconventional marriage as in service to their "responsible hedonism" and not to reforming an institution whose expectations are even more locked in now than when the characters mocked it on *Sex and the City*.

I suppose that lock-in is the predicament of all culture, as arbitrary mores and traditions acquire the air of not only convention but also common sense. I can't advocate here for everyone to throw off the bounds of traditional gender roles because the only people who would take up that charge would be those with enough privilege to evade their expectations in the first place. I sometimes find myself playing the judgmental feminist, shaking my head at women who get married right out of college, take their husband's name, have three children under three, or choose not to work outside the home. At the same time, I know from experience: it's not a choice. What once made *Sex and the City* seem so progressive rings hollow to me now, with its characters' ambivalence toward marriage as further proof of the postfeminist doctrine that women deserve freedom only if they can afford it. The reasons people are cornered into taking on these traditional roles are manifold, and they overlap with the most glaring problems in our country: no universal healthcare, a housing crisis, the disappearing pool of middle-class jobs. The COVID-19 pandemic pushed mothers out of the workforce in huge numbers, conscripting them without asking as an army of surrogate educators when schools moved to online classes. This points to the most basic reason that women are still chained to the home sixty years after the Second Wave began: child-rearing and maintaining a home *are* work, and it needs to be done by someone.

A true politics of pragmatism would pay people for the labor they're already doing, which is why it is a shame that "Wages for Housework" has all but disappeared from the catalog of feminist slogans. In a utopian future we would have labor unions and governmental income for caregivers as well as universal healthcare, free daycare, and technological innovations that would make pregnancy safer, give parents options for how they gestate and deliver children, and expand their fertility windows. Perhaps some of the trillions in technology spending could be diverted to these ends from the defense budget and AI companies generating pictures of naked women with messed-up hands. But wages for housework would be a good place to start.

If conservative forces think it is proper and natural that women stay home and take care of their children, then they must pay them for it!

Neoliberalism's First Lady, Margaret Thatcher, famously said that there was no such thing as a society, only "individual men and women and families." I could not write a more horrifying encapsulation of the alienation and isolation that Third Way politics have bred. In this scenario, the family is the one respite we as social animals can have from the loneliness of life as a capitalist agent, with the broader community dissolved to reveal only other individuals to compete against. That's why I can't fault people who cling to family and their role within it as a bolster of joy against the winds of the world. It's the same with the comfort and delight that nostalgia brings. I often see posts on Instagram exhorting me to "let people like things" or "give people their fandoms, since the world is falling apart." I am afraid, as a professional cultural critic and full-time asshole, that I cannot. But I get it. I have two *Star Trek* stickers on my laptop, and I love being married, even if I sometimes have problems with being a wife. Despite being forced into marriage by my employer, our courthouse wedding was a deliriously happy occasion, and I was and am filled with gratitude to have found a brilliant, kind person to illuminate my days. As I was working on this piece, he came home with a pristine copy of *Star Trek: The Next Generation Companion* that he bought from a used bookstore, containing synopses of all the episodes. I held it to my breast, marveling at my luck for acquiring this treasure and the perfect person who found it for me. Thank God, at least, for small pleasures. There seem to be fewer all the time.

5

REAL TIME

MY *ANIMAL CROSSING* ERA STARTED LIKE IT DID FOR anyone else who thought they were too smart, old, busy, or female for video games: the April 2020 COVID lockdown and its attending desires for normalcy, routine, distraction, and a way to spend the long days indoors. The *Animal Crossing* series had been a hit for Nintendo, but its 2020 release, *Animal Crossing: New Horizons*, was a perfect storm of anticipation (there hadn't been a new game in the franchise for seven years), buzz, and the good fortune of coinciding with a global health crisis that ground many people's routines of work and school to a halt—eventually leading *New Horizons* to become one of the bestselling video games of all time. For the unfamiliar, in *New Horizons* the player is mortgaged a home on a deserted island by a capitalist tanuki named Tom Nook. The game has no narrative beyond the goals and milestones that come with developing the island: paying off and expanding your home; decorating your island and house; growing flowers, trees, and crops; catching fish and insects to donate to the island museum; recruiting and replacing your anthropomorphic animal villagers; selling fish, insects, and basically anything else to the island store; and, of course, buying the seemingly endless furniture, objects, and clothing items on offer. Although I would venture that most of its players are adults, *Animal Crossing* is a kids' game, and the characters, environments, and design in general are infused with an intoxicating cuteness.

My husband dropped sixty dollars on *New Horizons* when it came out, and initially we were going to play it together. After approximately one night, I had commandeered the Nintendo Switch and would play *Animal Crossing* for something absurd like six hundred hours that spring and summer of 2020 before I eventually abandoned my island. I could look up the exact amount of time on my Switch, but there are a few complications: first, I don't want to. I have never understood why video game consoles log the number of hours you've sunk playing games, as if I want to know how many cosmetics licensures I could have gotten in the same amount of time. And second, I've started playing the game again.

I never considered myself a "video game person," and even so, they have somehow managed to waste vast swaths of my time. As a teenager I would play puzzle games on Miniclip.com, particularly one called *Piranhas* that was so devilishly hard it took me a whole summer to beat it. My younger brother would watch me play, barking at me like I was an Olympic gymnast and he was my abusive, Soviet-bred coach. I remember him bursting out at me in anger once: "You're playing like you don't want to win!" Eventually I had *Piranhas* memorized and was able to play through all ten levels with my five lives intact. Throughout my twenties, I had periods of *Candy Crush* addiction where I would not only play it when I woke up and before bed and on breaks at work and while watching TV and during those random slivers of dead time while waiting in line but also for hours of what was supposed to be writing time in the middle of the damn day, unable to escape its infernal feedback loop. Even when I would run out of lives, I would wait the ten minutes in a state of tweaky agitation until one reloaded.

I say this to explain my reasons for avoiding playing any "real" video games—that is, complex games played on a PC or console. Of course, this decision was rooted in a value judgment that may or may not be fair: video games are a waste of time. But I have always found creative and perverse ways to waste my time, like rewatching YouTube videos and reading my own tweets. My real trepidation about video games was my susceptibility to them. When my husband bought our Nintendo Switch, our friend lent us her copy of *Mario Kart*. I later found out that she not only loved this game but excelled at it, having developed an almost Zen merging of mind and game. It turned out that this was the exact reason she had lent it to us. *Mario Kart* was so entertaining that it had essentially ruined her life for a short period, leading her to play it for hours every day while hypnotically vibing to a playlist of dance music called "Karting." She had to get the game out of her house to be safe from its seductive power.

Why is it so easy to be taken in by such seemingly simple and even stupid games, so that my friend, who, for what it's worth, has a PhD, could be temporarily ruined by *Mario Kart*? This dissonance is an essential source of frustration about gaming. Games hijack our brains and control our behavior, implanting intense desires in us for meaningless rewards, and that is often the reason we enjoy them. As Tom Bissell writes in his 2011 essay collection, *Extra Lives: Why Video Games Matter*, playing a video game is an almost symbiotic experience, in which "your mind, and your feelings, become as seemingly crucial to its operation as its many millions of lines of code." Even as you are playing the game, the game is playing you. If Bertolt Brecht created games (as, if he were alive today, he surely would) that drew players' attention to the fact that they are like rats in a maze, easily herded using bits of food and electric shocks into participating in a narrative that they would find stupid, childish, or hackneyed if they encountered it in another context, he would be either impaled by the Twitter mob or hailed as the next indie gaming genius.

Gaming is an emotional medium (or, as the philosophers might call it, an *affective* medium), relying on mood, worldbuilding, and immersion to create an arc of emotions in the player that cannot be explained in a synopsis. Emotional power has always been a source of suspicion about new technological genres or ways of enjoying art: critics saw film and television as deleterious influences because the immersiveness and realism of their worlds made them addictive spectacles. Even the rise of reading silently in the Renaissance was viewed as suspect for being essentially antisocial. Ideas and images were transmitted privately, causing a feeling of such intimacy and excitement that people could be easily manipulated by this relationship forged between writer and reader, or so the alarmists thought. Of course, this advancement in reading and typography *did* go along with the development of modern media and massive re-alignments in politics and social hierarchies. Many people were inspired—or manipulated?—by what they read to, you know, join new religious sects or declare independence from the king of England. There is a common critique of art and media that they manipulate their audiences, which sidesteps the difficult fact that that is exactly what they are designed to do. What higher praise could there be for a work of art than "it changed my life"? But at least with *Animal Crossing*, there is something different at work. The game isn't trying to change your life. It's providing you with an alternate one.

The central tech of *Animal Crossing* is the real-time clock (RTC), which simulates the natural course of days and seasons on your island. The sun rises in the morning and sets at night, and different creatures are active at different times of day. There are new fish and bugs to catch with each new month. In the fall the trees turn orange, and in the winter, it snows. This was the game's initial inspiration, inspired by the RTC Nintendo had added to its 64DD, a disk drive intended to modify the Nintendo 64 that was such a flop it was sold for a short time in Japan before it was quietly discontinued. The RTC (which was also included in all of Nintendo's later, successful consoles) inspired *Animal Crossing* designers to create a relaxing game that would unfold at the pace of life, with an emphasis not on reaching targets or winning levels but on small daily delights and discoveries. There's an emphasis on delayed gratification: if you plant flowers or trees, you have to wait for them to bloom, and there are frequent occasions where even if you've bought something or received a gift from one of the island's visitors, you have to wait until the next day, when it will be mailed to your house. I guess this is supposed to make the player focus less on greedily acquiring and more on enjoying their island in the moment, in addition to being an incentive to log off and try again tomorrow. But anyone who has played *New Horizons* knows it doesn't work that way.

The daily tasks available in *Animal Crossing: New Horizons* are so many and so varied that it can easily take three hours just going about my daily routine. There are hundreds of flowers to water, trees to shake to find hidden items, mystery islands to visit, villagers to greet, and weeds to remove, which is not even to mention the fish, bugs, and sea creatures to catch if one is trying to make fat stacks of the two kinds of in-game currency. It is so easy to get sucked into for such endless stretches that I have actually had one of my computer-generated animal villagers gently suggest that I drink water and meditate. The frustration of my wishes—having to wait until something I need is delivered the next day, for instance—has the paradoxical effect of making the game even more enticing. I would rather fuck around in this world where I will eventually get what I want than go back to my real life where reward is less assured. So even if I have nothing left to do for the day, I'll invent something: digging up all my flowers and planting them somewhere else; making fish bait to lure the giant fish that can only be caught at the pier; buying all the clothes I don't have at the Able Sisters shop. Or, if none of that satisfies, there is always another option: time travel.

✳

About as soon as *Animal Crossing* was released, with its ground-breaking vision of a slow video game, players were figuring out how to manipulate its RTC to get the things they wanted without having to wait. In *New Leaf*, *New Horizon*'s predecessor, a mole named Resetti would burrow out of the ground to berate you for resetting the game's clock, making clear the game designers' stance against time travel. Time traveling had no *real* consequences, however, beyond Resetti's anger and empty threats. This tension—between those who believe that time travel goes against what makes the game fun and special and those who believe it is crucial to unlock all that the world of the game can do—is the defining debate of the *Animal Crossing* community.

It may seem trivial to argue over "cheating" when one is only cheating the game's computer, but as Mia Consalvo writes in her prescient 2007 book, *Cheating: Gaining Advantage in Video Games*, this kind of conflict has existed since the first cheat codes were inserted in games. Consalvo speaks of games as creating a "magic circle," a set-apart space with an alternate order, time, and physics, which is one theory for the immersive power games have on our psyches. What delineates the magic circle is a set of rules that are different from the rules of ordinary life; one must abide by them in order to stay within the magic circle's bounds. However, with video games, Consalvo writes, "while it may be helpful to consider that there is an invisible boundary marking game space from normal space, that line has already been breached, if it was ever there to start with." The prevalence and familiarity of cheat codes and the great variety of other means for cheating, like time traveling, have for most players already punctured the bubble of the magic circle—or maybe expanded it.

Animal Crossing is narrativeless and emphasizes design, creativity, and discovery, so of course players manipulate all its mechanics, not only the RTC but also using hacking and in-game loopholes to explore the limits of the game world. There is no rule against flooding your island with a giant lake, as one video with eight million views on YouTube demonstrates. Sure enough, when *New Horizons* was released, it lacked even a fourth-wall-breaking mole to dissuade you from time travel, implying a weary acceptance on the part of Nintendo. And time traveling in *New Horizons* is as easy and precise as adjusting the clock in the Switch's system settings, making it almost irresistible.

With the first island I made, in the spring of 2020, I avoided time traveling for months, puritanically judging others who couldn't play the game from morning until night, ignoring emails, having their camera off during Zoom meetings so they could be harvesting wood and iron from mystery islands at the same time. The best argument for the game allowing time travel is the practical one, that many players have commitments that mean they can play the game only for short stretches, perhaps late at night, so they would progress slowly and even be completely excluded from seeing certain creatures or taking part in events that were tied to specific times of day. This was not my reason for eventually breaking down and messing with the game's clock. It was plain old greed, specifically for the shooting star fragments that wash up on your beach the night after a meteor shower. These can be used to make some of the most enchanting items in the game, including a collection of witchy zodiac furniture that would have made Aleister Crowley slaver.

Meteor showers are unpredictable, and shooting stars are

easy to miss, indicated only with a subtle silvery sound and quick streak across the sky. Through time travel, once I had wished on one shooting star, it was easy to turn the clock back a few minutes and wish on it again and again, until I had racked up as many star fragments as I could collect for the night. Once I opened this Pandora's box, of course, I wasn't satisfied with going a few minutes back in time. I started brazenly venturing forward and back to look for meteor showers, at times going weeks or even years into the future, which caused my island to grow over with weeds and my house to become infested with cockroaches. After I had fucked up my island this way one too many times, I decided it was my sign to bow out gracefully and didn't touch the Switch for two years. When I told my fifteen-year-old cousin that I had gotten burned out on the game, he said, "Time traveling?" smiling in sad amusement that I had made such a textbook mistake.

Time travel forward two years to 2022, and COVID-19 is still raging after half a dozen uncontained waves and variants, although its impact is blunted by life-saving vaccines. This is when I finally caught it, after spending around a half an hour unmasked in a crowded bar. I went to Easter brunch and infected five of my friends before testing positive for COVID the next day. The brunch crowd put me in their recuperation group chat, causing me pangs of guilt every time they messaged for being the vector that had caused their suffering. All of us recovered fairly quickly—I felt better within a few days and tested negative exactly one week later. But by that time, I was already deep into building a new island in *Animal Crossing*, with

COVID and its guidelines for quarantine being the perfect excuse to extend my stay in bed and in the world of the game.

I started time traveling more quickly this time around. Initially I did it out of desperation to avoid a koala wearing a leather jacket named Eugene who had shown up at my campsite to live on my island. I desperately set the clock forward and back, willing the game to spawn a new villager for me, but every time I visited the campground, Eugene would be there, unaware that we had ever met before. Eventually, after reading *Animal Crossing* fan sites and forums, I resigned myself to Eugene. But once I had done this, I found that many of my daily tasks had been reset: I could shake trees again, dig up new fossils, hit rocks, find the glowing spot where a bag of money could be buried to create a money tree. I had doubled the happy chemicals the game provided through a simple adjustment of the system controls.

After this, the lure of time travel was too much for me to overcome. I was in monomaniacal pursuit of a five-star island, the highest achievement in the game, which indicates that you have planted, decorated, and terraformed your island within an inch of its life. This meant going back and forth, usually within one or two days, to try to find new items to buy in the island store, grow new flowers and trees, and finish construction projects like bridges without having to wait until the next day to start a new one. This is when the experience became hazy for me. The first few weeks of playing *New Horizons* chart a trajectory wherein the player is reaching new milestones every day: upgrading the shop, the plaza, and the player's house; building the museum and clothing store; meeting new nonplayer characters (NPCs); and eventually unlocking terraforming and other special ways to customize your island. I had disrupted this trajectory through time traveling, experiencing it all almost simultaneously. When played properly, *Animal Crossing* is a game designed to keep you grounded, connected to the cycles of nature, with breaks and mindful moments built in to allow you to take in the sheer beauty of the game's art. But played at the accelerated pace that I was going, it had the opposite effect.

My real house, with the real laundry pile growing in the corner and the real dishes in the sink, started to seem less real than my house in *Animal Crossing*. My real, parched houseplants seemed less in need of watering than my acres of flowers within the game, and any work I needed to do in real life was subordinated to the work I put into maintaining my island. It's not that I believed my island was real or had forgotten that it was a dumb Nintendo game made for kids. It was more that the real world started to appear just as fake to me as the game, with emails from my therapist, my utility provider, and my literary agent feeling as pointless as the pablum my villagers sent along with gifts to my mailbox every day. I treated all the messages in both of these inboxes the same way: deleting them unread. This was the same month in 2022 when news leaked that the Supreme Court was planning to overturn *Roe v. Wade*. Adding this to the monthly mass shootings, the flurry of laws banning Black history in schools and restricting trans healthcare, and, oh right, that insurgency at the U.S. Capitol, and the American political situation started to feel less like "partisan polarization" and more like the rumblings of something that rhymes with "drivel bore."

Perhaps I was responding to the expectation of business as

usual—I still had to write, send emails, pay bills—when the unabating pandemic, inflation, housing shortage, corruption of American democratic institutions, and threat of far-right violence made life so painful. The illusion of normalcy that we were all forced to act out felt as artificial, as far from real importance, as the daily cycles of life on my *Animal Crossing* island, while also being far more onerous and unfair. Although my house in *Animal Crossing* cost millions and millions in the game's fictional currency, at least I could pay it off by selling mosquitoes and trash.

At first, I told myself I was using the time I spent playing the game to think about this essay and others I was planning to write. And this was true: I binged video essays on YouTube, listened to music I wanted to write about, did some soul-searching and crying, all with the Muzak of the *Animal Crossing* theme playing in the background. Then something, for lack of a better word, *switched*. I was playing so fervently my eyes were drying out, and I was getting days-long headaches that I knew were caused by the game but weren't enough to make me stop playing.

There was also the arrival of Dark Thoughts. When I was a tween, I would play solitaire on my grandma's computer for so long I felt like Russell Crowe in *A Beautiful Mind*, seeing the mystical connections and patterns in the cards. In college, I played the classic mindless match-three game *Bubble Shooter* for hours, in a flow state so deep it was impossible for me to lose. But the brain massage the games provided came with the threat of Dark Thoughts, the chance that the patterns my brain followed to beat the game would become attached to a loop of self-loathing and anxiety that would cycle in my mind along with them. The Dark Thoughts became as addictive as the game, or as compulsive, a script I was forced to play out to its end, only to have it start again immediately. The best solution for this was to watch grisly true crime documentaries at the same time, replacing my Dark Thoughts with those of the *Dateline* producers, but at times this could backfire, leading to a bigger avalanche of shame for indulging in these two corrupting activities simultaneously.

The Dark Thoughts came to *Animal Crossing* without warning. I had been playing without shame, giving myself a break, letting myself think, when all of a sudden the only thinking I could do was about how fucked the world was, how little I could do about it, how I was doing the least productive thing possible by playing a video game all day, which was rotting my brain and preventing me from doing anything useful in the future. This shame and despair increased my dependence on the game, which was both my escape from the Darkness and the source of it. I was playing joylessly, brazenly traveling through time to acquire items, build up my island, and wring as much dopamine from the game as it could possibly provide. When I turned on the game one day and saw that a lily of the valley flower had appeared near my house, indicating that I had reached my goal of creating a five-star island (for the second time), I was mortified. It had been six weeks since I got COVID, and in that time I did nothing but play *Animal Crossing*. What had happened to me?

Don't get me wrong. I'd been through the whole dissociate-for-a-month routine before. But I had almost never had something that meant so little to me hijack my brain so completely and persistently as *Animal Crossing*. When I say I was not emotionally attached, I mean it. If my island were destroyed, I would go about starting a new one as impassively as an ant whose hill has just been stomped on. Not only that, there were many times when I was playing when I would rather be doing something else. I would see my animal villagers reading a book in the sun or going on a walk and look at them with envy, despite both of those options being open to me. Somehow, I was trapped in the game world, where there were always more crops to harvest, fish to catch, DIYs to make. There's an irony that this prototypical relaxing game can feel so much like work, an endless grind for more stuff and money with no defined goal or end, beyond death, I guess.

It's nice to feel like you know exactly what you must do next. The only kind of similar flow I've felt was working busy shifts as a waitress and simultaneously running food to table five, dropping the check to table six, and refilling coffee at table seven. I imposed my tasks in *Animal Crossing* on myself because they made me feel like I was being productive when I was being the opposite. Many critiques of the game, like if you search "Animal Crossing video essay" on YouTube, focus on the neoliberal labor model, where productivity and personal responsibility are paramount, personal and professional labor are elided, and consumer culture distracts from the fact that one megacorporation sells everything you buy. Tom Nook immediately calls to mind a tanuki Jeff Bezos, since pretty much all merchandise on the island is only available through the company store. You as the player do virtually all the work around the island, and Tom Nook rewards you in "bells" (one of the forms of in-game money), which you immediately return to him in a never-ending cycle. He also tries to bait you into ever-larger home contracts, so by the end you are millions and millions in debt and forever trying to get out of the hole. To put an even finer point on it, there is a "stalk market" in *New Horizons* in which one can buy and sell turnips at speculative prices.

This bothered me at first. I couldn't figure out what the game was trying to say. The ideology was a total muddle—you got points for both planting trees and chopping them down. A student of mine wrote a piece arguing that it provided a model for slow living, with its animal villagers who spend the day reading, exercising, or plopping themselves on the ground for a nap. But I thought it could be read in a different way, as a simulation conditioning players to accept our place as subjects of corporate overlords, not to mention the gamifying of the liquidation of natural resources at a time when extraction capitalism has pushed us to the brink of social collapse. The only reason any game is fun is because it is a feedback loop of reward and punishment, and like all feedback loops, games are teaching tools. Was it teaching us to quit worrying and love corporations? To treasure friendship and small pleasures? To always be working, producing, extracting? Or to slow down and enjoy the view?

The most compelling illustration of this confusion of themes is the glaring fact that some of the animals are animals and others are people. The player has a human avatar, while your villagers are cartoony, fantastical, anthropomorphized animals who talk and wear clothes (although, in Porky Pig fashion, they cannot wear pants and are most often nude from the waist down). But the fish and insects you can catch in the game are hyperrealistic representations, clearly heavily researched to reproduce their coloring and movements accurately. Many of the species of animals featured in the game as villager characters are ones people kill and eat, at least sometimes—cows, deer, chickens, ducks, octopuses, frogs, alligators—but there is little acknowledgment of this in the world of the game, despite the fact that you can catch realistic versions of frogs and octopuses in the lakes and oceans. This is the same dissonance we live with when we see ourselves as if we were not animals and think that gives us the authority over those creatures not endowed by us with personhood.

When the game came out, the famously provocative animal rights group PETA went lightly viral by publishing "PETA's Vegan Guide to 'Animal Crossing: New Horizons,'" in which it condemns fishing and catching bugs in the game and recommends that you post a bulletin reading, "ZERO TOLERANCE POLICY on speciesism. No fishing. No catching bugs. Respect all animals while visiting." Most people found this to be a hilarious example of the obnoxiousness and trolling that PETA has become known for. Almost no one took its critique seriously, and the near-universal response was that PETA should take a chill pill because, after all, it was "just a game." But was PETA wrong? The article seems to bait us with outrage at PETA's killjoy attitude, though it does accurately draw attention to the ironies of the game. "It's disappointing that a game in which villagers from all different species . . . coexist harmoniously with humans encourages abusive behavior toward fish and insects," it reads. "Instead of being recognized as the living, breathing, feeling individuals they are, they're presented as forms of entertainment for the other villagers."

At this point you may be suspicious that I am one of the crazy animal personhood people who think zoos and animal testing labs and cattle ranches and the fishing industry should be eradicated. You would be right. I believe that we need to fundamentally alter how we think about and relate to animals if we are to evolve human consciousness and protect the ecosystems that support life on Earth. People always want to treat animal rights activists as hysterics, I think because the magnitude of cruelty toward animals and destruction of their habitats is more than most can face, particularly when almost all people "love animals" in some capacity. It's a lot easier to act like PETA is being insane—what kind of a *loser* with *no life* would even *consider* the well-being of *fake fish* in a *stupid video game*—than to acknowledge that there is something uncomfortable and even disturbing in *Animal Crossing*'s relationship to animals, and that most people who play the game notice it. Not that I am any better than your average *Animal Crossing* enjoyer. Despite my sympathies for PETA's position, I fish and catch insects and swim for sea creatures in the ocean, and at this point I have caught so many virtual sea bass, one of the least sustainable animal species sold as food, that I should probably be placed on PETA's most wanted list. I also chop down trees and mine iron from rocks with the zeal of a nineteenth-century robber baron, and I feel guilty about that, too. One of the greatest environmentalist guilty pleasures of the game is going to a "mystery island," which are uninhabited islands you can fly to in order to harvest resources and catch creatures, chopping down all the trees, destroying all the rocks, and picking all the flowers so you can force high-value insects into palm trees, where they are easy prey. My vegetarian ass has done this for hours!

I was always uncomfortable with the extractionist ethic that courses through the game, where development is the only goal, to turn an uninhabited island into a manmade environment. And the thing that disturbed me the most was that this exploitation was so fun, so addictive. Was I indulging in a colonialist fantasy of abundance, that there will always be new frontiers to plunder, more resources to exploit when you have sucked your current environment dry?

In his essay "Colonized Play" from the anthology *Video Games and the Global South*, Jules Skotnes-Brown notes that the frontier has long been a fixation of the video game industry, both in its subject matter—space, the old west, a desert island—and in a figurative sense, with the industry romanticizing itself as generating new spaces to discover in a world that has been fully mapped and conquered. But this explorer ethic is culturally constructed. As Skotnes-Brown notes, "Since most mainstream video games are produced and disseminated in the 'developed' world, they are spaces in which primarily ex-colonial nations can continue to 'conquer' the 'other,' even in postcolonial periods."

This critique cast an unattractive light on many of history's most popular video games, where you use a map to explore an unknown land, collect resources, and fight or kill the hostile creatures who make their home there. Skotnes-Brown examines the "sandbox game" genre, which *Animal Crossing* could be classified as, where the player is encouraged to build their own environments and narratives, rather than having them imposed by the game. He provides a surprising analysis of the wholesome kids' game *Minecraft* that could do just as well to address the politics of empire in *Animal Crossing*:

> The player arrives, like Robinson Crusoe, into a *terra nullius* and [the game] encourages him to "improve" this land—by clearing jungles, draining marshes, building infrastructure, and mining minerals. Its inhabitants—hostile monsters or local villagers—appear simply as obstacles in the path of development or as resources to exploit.

As Skotnes-Brown notes, the obsession with maps in video games in general is related to the political origins of cartography in the age of discovery, where projects of mapping and making land legible went hand in hand with making it exploitable.

One of the primary reasons to catch live fish and bugs in *Animal Crossing* is to display them in your museum along with fossils and pieces of art. These exotic specimens are not a complex ecosystem but individual types to classify, study, and eventually gawk at behind glass, so human edification becomes an unassailable goal, one that happens to be served by capitalist development. The game unwittingly wades into the political problems of museums, many of the great ones having been financed by the plundering of natural resources and then filled with plundered artifacts. Their function is less education than absolution, with theft and the decimation of species transformed to serve an idealistic vision of progress for the common man. Donating those artifacts for the benefit of the public also makes them the public's problem.

The mad diversity of the flora and fauna in *Animal Crossing* often preoccupied me as I played. What was I being lulled into accepting as I labored on this island for forty hours a week plus overtime? Like in most games, I suppose, the simplified world lent itself to ideological convenience. It is easier to dismiss the rights and needs of animals when they are reduced to types to be collected, logged, and liquidated, and they never, ever inter-act with one another. A great white shark in *Animal Crossing* will not eat a tuna. Bees do not exist in communal hives but spawn spontaneously on flowers and then disappear into the ether if you approach them the wrong way. And creatures from every corner of the globe make their homes around your island, including super-rare fish like the coelacanth and bugs that exist only on the island of Madagascar. Even the most casual David Attenborough viewer will know that this is not the correct way to view animals, as if they could be transplanted as easily as humans from the habitats that formed them. But I will admit it is enchanting through the absurdity. What a thing to see an emperor butterfly as big as your head alight on a psychedelic purple tulip, its sapphire wings perhaps picking up the electric blue of a *Rosalia batesi* beetle, when these two creatures should be seven thousand miles apart. This experience is beautiful, and *Animal Crossing* is the only place where it is possible.

In this way, I see the Tom Nook character as more of a utopian than a ruthless capitalist—not that it's necessarily a compliment. Utopians are dreamers who would rather wish away impossibilities than reconcile them, with their deepest-held delusion being that they can solve any conflict through the force of their charisma and hugeness of their vision. I thought of *Animal Crossing* (and not only because I was always thinking about it) when I read the Argentine author Adolfo Bioy Casares's 1940 sci-fi novel, *The Invention of Morel*, about a fugitive who seeks sanctuary on a bizarre and mysterious abandoned island, with the only hints of its recent former inhabitants being in three structures that remain: a museum, a chapel, and a swimming pool.

Our unnamed narrator is surprised one day to find that the previously silent island has become inhabited with vacationers, who seem normal in every way except that they cannot see or hear him. In a twist that has been rendered predictable from countless *Twilight Zone*, *Star Trek*, and *Black Mirror* episodes, it turns out the people our narrator sees are holograms, super-realistic recordings taken by the inventor Morel who are playing out their time on the island in an eternal loop. Morel's invention is truly grotesque because it is fatal to those he records, whose bodies quickly wither and rot away.

The book is about immortality, particularly in the face of what we would now call tech, which makes monuments of us all. Bioy Casares loved the silent movie star Louise Brooks, and she was the model for the ominously named character of Faustine in *The Invention of Morel*. He was inspired by how film as a medium could deify and flatten Brooks, so that she was both more and less than a human woman. The book can be read as an ironic statement about love and infatuation, where this one-way connection, from fan to star, becomes less taxing and complicated and therefore purer than any real love affair. In the age of the parasocial relationship, where people carry on deep though ersatz friendships or even romances with influencers whom they've never met, this plot feels ever more relevant. Sorry for the spoiler, but in the end our narrator chooses suicide by hologram, recording himself so he can be forever with the beautiful Faustine (a deal with the devil indeed), whose image he has fallen in love with. This is the only way they can be together at all, in a kind of perpetual performance. The narrator imagines the unlucky person who will happen on this island next and see his recording next to Faustine's and assume they were once there together, not knowing the perverse palimpsest they are really seeing.

In *The Invention of Morel*, the island is unsettlingly lush and abundant, covered with bizarre plants that grow impossibly quickly but decay and die the second they are plucked. It made me think of the environment of *Animal Crossing*, where the simulated plants and animals are uncannily ordered and self-contained, so unlike the churning of the natural world, where every element is interrelating and overlapping, forming layers of life that stretch from deep underground to the tallest tree canopy. More pointedly, though, I recognized how Bioy Casares's characters are living an endlessly looped pseudo-life. The images captured on Morel's machine are like NPCs, the characters the player encounters in a video game to give quests, hints, or important objects, who exist solely to help the player along.

(Now I'm imagining some highbrow indie developer adapting *Morel* into a game where you would spend your days building a shelter in a swamp, evading the notice of the evil doctor as you attempt to uncover the mysteries of his plot, only to learn, in a metacommentary on the gaming genre, that the doctor and his guests whom you have been either hiding from, observing, or sending secret messages to were mere shades: you were alone the whole time.)

Bioy Casares's novel speaks to the solipsism of the video game medium, which caters to each of our dreams of being not only the main character but the only person who matters, who thinks, who desires, who lives a full inner life. This enforced narcissism is related to the loudest critique of video games, that most of them are bloodbaths where players, many of whom are young men, can act out their violent fantasies in an arena that is not only consequenceless but full of emotional rewards for that behavior. As Bissell notes, first-person shooter games have a tangible overlap with real-life violence, though not in the way that many people assume. Violent video games were a source of perennial handwringing in the 1990s, with parents fearing that they would spur impressionable children to act out real-life atrocities. But it was the purveyors of institutional violence who were making use of them, with the popular games *Battlezone*, *Doom*, and *Counter-Strike* used as training or recruiting tools by the U.S. military and Chinese antiterrorist police forces. The ranks of multiplayer shooter games are filled with ex-military guys, Bissell writes, and when he was embedded as a journalist with the Marine Corps during the Iraq War, he found "nearly every young enlisted Marine [he] spoke to was a shooter addict." So grind the gears of culture, where what we like is influenced to an uncomfortable degree by exchanges of power on a scale we can scarcely comprehend. Yes, it is disturbing that the graphic destruction of humanlike characters seems to be inherently satisfying to millions of people, but why do our critiques stop there? Let us try, if we can, to cut this problem off at the root.

The highest ideal of late capitalism is total individual agency and self-determination—as long as you accept the totalizing framework of consumer culture, the pursuit of wealth, and the nuclear family, an invisible ideological hand as all-powerful and invisible as a video game's engine. One of the greatest pleasures of *Animal Crossing* is its retail therapy. You are encouraged to buy things not only in the island shop, the clothing store, and an outdoor market run by a hippie dog on a nearby island but also "online," because, perversely enough, your character has their own smartphone where you can order even more items. This is so fun that it distracts from the fact that after a while this is basically the only thing you can do in the game, an endless cycle of acquiring, hoarding, and liquidating items. This eerily mirrors the state of many of our lives in the twenty-first century, where we are free mostly in the sense that we are free to consume—and each person's consumer decisions are considered sacred, regardless of the effect they have on others. "It's a free country," I was told as a kid on the playground when I complained that someone was doing something mean, disgusting, or annoying. Indeed, a person is free to buy an AR-15 but is not free from the fear of mass shootings. We are not free from the excesses of the superrich, even when they are hoarding resources and destroying the environment. *They* are free—and many of them think they should be free from criticism, too—because they earned it with their wealth. Freedom is not a birthright, only another consumer good.

Rafael Miguel Montes and Andrea Ann Campbell posit that video games are an essentially postmodern form that have from the beginning been obsessed with the activity of consumption. They point to the symbolic significance of Pac-Man greedily gobbling his way through level after level. Video games reached cultural ascendancy in the late 1980s, at the same time when consumer capitalism cemented its stranglehold on the globe, creating one massive economy that every human was subject to. This meant a hugely eclectic marketplace, where one could have their pick of products from around the world. (Nintendo, the Japanese company that produces *Animal Crossing*, is without a doubt one of the winners of globalization.) But it also meant that global consumer culture effaced local or national identity. Since the philosopher Jean-François Lyotard wrote about this phenomenon in 1984, this has only become truer. Modern citizens often base identity around our tastes—in fashion, music, food, or video games—more than our religious or political commitments, careers, or ethnic or geographic backgrounds. Or perhaps we wouldn't see ourselves as constructing our own identity in this way, but we judge others by what they project with *their* consumer tastes.

Montes and Campbell see video games as re-creating this system of consumption-formed identity, focusing especially on the popular computer game *The Sims*, in which a player designs a family of virtual characters and is responsible for their productivity and happiness, building a narrative through the choices they make for their characters. The player must care for their Sims by making sure they are clean and fed but also by attending to their "happiness," which is achieved by buying them more luxurious in-game objects to make their lives easier and more comfortable. To Montes and Campbell, this is a bizarre compression of Abraham Maslow's famous hierarchy of needs, essentially exchanging a complex, elusive, and abstract idea like happiness for a simple one: consumer satisfaction. This happiness is even creepier when one considers the satisfaction the player is supposed to receive from it. It is as if the game's designers (and the company that produces it) are not only preaching the philosophy that happiness can be bought but prescribing feelings to the player, too. Your Sims are happy. Why aren't you?

There is something grim about the picture of the *Sims* player as puppet master or fickle god, alone in their bedroom, holding the fate of their digital children in their hands, perhaps grinning in smug pride when their characters reach a certain achievement or choosing sadism instead, locking them in a room with no toilet until they wet themselves or forcing them to swim laps in a swimming pool with no ladder. This is a fate as hollow as Morel's, who is so driven to trap other human beings like exhibits behind glass that he has no choice but to reduce himself to one of his specimens. The truth is that even though video games are an emotional medium, they can't *give* feelings to their players, except maybe in the most pale and counterfeit way. It is true that *Animal Crossing*, a game about friendship, gave me the feeling of something like company. Like happiness in *The Sims*, friendships with your animal villagers in *Animal Crossing* are codified and concretized, and they are built by talking with them and (especially) giving them expensive gifts. When you reach the highest level, the villager will give you their picture, and I lavished gifts on my villagers and felt a swell of pride when I received that coveted object. But it was pride only: achievement unlocked. I felt no love or companionship from my digital friends. I noticed that I often played the game when I was lonely and that it was isolating me from my partner, friends, and family, thus making me lonelier. There was something wrong with this pattern, but I realized later that the problem wasn't with the game. It was with how I was playing it.

With its 2.0 update, *Animal Crossing* included a curious new feature, in which players could record their island as a "dream" and could visit the "dreams" of other players. From the beginning the game was intended to be played socially, with other players either in the same room or around the globe, and Nintendo added many features that encouraged you to visit your friends' islands. But there was vulnerability in allowing people to visit your island, especially if the other players were strangers. If you wanted people to experience the island you had worked so hard on, you opened yourself up to them trampling your flowers, ransacking your valuables, or leaving trash lying around. Developers solved this quandary with Dream Islands, where others can interact with an image of your island while leaving the real one untouched.

Despite understanding the need to protect one's island from marauders, thus the negative necessity of Dream Islands, I didn't understand its positive use. What was the point of visiting Dream Islands? I was so confused that I googled "what's the point of dream islands" and found a forum question with this exact title and an answer that began succinctly, "The point is to look around. You're just looking at stuff." Until this point, I had seen going to other islands purely as a means of exchange, a way to get stuff my island didn't have, which made Dream Islands moot. Although you can interact with items in Dreams, you can't take anything home. But once I began to "just look at stuff," I realized that I had not only missed the point of Dream Islands but of the whole game.

The first Dream Island I visited that changed the way I saw the game was a masterpiece called Dreamy Moon, a stoner dreamscape in neon shades, contrasting motifs of lime-green aliens and tie-dye with augustly terraformed cliffs and water features, liberally adorned with the game's coveted lunar items, which include a giant floating replica of the moon itself. I was struck by how difficult it would be to perform some of the mundane tasks that I had become so used to laboring away at for hours each day. It would be almost impossible to fish in mountain streams, where some of the most rare and valuable creatures are found, and one couldn't shake pine trees on this island since there were none. This island was made to maximize beauty and pleasure, not the ease or speed at which one "finished" the game. Why would one want to finish their time in a Xanadu such as this?

What perplexed me, though, was how the creator of Dreamy Moon had gained access to so many of the game's rarest and most expensive items to create such a paradise. To get a giant floating moon, of which there were at least three on this island, one had to luck out and receive a "recipe" for how to make it from Celeste, an owl who visits your island one night a week at most, and, in order to create it, hope that you have fifteen star fragments and one large star fragment, themselves a huge pain in the ass to collect, as I detailed earlier. This mystery was solved when I happened upon a YouTube video explaining the concept of treasure islands, a trend in the *Animal Crossing* community that blew the game's economy wide open.

These were created using hacked Nintendo Switches, with the consoles mysteriously modded such that the player had access to the catalog of every item in the game. The proprietor of the treasure island would then lay out items on their island in tidy rows for visiting players to stuff their pockets with. Though some owners of treasure islands asked for a small membership fee to access islands not so picked over by the treasure-seeking hordes, by the time I discovered them, the number of treasure islands was so huge that one could almost always hop on one for free. Even more luxurious were the Discord servers run by concierge-like robots, where I could specify the exact items I was looking for and then, with a special code private messaged to me, arrive at the island to see my order laid out at the entrance. At the start of the *Animal Crossing: New Horizons* cultural phenomenon, many players had been swindled by ruthless traders asking actual money for virtual items in the game. Treasure islands more or less put a stop to that, ringing in a golden age of community and creativity in the game. Once rare *Animal Crossing* items had become so abundant that their market value matched their real-life value: nothing. And why shouldn't they? It was, I realized for the first time in my months-long addictive stupor, *only a game.*

I had made the crucial mistake of playing the game not only alone but without the pool of information available from a broader community of players, which would have helped me out of the maze the game had trapped me in months or even years earlier. Of course I had sought outside counsel, like looking up prices of items or creatures on the *Animal Crossing* wiki, but beyond this encyclopedic knowledge, I had not actually become an expert in the game *as it was currently played*. To do that, I would have had to consult the massive community of players on YouTube, Twitch, and Discord, which, ironically, I had scorned as a waste of time.

Ten years or so ago, when I worked at a boarding school in Southern California, it never worried me that the teenage boys in my charge would spend hours gaming on their PCs instead of doing their homework. It struck me as a bad sign only when I realized that they were not playing but watching YouTube videos of other people playing. One boy who had gone to a rehabilitation camp for video game addiction the previous summer would watch these play-throughs for hours, as a way of white-knuckling it through the school year. With the rise of the video streaming platform Twitch, which began exclusively as a platform to watch other people play video games, this kind of spectating transformed from a niche pastime of doofus teen boys to an increasingly legitimate form of media. I made peace with it as a big-brother effect, not in the Orwellian sense, but in that it is fun and relaxing to watch a seasoned player with greater knowledge, instincts, reflexes, and fine motor skills than you have achieve greater heights in the game than you could hope to achieve on your own.

I truly understood this once I started watching *Animal Crossing* masters on YouTube creating more beautiful, intricate, and inventive islands than I could have dreamed of. They made Tokyo city streets, medieval pubs, jungle outposts, ice palaces.

One such genius had used the game's built-in perspective to arrange floating items in such a way that their shadowed silhouette resembled Howl's moving castle. Everything was customized, every detail attended to. None of these players were concerned with shaking trees every day or catching every possible fish to fill their museum—why bother, when, if they wanted to, they could order one of every fish from an order bot? The point of the game had shifted under the weight of their resourcefulness and creativity. It was no longer about friendship and the daily cycles of life but about decoration, storytelling, and engineering an experience, so that Dream Islands, rather than a random, peripheral add-on, became a central feature.

It was obvious when I saw the awe-inspiring beauty of the islands that these elite players were creating (some of whom were doing it more or less professionally, making money from Twitch or Discord memberships, YouTube views, or Patreon subscribers) that despite the hundreds of hours I had spent playing the game, I had not even approached their sophistication or expertise. It was as if we were playing two different games: I had been *Animal Crossing*'s dupe, believing that the ultimate achievement was a five-star island; all the while people were doing things with the game that its designers would have never thought possible. This is exactly the role of what Consalvo identifies as paratexts in gaming, as she charts the symbiotic growth of supplementary media like magazines, books, forums, blogs, and videos alongside the video game industry itself. These paratexts might provide players with help when they're stuck on a level, disseminate knowledge of cheat codes and other hidden features, or give a bird's-eye view of a game's levels. Most crucially, they give players the opportunity to talk to one another, share strategies and innovations, allowing them to reclaim agency from the game's seemingly immovable mechanisms and choose how they want to play. Through this collaboration, paratexts become a means for adaptation, a way to transform games from fixed, unchanging documents into something as flexible as the community of players, able to be played in more ways and for more time than they would have otherwise.

A vast field of paratexts sprang up with the release of *Animal Crossing: New Horizons*, including YouTube channels, Twitch streams, wikis, fan Discord servers, treasure islands, and modding communities, so the question of cheating on *Animal Crossing* soon outgrew the argument over the ethics of time traveling. One of the central tensions in Consalvo's book on cheating in video games is that video games do not have rule books, only engines, computers that delineate the limits of a virtual world. Knowing this, there should be no such thing as cheating in video games; anything that is possible within the limits of that world is fair game. But these limits are more porous than they first appear. There may be built-in cheat codes that give the player an advantage, ways to manipulate the gaming console itself (like with time travel), laborious workarounds that the game designers never considered, or hacks and mods that alter the engine itself. There is a tension—seemingly set up by the video game industry, which invented cheat codes and Easter eggs—between playing creatively to push the possibilities of a game's world and playing as well as possible on the game's own terms, which will likely require more time, tedium, and raw skill.

The idiosyncratic melding of these two forms of play—a tension between cheating and following the rules, or finding ways to manipulate the game mechanics and ways that the game mechanics manipulate you—form the true shape of any game. The fact that cheating in video games is inherently ambiguous and socially constructed, then, has heavy implications for the medium of gaming itself. After all, to return to the magic circle, rules are all that typically constitutes a game. There has never been an art form more labile or prone to its audience, so that the experience of playing may take years to form a stable shape, as communities and paratexts delineate a game's "real" rules and boundaries.

This may be why it is so hard to write about games, despite them being a nontrivial part of so many people's lives, including people who are supposedly too old, smart, or female to enjoy them. Games have influenced novels and movies, with their hero's journey structures and metaphor-laden mechanics like a "health bar." They serve as a heightened illustration of both the power and the absurdity of fiction: flattened, limited worlds created by fallible people that nevertheless make it possible to live impossible lives. But until recent years Bissell's book was one of the few popular nonfiction volumes dedicated to the problem of video games as text, and despite the breadth, intelligence, and delight that *Extra Lives* offers, he often struggles to come to conclusions about them.

He wrestles with the stupidity of video games: their lack of originality, the alternating inanity and insanity of their plots, the boring, leaden dialogue, and the mysterious fact that this stupidity is irrelevant to whether a game is good, when it wouldn't be in any other art form. It may be that the industry is doomed to a lowest-common-denominator approach to anything resembling story: games take tens of millions of dollars and years to produce, and therefore they need to appeal to the widest possible audience, meaning that they are usually genre pastiche, set in already familiar worlds cribbed from *Lord of the Rings*, zombie movies, or *Star Trek* and/or *Wars*, with stories that must be able to be understood and enjoyed, to paraphrase a board game box, by kids ages eight to eighty-eight. They are, furthermore, generally created not by writers but engineers.

This doesn't explain, though, why these games are so compelling or even addictive to people who would have found their silly plots and derivative story worlds tiresome in a movie or book. Games defy the primacy of content, particularly since many are built on similar engines differentiated by "skins": visual styles, story worlds, and plots that superficially distinguish them from one another. It is foolish to seek the meanings of games solely in this subject matter, as I had striven to do when I was pondering the attitude of *Animal Crossing* toward speciesism and work. It is funny to me to read back these pages where I refer to Tom Nook as a utopian, as if he were the game's Morell-like author and not simply a shade within it. I had created this narrative that imbued Tom Nook with power, which I had obeyed like a hologram doomed forever to enact my demise. And yet, there is still something that rings with significance in my reading of the *Animal Crossing* utopia. Utopians, from Thomas More to Walt Disney, are often authoritarians whose vision of the perfect society hinges on other people behaving exactly as the mastermind wishes. The foil to this impossible vision of a restored Eden is the messy process of emergence that characterizes human society, where genius is the result of friction and heaven is other people—as is elegantly illustrated by the exuberant and organic community that transformed *Animal Crossing* completely.

Meaning is made in video games through a dialectical vac-
illation between the game-as-product to game-as-process (to
borrow terms from Consalvo) and back again. *Animal Crossing: New Horizons*, the product, is about laboring daily to earn
the cushy island life provided for you by the corporate overlord
Tom Nook, the pleasures of which are abundant but somehow
never enough. (The metaphorical link between the totalizing
authority of Nook Inc. and Nintendo, which could be seen as
its parent company, is obvious.) But every paratextual innovation in *Animal Crossing* has been geared at resisting this authority. If one sees games as training tools, it is heartening that so
many players have collaborated to refuse the obeisance of the
ideal capitalist subject, conspiring instead to give everything in
the game away for free.

One of the first major paratextual expansions of the world of
Animal Crossing: New Horizons was Nookazon, a website where
one can trade in-game items. The site was one of the first ways
to "order" items that weren't available to you before the invention of treasure islands or order bots. Despite easier ways to get
in-game items, Nookazon is still very popular, mostly because it
is incredibly fun. The first time I used it, I listed a villager who
was leaving my island, an adorable white goat named Chevre,
for free. The girl who contacted me wanted to give Chevre to
her best friend for her birthday. I arranged wrapped presents
around the entrance to my island for when the birthday girl
showed up wearing glasses shaped like a cake with candles. She
was so thrilled to get Chevre for free that she left me a pile of in-
game money, which was somehow different from if I had asked
to be paid. "HAPPY BIRTHDAY," I screamed at her, and I was
on an altruistic high for at least an hour afterward. How strange

to think that I was only interacting with pixels on a screen: the Nookazon interface, the messages I sent, Chevre, the presents and the paper I wrapped them with, the birthday girl's outfit, the money she paid me, my island, my trees, my flowers, my villagers. This was the beginning of my way out. I knew more clearly than ever that it was just a game, but for the first time in the *Animal Crossing* world, I felt something real.

6

TEEN PEOPLE

PART I: GOLDEN AGE

This one's got to start in my bedroom. Moscow, Idaho, 1998. In my plastic choker and pajama pants, in my inflatable chair, I slick on Dr Pepper Lip Smacker and array my magazines around me, their bindings worn white from repeated readings. I humbly invoke the spirits: *Oh Britney, oh Brandy, oh Usher, oh the Chrises, Justins, and Nicks of the boy bands, oh Dawson, Joey, and Pacey, oh Carson Daly, you are old enough to be my dad.*

I've been thinking a lot lately about these icons of my childhood, the ones whom I don't want to feel nostalgia for but do anyway. They inhabited my television, they were at the two-screen movie theater near my house, and they were in the magazines I bought, subscribed to, pored over, and hoarded. My mom says my magazine collection is probably still in the family's storage unit, but I have never had the gumption to spelunk in there and find them, with the added complication that if I were to find them, they would become my responsibility.

In my teens, I had them all meticulously organized in file cabinets that my librarian dad brought home from work, and there were hundreds, spanning a decade and at least a dozen different titles. They must weigh a ton. I would have to wrangle the file cabinets into my car and sift through the magazines, and then what would I do with them? Take them to my house?

Not wanting to deal with them, but not wanting to let them go. That is more or less the predicament I find myself in with most of the pop culture from my childhood. For years, when people asked me about this book, I told them I was writing about teen magazines. This answer feels laughable now that the book has experienced mission creep so dramatic that it is also about the fall of empire, late capitalist cults, twenty-first-century gender trouble, and the transformation of entertainment in the age of the internet. I *have* been writing about teen magazines, though, day after day, mining the vein that contains all the handkerchief-hemmed prom dresses and butterfly clips, *Dawson's Creek*, *The O.C.*, and the cloud-printed pillowcases from the Delia's catalog, in thousands of words that will never see the light of day. But at the same time, I am not doing what I said I would. I am not going to my family's storage unit and finding my magazines. I am not spending my time looking at old magazines, conducting interviews with current and past magazine staffers, or researching the magazine industry. Sure, I've done some of that, but at a certain point I started winging it, spinning out into reminiscences of my isolated childhood in Idaho and how it was nevertheless imprinted with mass culture, particularly with the demographic ascendancy of the millennial, which happened around 1998.

This was also the year I started reading magazines and

roughly the same time I started watching MTV around the clock. I thought that I had entered a world of pleasure designed just for me, which I had, though of course I could not understand the implications of being so catered to. This is why my piece "about magazines" has become about millennial complicity with the machinery of marketing, among, I hope, other things. I grow increasingly uncomfortable with the fact that my marching orders were mailed to me by *YM*, *Teen People*, *Teen Vogue*, *Elle Girl*, *CosmoGirl*, and *Seventeen* every month, and I more or less obeyed.

In second grade, I passed the ultimate marshmallow test, hoarding my two-dollar allowance for an entire year to buy a tiny $100 TV at Wal-Mart. Fair being fair, my parents rewarded this act of willpower by letting me have the TV in my room and giving me zero boundaries on what I could watch and when. My favorite shows immediately became the trashy talk shows that played after school, hosted by Jerry Springer, Ricki Lake, Sally Jessy Raphael, Maury Povich, and Montel Williams. On these shows, teens were wild, or they were witches, or they were pregnant, or they thought their mothers were "Too Fat to Dress Like That." These antisocial, violent, loudmouthed, Satan-worshipping teens were like sirens singing me toward the dark side of adolescence, to a freedom that could be mine in only a few short years, though I knew, deep in my heart, that I would not avail myself of it as they had.

I didn't start consistently begging my parents for magazines until I had completed my premature transition to teenhood, worshipping especially at the altar of MTV. I started waking up at six a.m. to watch its *Spanking New Music* block of music videos and was switching more often from Nickelodeon to watch Puck's cruel and erratic behavior on reruns of *The Real World: San Francisco*. MTV between the years of 1998 and 2004 was probably the last moment youth culture revolved around the TV schedule. Like kids in the '50s running home to watch Elvis gyrate, everyone I knew watched MTV's daily musical countdown show *Total Request Live*, which featured millisecond snippets of popular music videos that the viewers had supposedly requested along with celebrity appearances and live performances, all in MTV's Time Square studios, where outside you could see a gigantic mob of teenage fans waving signs. *TRL* took on treacherous stakes in 1999 when it cooked up a rivalry between the two most popular boy bands, NSYNC and the Backstreet Boys, over whose single would be retired from the countdown first. They traded the number one spot from April to August. Eventually the Backstreet Boys' "I Want It That Way" defeated NSYNC's "I Drive Myself Crazy." No one was surprised. It was the Backstreet Boys' best song and NSYNC's worst.

My hometown of Moscow, Idaho, is a university town two hours from the nearest major airport. The atmosphere, though rural, was not cultureless. I remember being exposed to all kinds of earnest arts programming like folk music and jazz festivals, craft fairs, and numerous used bookstores where I could buy any Agatha Christie book I wanted. Thanks to the presence of the University of Idaho, I had classmates from China, Saudi Arabia, Pakistan, Malaysia, Gabon, and Jamaica. My town was more accurately *pop cultureless*. No famous music act would ever have come close on their tours, and even the Top 40 radio stations seemed to lag mysteriously behind MTV. People there dressed carelessly, in free t-shirts from 5k races, fishing vests, or ugly embroidered denim shirts, the better to bike fifteen miles in each morning, as my dad did.

My parents are eccentric and anti-materialistic, while also collecting all kinds of random junk, so our house was cluttered, colorful, and ridiculous. This might be their essential contradiction: their asceticism and love of stuff; their tendency as early adopters and their inability to keep up with the Joneses. My parents are both university librarians, and my mom had a laptop where she would check her email and play solitaire in bed while watching TV, long before my generation made this a venerable after-work tradition. And yet our home computer was a DOS-prompt library hand-me-down until I was in junior high. Its only game was a basic typing tutor that I played for hours on end, so my computer teacher was stunned with my proficiency. When I was a tween and the '90s were dangerously close to over, we finally got a proper '90s home computer setup, this one another hand-me-down from my mom's coworker that ran the already outdated and slow-as-hell Windows 95. We had dial-up internet for free through the University of Idaho, and it was terrible, taking forever to connect and disconnecting several times an hour when I was trying to talk to boys on MSN Messenger. My parents had perfectly fine computers they could mess around on at work. At home, the TV and the magazine reigned supreme.

I don't know if being professors made my parents value cultural capital basically to the exclusion of real capital, but I think we all felt adrift, our household an island in endless rolling farm fields undulating like a lonely sea. You see, my parents, and especially my mom, are pop culture obsessives who were enthusiastic consumers of everything from James Joyce to *Judge Judy*. Our shelves were lined with the works of midcentury British humorists like Kingsley Amis and Barbara Pym. My parents were filled with acid contempt for anything amateurish, quaint, or ill-conceived, reducing 100 percent of the cultural programming provided by our small-town Svengalis into laughingstocks to be ridiculed for days and months on end. On Christmas Eve, my mom would listen to her CD of Kathleen Battle and Jessye Norman singing carols at Carnegie Hall, and I could practically see the veins in her temples recede with the opera singers' sure and merciful training.

Despite enjoying the anonymity and freedom that living in a remote town of eccentrics afforded us, my parents and I (and I assume my brothers, too) all longed obscurely to be somewhere else. That somewhere was the center of things, where culture was made and traded, where good and bad were decided, where people understood every reference: high and low, new and old. It should surprise no one that we were a Magazine Family. My grandma paid for our subscriptions to *Ranger Rick* and *Highlights* from the time my brothers and I were toddlers. When I was in elementary school, she got me *American Girl* magazine. My parents got *The New Republic* and *Rolling Stone* and *The New Yorker* and *Vanity Fair*.

All this criticism consumed yielded more criticism. Opinions were the coin of the realm in my family, the wittier and meaner the better, which is probably the rather Freudian source of my writing career. In my family I am considered the unopinionated and uninformed pushover. Perhaps I am on some sad quest with each piece I write to prove myself as devastating as they. But I also think we derived a familial safety from absorbing ever more words and pictures into our brains. My magazine cramming was probably not so different from when my little brother read *The World Almanac* every day on the bus to elementary school, memorizing the world's longest rivers and the number of chickens in Illinois.

When I was a child—that is, before I got my TV—I would leaf longingly through the fan magazines at the grocery store like *Bop* and *16* and *Teen Beat* and *Tiger Beat*. These were supposedly for teens, though I cannot imagine they had many readers past the eighth grade. Most of these had been around since the '60s to cater to tween girls' burgeoning libidos and taste for beautiful, soft-featured boys. At the time, the covers of every issue of every one of these magazines glowed with the sunny aura of Jonathan Taylor Thomas (or JTT, as we knew him), the child actor who played the middle son on the sitcom *Home Improvement*. He also voiced young Simba in *The Lion King*, and he resembled him, with deep tan skin and a golden butt cut framing his face like a mane.

These magazines were almost all images, designed to be ripped out and plastered on a young fangirl's walls. They would hold meta contests for which readers' rooms were most thoroughly wallpapered with images of JTT or Devon Sawa. I remember when the tween magazines started making Sawa's picture larger and larger on their covers and JTT's smaller and smaller. I was dismayed, since I found Sawa less cute, despite his hunky turns in *Casper, Little Giants*, and *Now and Then*. This was part of a larger shift in the culture, though I didn't see it then. Sawa had the same blond haircut as JTT, but he looked like Leonardo DiCaprio, an edgier late '90s heartthrob. This may have been my first experience of generational disdain, the feeling that the culture is both passing you by and painfully mistaken.

My first magazine obsession was the mostly forgotten title *Twist*, which started in late 1997, a new contender for the freshly discovered millennial market. I bought its third issue by chance in the grocery store, and I still have no idea what drew me to it. Its cover star was Fiona Apple, but my Fiona Apple phase didn't hit until my freshman year of college, when I would ride the bus listening to *When the Pawn . . .* on my iPod and sighing. If *Twist* sounds familiar, it is probably from its later incarnation as a fan magazine for preteens à la *Tiger Beat*, with covers crowded with random assemblages of pop idols, that somehow existed until 2016. I'm talking about its glory days, from 1998 to 2002, when it was a frothy and hilarious teen magazine with a good budget, chock-full of personality quizzes and jokey sidebars with titles like "Signs Your Crush Is a Moron."

I recently ordered an issue of *Twist* off eBay, where they are depressingly hard to find. As it has so dramatically in recent years, the cult of Britney Jean Spears came through again, producing a pristine copy of the September 1999 issue with Britney smiling from the cover for the only moderately stupid price of $24.99. The writer Joy Williams said that the smell of Ivory soap is the madeleine of American experience, but I would haz-ard that for American women born before 1994, there is a sim-ilar time warp that comes with beholding a magazine you read with extreme interest twenty years earlier, completing all the quizzes, trying the flirting advice with disastrous results, mem-orizing the answers Britney provided for reader questions, like when she said that she doesn't ride her four-wheeler anymore because she has a car now. Even the Gillette razor advertisement on the back cover, where a blond model is swathed in a sheet of seafoam silk, reawakened my longing for that tender time, the beginning of my seventh grade year.

When I bought my first *Twist*, I was ten, a worldly and mis-erable fifth grader stranded in the realm of children. I remem-ber holding it in my hands in the grocery store and feeling like my life had led to this moment, a rite of passage I hadn't been anticipating, when I would open a teen magazine and feel spo-ken to. It's hard for me to explain the transition that occurred inside me when I discovered magazines, but it was like my iden-tity had come into full flower once I had a trellis to train it on. I read and reread this issue, so that it was soon covered with food-stained fingerprints and rippling with water damage from the bath. My heart stopped in my chest when I finally spotted the next issue on the newsstands, and I greedily snatched it up. Shortly after that, I started hoarding other magazines, too, to get me through the long month. (Woe be to me when they did joint issues that were supposed to last me two months.) *YM* was my second favorite, a big, glossy institution with great cover stories, but I would eventually add *Elle Girl*, *CosmoGirl*, *Teen Vogue*, *Teen People*, and, if I was really desperate, *Seventeen* or the lamely wholesome *Girls' Life* to the rotation. Soon I was attuned to the rhythms of the newsstands, my month revolving around the time when the magazines would turn over, a whole rack of new issues glistening in the fluorescents. Even after I had coerced my parents into subscriptions for *Twist* and many other magazines, I still anticipated when new issues dropped, always eager to add more titles to my stable. Ideally, I would have had a rotating cast of thirty magazines, so I could read a new one every day. My subscriptions often lagged irritatingly behind the newsstands, so I would take the opportunity to peruse ones that had yet to be delivered to my house and sometimes bought them, too, so that my parents were paying for two copies.

In the late '90s, cultural commentators had a new bone to chew on: dissecting the interests, concerns, likes, and dislikes of a newly discovered demographic. They were called the millennials, the oldest of them were teenagers, and there were seventy-two million of us in the United States alone. *Rolling Stone*'s 1999 feature "The Secret Life of Teenage Girls" by Jancee Dunn reports that since teen girls are "creatures of habit, they dearly love ritual, particularly going to the mall," and she spends a long scene shadowing them there. The piece was a pseudo-ethnography of burgeoning millennial teens, followed them as they ate fast food, talked about *Dawson's Creek*, and perused Spencer's Gifts. Dunn enthuses, "The mall! It's so much more than shopping. To a teenage girl, it is a weekly chance to safely reinvent yourself . . . All it takes is some baby-sitting money and a few twenties wheedled from Mom and Dad." This last sentence gets at the real reason *Rolling Stone* spilled so much ink following around a bunch of boring girls from

Connecticut. In short, the teens were spending tons of money on stupid shit, "the most style-conscious, splurged-upon, and media-immersed army of ragamuffins in history," as James Wolcott called millennials in *Vanity Fair* in 2003, quoting statistics that American teenagers "spent $155 billion in 'discretionary income' in 2000 alone."

Believe it or not, I remember reading the *Rolling Stone* article when it came out, and even at eleven I could sense the condescension. (I read the *Vanity Fair* article, too, and when Wolcott joked, "Welcome to the launch party for *Teen Vanity Fair!*" I mistook his tone and started looking vainly for where I could subscribe.) The piece attempts to balance tenderness with humor. It begins with one of the teens complaining that ABC had cut away from the Backstreet Boys' performance on *The View* because "there was a stabbing or something" and ends with Dunn retreating from the overwhelming energy of a sleepover where the chatter is punctuated by "dolphin-like shrieks." *If you hate kids so much, why are you writing about them?* I remember thinking. Some of my indignation must have resulted from hearing someone talking about me when they thought I wasn't listening. There was also embarrassment, and it persists, at how easily I was marketed to—you mean my trusted advisers at MTV and *YM* magazine just want my money? My billions?!

It hurt because the trend pieces were right, at least about some things. I did adore, enjoy, dream about, and fetishize the mall. I was enchanted by the giant malls I'd seen on trips to see my grandmas in Nebraska and Oklahoma, particularly delighting in department stores with their own escalators. You wouldn't believe how exotic suburbia appeared to me. If I could have bought everything on every spread of every magazine, I would have, and if I could have glided up an escalator like Cher Horowitz, my arms laden with Fred Segal and Contempo Casual bags, I would have. My only claims to virtue are that I had no money and, if I did, I would have had nowhere to spend it.

Moscow had a mall, though I once heard a sorority girl derisively calling it "the sMall." The sMall had very few stores, and the ones it had you would never have heard of. Its flagships for a long time were three fictional-sounding department stores: Lamonts, Emporium, and the Bon Marché. These sold the limited stock of trendy clothes available within the Moscow city limits, like Tommy Hilfiger baby doll shirts, Mudd jeans, and clownish JNCOs that were so baggy they made skater boys look like they were wearing a Mormon mom's jean skirt. My parents were not about to shell out for any of these brands, and they would not have looked right on me anyway, since with puberty I seemed to have passed from the children's section to matrons, with no stopover in juniors.

My brothers and I wore clothes from Wal-Mart, garage sales, and an outlet store called Sylvester's, whose strange-smelling merchandise seemed to have fallen off a truck. Luckily, many of my classmates did, too, including some whose parents, like mine, were professors drawn to academia because they'd never have to apologize for their eccentricity. But this does not mean that we spent any less time at the sMall. From the time I was in elementary school, my friends and I would roam its one long corridor sans chaperones, making mischief in department store dressing rooms, throwing things in the ugly brick fountain, setting off all the Big Mouth Billy Basses in KB Toys, breaking ornaments in Hallmark, spending three minutes and three quarters on *Ms. Pac-Man* at the arcade. When I was in junior high, the sMall got a Bath & Body Works, and we were in there for hours, washing our hands. It's funny to me to think about our "buying power," since the mall was as much a source of free fun as fun you could buy.

Sure, we bought things. We bought little things like goldfish at the nasty and crowded pet store, key chain hand sanitizers at Bath & Body Works, lipsticks from Rite Aid. I suppose those purchases contributed their small drops in the $155 billion bucket. But a magazine was the best thing your three dollars could buy at the sMall, because it was a purchase of purchases, facilitating fantasies of consumption that were almost as satisfying as the real thing. Like the mall, its purpose was to make spending money as easy and appealing as possible, but its pleasures were ineffable, an end in themselves.

When I spoke with a former *Twist* staffer, they told me that they had wanted to create a teen magazine that was funny, refreshing, and tongue-in-cheek—or, as a shorthand, "Like *Sassy*." It's difficult to overstate the influence of Jane Pratt and her groundbreaking teen magazine *Sassy* on the entire teen industry. By the time I was buying magazines, Pratt had already moved on to creating her magazine for adults, *Jane*, in 1997, getting out of the teen game right when everyone else was getting into it. But *Sassy* had already changed everything by capitalizing on cool in a way that no teen magazine had ever done, its shining moment forever immortalized with its legendary 1992 cover of Kurt Cobain and Courtney Love. The teen culture of generation X in the early '90s appeared enviably intellectual and avant-garde, dominated by college rock and enfant terrible filmmakers like

Harmony Korine. *Sassy* still shines like a beacon of this golden age of alternative teens. Carl Swanson wrote in *New York* magazine in 2012 that bands like Sonic Youth used *Sassy*'s offices as a "clubhouse," and Chloë Sevigny was an intern there.

Pratt's own legend goes far beyond *Sassy* (and her later editorial ventures, *Jane* and the website xoJane, too), as a figure so eccentric and glamorous that she could rightly be called the gen X Diana Vreeland. In the '90s she was almost a household name, in tabloids and on red carpets with her famous besties like Courtney Love, Michael Stipe, and Drew Barrymore, *Jane*'s first cover model and Pratt's rumored lover. Almost all stories and profiles about her paint the picture of a lovable basket case who has been known to throw conversational pipe bombs like insisting that she has psychic powers.

It is impossible to extricate Pratt's real genius from her eccentricities. In Swanson's profile, Pratt says that her "emotional age" is fifteen and that almost everyone's true age is sometime in adolescence, when our identities are catalyzed inside a centrifuge of pain, humiliation, passion, and aspiration. To successfully appeal to teenage girls, the best magazine editors and writers were deeply connected to their younger selves, forming a band of grown-up girls writing in practically the same voices since their teenage diaries. I can relate, since reinhabiting my childhood magazine obsession makes me feel so at home that I have been doing it aimlessly for three years, with no end in sight.

Probably Pratt's greatest innovation was her insight that readers would connect with a magazine more if writers and editors were not treated as anonymous providers of copy but as a cast of characters they could follow month to month. The former executive editor of *Jane* told *New York* that the characters Pratt was looking for were not from the traditional Ivy League to magazine internship pipeline: "We had people who played in bands or made clothes," he said. "We didn't want traditional people; we wanted freaks with a point of view and talent." This was the stroke of genius that led Pratt, when staffing xoJane in 2016, to discover Cat Marnell, disgraced beauty editor formerly of *Lucky* magazine who at that time was doing as much PCP as she possibly could. This period Marnell describes in incredibly entertaining detail in her drug memoir, *How to Murder Your Life*, surely one of the greatest books of the last decade. Pratt was looking for an "unhealthy health editor," and even strung out, Marnell could see that she perfectly fit that bill, having worked at Condé Nast titles for over a decade as her addiction spiraled out of control. Marnell's outrageous and brilliant blogs for xoJane, like the one where she said she used Plan B as her only form of birth control, made her the talk of the Twitterati, though anyone could see that she was walking a tightrope. She writes in her memoir that after making some casual references in an email to doing heroin, she was confronted by Pratt and human resources, who demanded she go to rehab. This Marnell saw as a betrayal: Wasn't it her candor about her drug use that was driving huge amounts of traffic to xoJane?

In a way, Marnell was complaining that she was just playing her part. And in another way, Pratt was complaining that her performance had become boring. "From a writing standpoint and a character standpoint, I wanted there to be an arc to this," Pratt told *New York* about Marnell, revealing the mistake that so many people have made with Marnell: thinking she would eventually get off drugs. But it must have hurt when she was being exactly who she thought Pratt wanted her to be, not just as an editor at xoJane but as an erstwhile *Sassy* girl who had studied at Pratt's feet since she was a preteen. Pratt was Marnell's blueprint when she got into the magazine industry as a weirdo who did her own thing, but *her* particular thing was too much even for Pratt. In the end, Marnell quit xoJane and went on to write even more gonzo ramblings for *Vice*. She was a literary star by that point, or at least a lightning rod, not a lowly staffer unboxing PR gifts and taking messages. Pratt's instinct for creating characters had collided with a new world of internet celebrity, an influencer era that she herself godmothered in.

It's telling that Marnell, despite her calamitous end at xoJane, still compares Pratt's genius with that of Andy Warhol. Pratt cultivated her own celebrity, and she said at the time of *Sassy* that she was finally the popular girl she had never been as a teenager. But she also was interested in celebrity conceptually, how a magazine could be a vehicle to create stars by telling stories. But navigating the pop culture pressure cooker is risky for any Svengali, even ones for whom it is a medium to explore the nature of fame and persona. Narratives online spiral quickly, not like the controlled storylines Jane could orchestrate through the issues of her magazines, and they were collaborative, with the gossip and outrage readers generated setting the terms of the conversation. On social media, the reader participation Pratt championed in the early '90s had outrun her in an anarchic orgy of content, produced and consumed by everyone, with little need for editors, tastemakers, or even a celebrity class. Despite being a new media pioneer at xoJane, Pratt talked about her discomfort with not being able to read every article that the site published because of the volume and speed of internet publishing. In the year 2000, when reality TV was still in its infancy, all the commentators were quoting Andy Warhol in wonder, as if he had been joking about our fifteen minutes of fame, as if there was anything else we could hope for from America.

After the seismic influence of *Sassy*, American teen magazines took on a new commitment to candor about sex, drugs, and relationships, along with discovering the lure of reader-generated content, which made magazines both more intimate and more sensational. It was inevitable that clean-cut American newsstands would soon discover their taste for the disgusting. This is when the iconic embarrassing stories sections were born, starting with *Seventeen*'s trailblazing Trauma-Rama in 1994 and becoming the defining feature of teen magazines in the '90s and '00s. Trauma-Rama was quickly followed by a similar monthly column in *Seventeen*'s biggest competitor, *YM*, and in basically every other one of the slew of teen magazines started in the next ten years. An editor from this era told me these were the most popular pages in every magazine she worked at and that there was a minor scandal when a new editor in chief at *YM* tried to discontinue its embarrassing stories column. After an outcry from readers, it was quickly reinstated.

The stories were practically identical across magazines. It was always getting your period in class, at church, or in the swimming pool; vomiting all over your crush's shoes or your SAT; clogging toilets, peeing your pants; your nasty little brother sticking tampons up his nose and blowing up condoms like balloons. People will say that these stories were made up, and they probably were, but they were by readers, not magazine writers.

These stories, true or false, were how kids talked to other kids about the things they feared most, the ultimate subject of almost all of them being the normal functions of their bodies. These confessions served as release valves among pages and pages of prom dates and big white smiles, and they pointed to the emotional vortex constantly threatening the carefree fun that was supposed to be the essence of teen culture. The creator of Trauma-Rama later told Jezebel that she regretted how much the section emphasized periods and other bodily excretions, but it was undeniably a stroke of genius to probe that constant teenage condition, embarrassment, and its even more toxic corollaries, humiliation and shame.

In September 1999, when I was reading and rereading the same *Twist* Britney issue I later bought off eBay, I had just started the seventh grade, having gone to the fancy hairdresser in the sMall with a picture of a choppy bob from *Twist*. I then attempted to dye my dark brown hair "strawberry blond" with box dye from Wal-Mart. It ended up macaroni yellow. This was all part of a broader reinvention I was undertaking by skipping sixth grade and going directly to the junior high across town, leaving my childhood in the dust. I had been in a class of eleven at my elementary school, most of whom I had known since I was six, and I was desperately tired of them all. I had formulated a theory in second grade that you learn nothing of value in the even-numbered years of elementary school (first grade curriculum: learning to read; second grade curriculum: making hand puppets), and with this in my back pocket, I asked my parents to help me escape. This was as easy as talking to the principal. Turns out no one really cares if you go to sixth grade.

This was my chance, I believed, to become the lissome teen

of my destiny. Having internalized dozens of Baby-Sitters Club novels, I had developed an unrealistic image of the income, dating habits, wardrobe, and social freedom of the average American seventh grader. (I hoped my new hair would evoke the awed jealousy inspired in the rest of the Baby-Sitters Club in *Mary Anne's Makeover*.) Add teen magazines to this mix, and I was convinced that leaving elementary school was essentially my graduation to adulthood, which I guess was why I bought a funereal black satin purse at Wal-Mart to take to my first day. When I got there, I realized that I had badly miscalculated, and I was the only child there in a black miniskirt and high heels carrying a handbag. There was more trauma-rama that first day. The school bus took a bizarre route miles out of the way, and I was twenty minutes late to my first class. I couldn't find any of my classrooms or open my locker, and I have a distinct image in my mind of tripping on a rug and accidentally tossing my purse into the trash.

After this, I was embarrassed nearly all the time. I got rid of the purse, but as any teen magazine could illustrate, there were so many other faux pas to commit, so many opportunities for humiliation. My haircut was related to the debacle of my school pictures, in which errant chunks of my highlighter-colored strands stuck up like devil horns, and I am doing a cross-eyed, Frankenstein's monster smile. "That is the worst school picture I have ever seen!" my friend exclaimed when she saw it. Still, I dutifully gave them out to my friends and charitable popular kids to hang in their lockers. The worst day was when I slipped on the huge staircase near the front door and skidded all the way down on my butt, in the process flinging my flute over the railing. It seemed everyone in the school was there, laughing or staring at me in shock. A nerdy ninth grader rushed over and asked me breathlessly, "Is your flute okay?"

I had once dreamed of traveling to different classrooms all day with different teachers and people in each one, but keeping track of where I had to be and when and what to bring was more challenging than in my fantasies. I couldn't remember to write my name on my paper, and I was always getting my sixth and seventh period classes mixed up. I made friends easily, at least, something I can only attribute to everyone else in their first months of junior high being as big a mess as I was. This was the first time I loved school, finding the constant social stimulation endlessly interesting, if stressful. In my diary from this time, the first line reads, "Hey! I love junior high, it's the absolute best thing ever." After that, all I write about are my rotating crushes ("We've been in jr high for what, three months now and I've already had like 15 separate crushes") and the different friends I'd made in band, in English class, and on the bus. My writing is clearly influenced by the teen magazine voice, constantly punctuated with direct addresses like "Weird, huh?" or "Too cool" to an imaginary audience. The entries are cheery and positive, constructing myself for myself as someone with loads of friends and many potential suitors, who made hilarious quips in class and knew every answer at her Knowledge Bowl meets. I would end entries with "gotta go" or "can't write now" as if I had somewhere important to be.

Sometimes I would write about hating my body or problems my older brother was having, but I invariably ripped these pages out, never wanting to confront those thoughts again. You would think in the hundreds of embarrassing stories I'd read, I would have learned that adolescence is universally awkward and painful. Instead, I took them as cautionary tales, with the worst-case scenario being that other people found out about, much less witnessed, your shame.

Any American woman my age will remember the glut of teen magazines that entered the market in the late '90s and early '00s, having been spun off from adult publications and catering to the mini version of those adult readers: *Teen People* for young gossip hounds, *Teen Vogue* for wannabe socialites. This was a giddy time, when month after month there would be *more* magazines on the grocery store shelf, more embarrassing stories to read, more ads for Hard Candy makeup and Diesel jeans, more quizzes about my celebrity soulmate, more facts about the casts of WB shows to memorize.

The most famous of the teen mag spin-offs at the time was probably *CosmoGirl*, the brainchild of the young *Cosmo* fashion editor Atoosa Rubenstein, who became Hearst's youngest editor in chief ever when she had the stroke of branding genius to scrawl "girl" in lipstick across the *Cosmopolitan* logo. (Almost all these teen sister publications closed unceremoniously in 2006, when I was turning eighteen. Only *Teen Vogue* lives on, though not in print.) Rubenstein was the queen of *CosmoGirl*, creating her own myth more intentionally than the editors of my other magazines. She would write these unbearably chummy editor's letters, often hearkening back to her teenage years, when she was the awkward child of Iranian immigrants with a massive halo of frizzy black hair. She lavished care on her readers, like the cool babysitter you could only dream of, assuring us that she was proud of us, believed in us, even loved us. I remember finding her familiarity off-putting—who was this lady who came into my life one day via the Tidyman's checkout line (oh, did I not tell you that the largest grocery store in my strange little town was called *Tidyman's*?) and was now trying to insinuate herself into my life like she had married one of my uncles?

Still, Rubenstein had my loyalty. When she left *CosmoGirl* in 2003 to take over as editor at *Seventeen*, I was dismayed, like she was telling me that even though she was divorcing my uncle, we would always be special friends. It began to seem like *CosmoGirl* wasn't really her precious passion project but a massive stepping stone in what was shaping up to be a career juggernaut. Rather than be affronted, I reveled in my attention being a prize worth Rubenstein's $1 million *Seventeen* salary. I kept reading *CosmoGirl* and read *Seventeen*, too.

It was a heady time, when all the marketing executives started to care about what I liked. In the summer of 2004, when I was turning sixteen, MTV aired Ashlee Simpson's reality show *The Ashlee Simpson Show* right before its hit *Newlyweds*, which starred Ashlee's older sister, Jessica. Ashlee's show purported to document her writing and recording her first album, *Autobiography*, as well as her first gigs. Watching the show back (which I have done three times in adulthood), it appears highly staged, probably including scenes of Ashlee scrawling the lyrics to her songs in a little spiral-bound notebook. But at the time it felt fresh and authentic, with Ashlee complaining that her label wanted to market her as a bubblegum teen star like Hilary Duff when she was drawn to edgier music. I went out to buy the album the day it released.

It's funny now to try to unpack how much of my Ashlee Simpson era was capitalist automatism on my part and how much of it was MTV and the Simpson sisters' dad/manager actually knowing what I wanted. It's rich how they were able to create the narrative of an artist taking on her label and fighting to make her own music in a project orchestrated by the label to sell records. They may have flown too close to the sun with that last trick, and the lies separating reality from reality TV would also lead to Ashlee Simpson's downfall. In October 2004, the backing track she was singing to on *Saturday Night Live* malfunctioned, giving the impression that Simpson had been lip-synching all her vocals. Singing to a backing track is a common practice on live TV appearances, but the media seized on the incident as the second coming of Milli Vanilli. The nepotism of her rise to fame, along with her secondary role as a reality TV star, led to the narrative that she was a talentless industry creation, the edgy brunette foil for her sister, the blond pop princess.

A few weeks after her *SNL* appearance, she was booed off-stage at the Orange Bowl, showing that the vitriol toward Simpson was not going away. After this, the teen boom began to die its slow death. Even in the Disney era that came next, stars were discovering before their sixteenth birthdays that tabloid scandals sold more records than purity rings. Instead of the gossamer, candy-colored world that magazine editors and music videos exactingly built, unadulterated access became the name of the game, with strange cases like the reality show *The Hills*, which was the first to leverage the dual roles its characters played: they were both the striving yet carefree twentysome-things of the show and the rich and famous TV stars covered in the tabloids. Naturally, when a group of San Fernando Valley teenagers calling themselves the "Bling Ring" decided to rob celebrity houses, they targeted a star of *The Hills*, Audrina Patridge. The robbers acted like they were owed a piece of the overexposed celebrities they targeted, which included the ultimate Y2K star, Paris Hilton. The reality star had become denuded of her status as a private individual, not a person with a job but a 24/7 commodity.

The Bling Ring is the sordid and inevitable outcome of this era of selling teenage girls to each other. I suppose Britney Spears's 2007 meltdown is, too, along with Lindsay Lohan's two DUIs, Mary-Kate Olsen's eating disorder, Amanda Bynes's social media meltdowns, and more other calamitous outcomes than I can list. These girls had carried the entertainment industry on their backs and were still surveilled, slandered, bodyshamed, and manipulated until they couldn't take it anymore. The sad thing is that Ashlee Simpson really did write all the great songs featured on her show. She has a writing credit on every song on all three of her albums. I still break out *Autobiography* on occasion and consider it a masterpiece of the 2000s guitar pop era, even surpassing Kelly Clarkson's *Breakaway*.

At the time of her *SNL* scandal, I was shocked at the glee people displayed at her downfall. I saw then that people wanted to hate her, that the snide attitudes teen pop singers had grown accustomed to had intensified to contempt, and that the same culture that was so fixated on ogling the bodies of these teenage girls would be quick to declare them talentless, stupid, and embarrassing. This era was full of parables for which girls not to be—don't be Jessica Simpson, the Christian bimbo singing sappy Whitney Houston knockoffs, and don't be Ashlee Simpson, the fake rock chick who has never listened to the band on her t-shirt—meaning that the girl culture that had once been so solicitous of me had become dangerous. How could it not be, when the gossip industry discovered that humiliating young women was more lucrative even than putting them on pedestals?

PART II: END OF AN ERA

Writers covering the new youth movement loved to point out that the late '90s teen explosion echoed the kiddie culture of the 1950s and '60s, when the word "teenager" was coined. In 1997, *The New York Times* described the incipient pop culture youthquake as "a blend of the 1950's and the millennium, with bright pop songs, interchangeable teen-age heartthrob stars and mindless yet ironic movies." As we might guess from the invocation of the 1950s, this was not necessarily a great turn in the representation of teenage girls, whose role models had gone from spunky eccentrics like Blossom or Clarissa Darling of *Clarissa Explains It All* in the early '90s to Britney Spears and all the other blond pop stars creepy journalists never tired of calling "nymphets."

Gen Xers at the time complained about the dumbed-down era millennials had ushered in, as if it were kids and not middle-aged media executives who were splashing hypersexualized teenage girls across every screen and newsstand. In Wolcott's 2003 *Vanity Fair* cover story, he says that then-seventeen-year-old Amanda Bynes had "ripened into full fruition" like the famously buxom 1960s teen idol Annette Funicello. (He doesn't call her a nymphet, though, saving that honor for the Olsen twins, "ancient souls in nymphet bodies." Barf.) There was a sense at the time that not only was this a new wave of youth culture but the ascendance of *girl* culture, centering on teen stars like Brandy, Britney Spears, the Olsen twins, and Lindsay Lohan. The lineups of teen-oriented networks like MTV and the WB were all targeted at girls, producing seminal shows like *Dawson's Creek*, *Buffy the Vampire Slayer*, and *Gilmore Girls*. *TRL* gave time to boy-oriented bands (as opposed to boy bands, which were obviously girl-oriented), mostly from the pop punk, rap rock, and crap rock genres. But this representation is like the exception that proves the rule: What could better show that *TRL* was a girls' domain than the supremely unappealing music and, indeed, band names of Limp Bizkit, Korn, and Hoobastank?

I had never considered that boys were left behind in this girl-power bum rush. In "The Secret Life of Teenage Girls," Dunn quotes an MTV executive saying, "The whole girl-power thing is huge. In fact, a lot of teen boys feel quite disenfranchised because they don't have as many role models." My first instinct is to roll my eyes, until I remember that only three years after this piece was written, boys my older brother's age went to Iraq and Afghanistan with their Limp Bizkit CDs and never came back. "These kids haven't had a war" was one of late '90s commentators' favorite lines to explain millennials' innocence and exuberance, never imagining that those qualities could be explained by the universal experience of youth. This abruptly changed in 2001, when American millennials went from spoiled babies in a prosperous and peaceful land sucking on MTV's saccharine teat to "the hope of whatever future the Bush administration manages to leave unwrecked," Wolcott wrote. September 11 demarcates the early and middle periods of the Y2K teen boom, a turn that, even if you are only looking at teen culture, was for the worst.

Millennial boys fared better in the post-9/11 teen landscape, in direct contrast to the plummeting respect with which girls were treated. Men and boys annexed huge swaths of the culture and jealously guarded them, on TV networks like Comedy Central and Spike TV, and especially in the video game industry, which grew exponentially in this era, helped along by the jingoism of the war on terror. But maybe a few boys held on to their earlier sense of grievance at being relegated to the margins of kid culture. Maybe as young children they watched the proliferation and success of music, shows, movies, and merchandise marketed to girls and meant to make them feel empowered, and noticed the dissonance between these messages and the compulsory heterosexuality, "edgy" humor, and explicit violence on offer in the media marketed to them.

This dissonance could serve as one explanation for Gamergate, the vicious and organized online harassment campaign against feminist media journalists, video game critics, and game developers (and a web of people associated with them) who questioned sexism in game storylines, the video game industry, and gamer space. The harassment started in 2012 and continued unabated for at least three years, and its echoes have lasted until now, even as its tenth birthday has come and gone. The quintessential Gamergater was a white male millennial active in online video game communities, and despite the violent misogyny and racism on display in Gamergate brigades and pile-ons, the men involved still believed themselves to be reasonable, seeing themselves as representing the position of the mainstream gamer, a white man who enjoyed violent, sexist games and did not think it was necessary to question them. When they argued against "social justice warriors" and "political correctness," of course they associated these things with women, since progressive media up to that point in their lives had always been chick stuff, and of course they feared "the one thing they had" (as many white male gamers have unironically described the massive video game industry) being taken from them by women. You see, our friends in the marketing department saw Bart Simpson in 1991 and invented a demographic profile for young boys that was outrageous, aggressive, childishly sexist, and horny. This meant that any men's media, particularly in the overwhelmingly male video game industry, must conform to these expectations for some men to comfortably enjoy it.

The massive size and hideousness of Gamergate took most people online by surprise, and it was a popular talking point and laughingstock, what with the cartoonish tantrums these grown men were throwing about a series of YouTube videos dryly explaining sexist tropes in video games. When looked at in the cold light of day, though, their anger was alarming, showing a stronger attachment to the caricatures of manhood they played as in video games and the violent acts they simulated than to the feelings of real human beings. Gamergate revealed a group of people who had allowed themselves to be shaped by the rubrics of their marketing demographic and were not about to give up that ready-made identity; who had come to conflate being a man and consuming in a manly way; who policed their friends' and brothers' performance of masculinity, judging others using the criteria the marketing department had handed them; and who were freaked out and embarrassed when their obliviousness and conformity were pointed out to them. People continue to be taken off guard by how easy it is for young men to be radicalized online, even though Gamergate directly prefigured actual fascist movements that started on the same sites. I am not trying to blame the growth of the video game industry in the '90s and '00s for far-right politics or violence, but it's the same with everything in the orgy of consumerism and marketing that the teen craze brought us: these violent delights have violent ends.

Cultural commentators writing the inaugural millennial trend pieces seemed to believe, despite plenty of indications to the contrary, that this juvenile cultural takeover was the result of an empowered generation with evolved beliefs demanding to be heard. The older people writing these articles theorized that these kids just love being marketed to ("They are open to the global marketplace," *The New York Times* wrote in 1997, whatever that means) as if it were a choice, rather than the end game in the development of marketing as a field, starting in the *Mad Men* era with the dawn of market research, the unholy intermingling of social psychology and advertising. As problematic fave Betty Friedan chronicles in her 1963 book, *The Feminine Mystique*, this was initially turned on the newly huge class of stay-at-home wives after World War II, who, having surpluses of time and intelligence and deficits of dignity, became the perfect marks for advertisers trying to offload appliances, cleaning supplies, and beauty products by speaking to these women as professional "home economists." This marketing was largely done through—what else?—women's magazines.

By the late '90s, advertisers had been training their targets on kids for decades, taking unabashed advantage of the most gullible and impulsive sector of the population (that is, until Fox News and Facebook discovered the disastrous power of the growing elderly population). Teen girls were seen as more covetous, emotional, manipulable, and insecure than boys, maybe because of the training regimen teen magazines put us through to keep us that way. Of course, as a ten-year-old, I was enthralled with magazines and MTV and the fifteen-year-old who worked at my after-school program and wore Dr. Martens sandals and shrunken sweater vests. This is because, despite initiating myself as part of the teen market, I wasn't a teenager. Everyone knows no self-respecting seventeen-year-old would read *Seventeen*, and I suspect that a huge proportion of the teen market was in fact under twelve. What I bought into more than anything was the Teenage Mystique, the exotic (and, indeed, erotic) pull of the teen girl I knew deep down I could never be.

Friedan's *The Feminine Mystique* was one of the first popular works of Second Wave feminism and is still the most cutting indictment of women's magazines that has ever been written. Friedan writes how, starting in the latter half of the 1940s and reaching its height in the 1950s, American women experienced a startling regression in the space they took up in public life, quitting their jobs, getting married young, forgoing college, and having more kids on average than they had in decades. All this reversed the trends in women's emancipation that had taken place in the 1930s and 1940s, when careers and education for women had grown not only because of jobs left open when men went to war but because of a feminist movement that was supported by popular magazines for women.

After World War II, though, it seemed that women's ambitions no longer reached beyond the front door of their suburban homes. As Friedan uncovered, this was a result of a vast system of social programming in which school curricula, magazines, and television advertisements redefined femininity, as embodied by women who were "young and frivolous, almost childlike; fluffy and feminine; passive; gaily content in a world of bedroom and kitchen, sex, babies, and home." With this in mind, the baby boom can be seen not only as a result of an influx of men into the beds of their wives but a hideous work of social manipulation by industries who wanted to create more American consumers.

Friedan called this ideology of womanhood the Feminine Mystique, a fantastical myth in which the "the highest value and the only commitment for women is the fulfillment of their own femininity." This tautology reinforced both the emptiness and the single-mindedness of this pursuit, where obedience is its own reward. Some of the men who returned from World War II were magazine editors, who unceremoniously replaced the women who had risen through the ranks in their absence. Male editors quickly developed relationships with social scientists who were creating empirical models of human manipulation. This was when magazines transformed from reading material to consumer guidebooks. "It is crammed full of food, clothing, cosmetics, furniture, and the physical bodies of young women," Friedan laments, "but where is the world of thought and ideas, the life of the mind and spirit?"

Unsurprisingly, Friedan was not a fan of teen magazines, either, seeing them as a further incursion of the Feminine Mystique, sexualizing girls through dating tips and beauty regimens, training them to see as suspicious any woman whose ambitions went further than wife and mother. It's no coincidence that the era of the Feminine Mystique and the advent of the teenager overlap: teenagers were invented in the 1950s as sexualized miniature adults, who were initiated into the standards of heteronormative middle-class life by going steady, holding jobs, and roaming around independently in cars. The Teenage Mystique of the late '90s and '00s imagined a teen who was both innocent and seductive, nubile and mature, earnest and snotty, smart and silly, ambitious and spoiled, aloof and popular, sporty and girly, knowing and naive. In other words, marketing departments had discovered that they could adultify children even as they infantilized adults. It was the best of both worlds—not only could those initiated into the stringencies of the Teenage Mystique do their part as, in Friedan's phrase, "thing-buyers," but they were also sexy to adult men!

Some may mistake the manufacturing of the Feminine Mystique for a frivolous concern when compared to other injustices of the postwar era, particularly when Friedan's shortsighted solution was middle-class (white) women finding fulfillment in work. But this reactionary ideology is related to all the others of its day, including the Red Scare, segregation, and American militarism. Think how magazines equated good women not only with the white beauty standard but with material situations that Black people were explicitly excluded from. In the '50s, Black women were more likely to work outside the home, and the apartheid policies of redlining had made "nice" neighborhoods synonymous with whiteness. White women served then and now as mouthpieces and worker bees for the dominant culture, but one of the Feminine Mystique's greatest coups was making women take themselves less seriously, encouraging them to doubt themselves in any arena outside the maintenance of their bodies, their children, or their home.

The Feminine Mystique systematically emptied the lives of American women to fill them instead with an ever-lengthening list of things to buy. This social campaign transformed the United States into a country centered on consumption, though women were still dogged for their shopping addictions. This development was crucial to the cultural imperialism that the United States undertook after this, which brought blockbuster movies and Coca-Cola to every corner of the world. American advertising had found how effective cultivating a sense of inadequacy in American women and children was for turning a profit. In overseas markets, this inadequacy was easy to manufacture with American supremacy. People in areas gutted by colonialism and warfare were told that the only proximity they could get to American wealth was contributing to it, by buying Coke, Levi's, and McDonald's.

Many see Friedan's diagnosis of "the problem that has no name" as jump-starting the women's movement in America, meaning that the Feminine Mystique as a system of social control had essentially backfired. Although Friedan and the women's movement would spark social change in the status of women, the lure of the Feminine Mystique is still with us. It is ingrained in the cycles of sexist backlash that have jeopardized the rights

Second Wave feminists fought for, including access to abortion and contraception. But it is also the blueprint for the increasingly invasive kinds of marketing we see today. Marketing is virtually inescapable now, and advertisers treated my generation as the guinea pigs in magazines, on cable TV, in the early internet, and in evolving forms of social media. Marketing has become harder to distinguish from "content" online, to a point that this distinction doesn't matter—it's all selling something, first and foremost social media users to one another.

Perhaps that's why so many people my age seem to be cracking at the seams. There are the social media archetypes, people we know from high school and college: the MLM #girlbosses, the tradwives, the boymoms and girldads, the five a.m. Peloton riders, the Disney adults, the Marvel adults, the people who seem to be traveling to another bachelor party each weekend. All this desperate posting often hides a hamster wheel of corporate work, side hustles, and body projects (Whole30 and 30 Day Shred) that we were told long ago was not only the path for fulfillment and happiness but the only path normal people could take.

The Bachelor and other romance reality shows have by the 2020s become postmodern allegories of the desperation of capitalist gender fulfillment. Many of the contestants (male and female) are social media influencers hoping to become online celebrities; to do so, they must convincingly pretend they don't care about the fame and are there "for the right reasons," meaning that they are longing for a simple life of family and children. This domesticity is a burlesque performed by these reality show contestants that they then are able to sell on Instagram, YouTube, and TikTok, sending an army of their followers to

Pinterest with the manufactured need for ideas for their gender reveal parties or man caves.

In a time when American families are pushed to the brink by a pandemic, inflation, climate chaos, and far-right takeovers of state governments and the courts, of course many people dream of domestic bliss, an uncomplicated life bought with good old-fashioned American money. But it's not only surreal real estate prices that have made younger people realize that the white picket fence was not a promise made to us in good faith. It's also that the very desire for that life was implanted into us, creating a false consciousness of capitalist striving that is at odds with most of the real yearnings of our animal bodies. As Talking Heads once said, "You may find yourself in a beautiful house, with a beautiful wife / And you may ask yourself / Well . . . How did I get here?"

When I was sixteen, I left high school and went straight to college, getting closer to my lifelong dream of being a teenage free agent with her own car who answered to no one. At that point, I was deep into fashion magazines, reading *Vogue*, *W*, and *Harper's Bazaar* every month, frequently supplemented by expensive French, Italian, and Japanese imports that I would buy in the campus bookstore and charge to my student ID, which I knew my parents would eventually settle up as an addendum to my student bill. (No university I have attended or worked at since had such a fanciful and permissive payment system, and after the damage I was able to do in the student union, I doubt my alma mater still does.)

Fashion magazines are the domain of the real magazine

freaks. They provide little practical advice, only showcase products that are prohibitively expensive, and are written in dense and inaccessible shorthand, assuming your familiarity not only with Gucci and Alexander McQueen but Demna Gvasalia, Alessandra Rich, and LVMH. *Vogue* and *W* are trade magazines and boosters for the fashion industry, with *W* being the public-facing sister of the fashion insider's bible, *Women's Wear Daily*. The fashion mags were where I was destined to end up: I didn't want to be instructed in the unattainable details of a wholesome suburban girlhood anymore. I wanted to be transported.

The years of my magazine obsession, which lasted from when I was between the ages of ten and twenty, consisted of occasional mental health crises separated by long stretches of normal misery. *Vogue* was a dream machine, stuffed every month with Mario Testino photos of Gisele jumping in Grecian dresses, pastoral and British-y editorials styled by Grace Coddington, and spreads inspired by urban life, with models in incongruous ball gowns photographed in front of New York scaffolding or on industrial rooftops. Each page was an escape into an ornate and impossible world, created with the utmost precision, indulgence, and expense. Believing I was a full-time citizen of these worlds, it started to seem strange that I was still expected to attend German class, drive my brother to play rehearsal, or go to work.

The fall of my junior year of college, when I was what I now recognize as a baby of eighteen, these fantasies leaned dangerously toward dissociation. I started charging dozens of magazines at the student union, stuffing my backpack with pounds of them that I took everywhere. I soon had no space for textbooks and no time to read them. I had to stop going to all my classes, too, since my time was taken up with magazines and ancillary activities, like looking at the snaps from fashion shows on Style.com, checking twenty street-style blogs a day (not to brag, but I was reading *The Sartorialist* when it was still on Blogspot.com), watching every episode of *America's Next Top Model*, and making collages from hundreds of tiny circles cut from tabloids or magazine issues I happened to have two of. My report card that semester showed a late withdrawal, an incomplete, and an F. (Somehow, I also got a B in Arabic.) I got the incomplete by pleading mental illness, and on some level, I knew I was overwhelmed and over it, having started college too young and been shut out from the perks that usually came along with it: camaraderie, sexual experimentation, binge drinking. But I didn't feel depressed—I couldn't bring myself to feel anything about my real life. I was floating in fashion, buoyed on a sea of Christian Lacroix tulle and Rick Owens leather.

Magazines were brilliant dissociative tools, though they would have nothing on the narcosis of the social media scroll. I would soon trade one for the other, though I didn't know it at the time. The year was 2007, and both my magazine era and the magazine era writ large were coming to a close. George W. Bush was elected when I was twelve and left office when I was twenty, meaning that my entire teenage years were inflected with the terror, depravity, greed, militarism, paranoia, purity culture, misogyny, and idiocy of that cursed presidency. I was already more or less disillusioned with mainstream culture when I was halfway through college, having been seasoned by the MP3 blogs to listen only to "real indie" and go see foreign language films at the art theater on campus. I started telling people that American cinema was worthless after 1940. The fashion mags were a good stopgap, seeing how they cultivated highbrow and rarified tastes, but my interests were starting to stray. Once I was accepted to a graduate program in poetry, I started reading *Harper's Magazine* and *The Believer* instead of *Vogue*. When I moved away to start school, I left my magazines behind, and it was almost like the previous ten years hadn't existed. I didn't miss them.

A person is very different when they're twenty from when they're twelve. But I was desperate to leave behind this season of my life. The day before Barack Obama was inaugurated, I rode around town on my bike like a dork listening to "One Day More" from the *Les Misérables* soundtrack, filled with a promise Obama had delivered on, if only for a time: hope. Other people I knew experienced a similar kind of elation, wandering around stupefied, hugging friends in the street, wearing t-shirts despite the January weather. It's just that it seemed like it might really be over, this cruel era we have come to know as Y2K.

CODA: HISTORY REPEATS

As I am writing this, one of the most talked about trends on the internet is the return of "Y2K thinness" after a decade or so of obsession with ultra-curvy bodies, influenced by the surgically enhanced asses of the women of the Kardashian family. Y2K, a fashion era retroactively identified by young people on the internet who don't remember it, encompasses the years from roughly 1997 to 2004 and is marked by the kitschy, juvenile chic of the teen boom, with trends including low-rise denim,

Juicy Couture sweatsuits, shrunken vintage t-shirts, and Chihuahuas as accessories. The glorified thinness of this era was a covert glorification of youth, a taste for pubescent gawkiness represented most often by the socialite Paris Hilton, who has the body type of a beautiful bipedal giraffe. Now as the ideal body seems to be resetting, Kim Kardashian herself has allegedly had her Brazilian butt lift reversed, and many celebrities are rapidly shrinking thanks to the seemingly miraculous appetite-suppressing power of Ozempic, a drug meant for people with type 2 diabetes whose widely publicized use for weight loss has caused shortages of it in pharmacies around the United States.

The suggestion that this change in body trends is due to the trend cycle and not a consistent fetish for thinness, which is now more easily achieved for the ultrarich because of medical and surgical advances, seems misguided to me. When Kardashian took the reins as top socialite from her former best friend Hilton at the tail end of the '00s, many ballyhooed the shifting of our beauty ideal from the long-limbed, bony blonde to the short, voluptuous, and "exotic" brunette. But if we remove our superficial preoccupation with these specific people's bodies, this transition shows complete continuity between the Y2K era and now, when Kardashian and her family have managed to create a billion-dollar empire by placing themselves at the vanguard of the nascent social media industry. In fact, many more Y2K trends than those from the world of fashion have continued into the present day, including the saturation of "nepotism babies" in our public sphere, with Kardashian and Hilton as two high-profile examples. The nepo babies of today have nothing on the socialites of the 2000s, who were not only the scions of the entertainment industry but the children of royals and the heirs of hotel and shipping fortunes. They dominated every gossip mag of this era by doing little other than sunning on their yachts, dating celebrities and each other, and clubbing in Hollywood. Unlike the nepo babies of today, Y2K socialites had few compunctions about their inherited privilege. Paris Hilton bragged in 2018, "I was the first one who invented getting paid to party," which isn't true, but it is a great thing to say.

And we mustn't forget our nepo baby president, George W. Bush, who has received an unfair pass for his catastrophic tenure in office simply because he seems less personally dreadful than Donald Trump, perhaps the most dreadful man on the planet. His presidency was an impressive convergence of disasters, chief of which was causing the deaths of one million people in his two criminal wars. It was also a neoconservative nightmare of bureaucracy and deregulation, so that he both created a brand-new executive department, the Department of Homeland Security, whose chief mandate was to surveil, profile, and harass in the name of preventing terrorism, and presided over a failure of financial oversight so profound that it caused the worst financial crisis since the Great Depression. Bush, the second Evangelical Christian elected as president (after Jimmy Carter), is responsible for the takeover of many of our institutions by the powers of Christian Conservatism, a cultural movement obsessed with female purity and patriarchal control. One can trace a straight line from the Evangelical Great Awakening to the eventual striking down of *Roe v. Wade*, the badly reasoned and embarrassing decision that was written, of course, by one of Bush's appointees.

Just as one can trace a straight line from the how-to guides, editorials, and well-disguised ads of the magazine era to the sea of social media content we now swim in. The addictive, instant, customized, and never-ending nature of the modern social media feed fulfills the dream of women's magazines after social psychologists began to see their potential: creating a world made of marketing, an endless source of new aspirations to be achieved or insecurities to be ameliorated in one click. When I started writing this piece, I thought I would be drawing a distinction between the beloved magazines I apprenticed under and the behated social media applications that eat up so much of my time each day, but it's come to seem like more of the same. Both the magazines and social media are in the business of offering a curated catalog of identities, each promising some kind of self-actualization. More often than not it's a hall of mirrors, with each way out revealing itself as nothing more than an endlessly refracting dead end.

My magazine era was a painful time. I see myself in my harrowingly dirty bedroom at my parents' house, a sixteen-year-old college student with almost no friends, confused about my sexuality, my body, and my worth, against a backdrop of what seemed to be the endlessly deteriorating trend of American life and politics. I am clinging to an issue of *Vogue* for dear life, becoming immersed, allowing it to transport me somewhere else, some strange fashion land where the only problem that mattered was finding the perfect pair of $300 mules that could be worn both as house shoes and for a night on the town. This helped get me through, answering my yearning if not quite fulfilling it, to a young adulthood where purpose and connection were finally possible for me. But now I know it could have been easier. If only in the frenzied pace of American culture in this century, with trends and talking points turning over like magazines switched out at newsstands at the end of each month, some still point had beckoned me, had grounded me where I stood on a square foot of ground, had told me that I had better pay attention because, as we bought things and gossiped and argued as if this world were made of purchases and scandals and squabbles, reality was constantly being destroyed and remade beneath me—not some papier-mâché dreamworld constructed by advertising executives to be entered through a trapdoor in my mind, but right here, life as I knew it, disappearing even as I write, vanishing to a point. I can see it now.

THE RABBIT HOLE

FOR THE FIRST PART OF MY THIRTIES, BOGGED IN A three-year-long depression, most of the books that could keep my attention were chick lit classics and celebrity memoirs. Meditation teachers say to imagine "a mind like the sky"; mine felt like a cage with steel bars a neglected chimp would rattle a cup across. When I was hungry, I would get stoned instead of eating; then I would read about the blond celebrities of my teenage years. "Did you read the Britney Spears book?" I asked a friend. "No," she said. "I read real books." I can't tell if my intellect has been so degraded by hours staring at my phone screen that I can no longer appreciate real literature, but these books feel not only real to me but important. Recent years have upped the ante on the anodyne, empty, inspirational celebrity book, and stars are now regularly naming names, giving receipts, getting vulnerable, and serving lyricism from some of the world's finest ghostwriters.

Sure, the main selling point is still the gossip, especially in Jessica Simpson's four-hundred-page tome, *Open Book*, where she provides enough incriminating stories about her celebrity exes to keep you entertained for weeks. But these books are full of just as many depressing details as there are frothy ones, like with Spears's horrifying account in *The Woman in Me* of the years she spent under a legal conservatorship as basically a prisoner of her parents, who controlled her medications, her relationships, her career, and her money. Another paragon is Jennette McCurdy's instant classic *I'm Glad My Mom Died*, where the Nickelodeon star turned writer (she did not use the help of a ghostwriter) describes the decades of abuse she suffered from her stage mother, who pushed her into the entertainment industry and was so codependent and controlling that McCurdy suffered from severe eating disorders and alcoholism before she reached adulthood.

These memoirs have ridden a wave of new compassion for the women of the era we now call Y2K, with adult millennials looking back to consider the toxic atmosphere we grew up in. It was inevitable that I would grow up with warped ideas about my body, sex, and power, shaped as they were by an atmosphere of both conservative Christian backlash and gonzo exhibitionism, which colluded to create a culture of violent sexual obsession with teenage girls. Women my age feel a kinship with the teen girls who were propped up as our heroes during this time, sensing they were at the epicenter of a storm of exploitation and abuse, something their books bear out. But our devotion to former teen stars is a double-edged phenomenon. We are both resentful of the pop culture of our childhood and forever marked by it, with residual programming from MTV and teen magazines instilling in us a celebrity obsession we have never quite gotten over. These books and the response to them are documents of these conflicted emotions. We are still invested in the stars of our youth, but we want to be told that their celebrity was a tragic mistake—that it was just as damaging for them as it was for us.

None of the 2000s tell-alls I read had quite the same impact as my favorite celebrity memoir of all time, *Down the Rabbit Hole* by Holly Madison, Hugh Hefner's "main girlfriend" during the filming of the 2000s E! reality series about life at the Playboy Mansion, *The Girls Next Door*. *Playboy* was a more consequential monument of my childhood than any of the teen stars of *TRL*, although I never saw it that way until the past few years. By the age of eleven, I was a tweenage magazine addict and insomniac who watched cable television almost literally twenty-four hours a day. With this media diet, I was already well aware of Hefner and *Playboy*. I knew that Pamela Anderson had gotten her start posing nude in the magazine. I knew its mascot was a rabbit, although I only recently learned that it was intended to represent not the female bunnies from the magazine but a jackrabbit, an amorous bachelor bunny. I even knew that it was a joke to say that you read *Playboy* "for the articles" but also that the articles were considered to be very good. I was eager to read it but too terrified to try to get my hands on one, not that it would have been difficult, considering they almost certainly existed in my house.

At that time, roughly at the turn of the millennium, I thought of Hefner as one of those old guys who was always on TV trying to project wealth by wearing silk pajamas, like Robin Leach or George Hamilton. I was more interested in "his girls," for latent homoerotic reasons but also because of the rarified dream they projected. There remains the seductive show business myth of a starlet being discovered, like fifteen-year-old Lana Turner being scouted as she drank a milkshake on Sunset Boulevard. Hardly anyone stoked this myth quite like Hefner. He wanted people to believe that he found and molded every model he worked with, plucking the hottest girl from every American high school, for which they adored him and owed him everything. In a way it is the most human thing in the world to long to have our specialness recognized by a keen eye, to shine out from obscurity and have someone tell us we do not belong down there with the normal people. Hefner intentionally spoke not only to men with *Playboy* but to women, too, encouraging them to imagine themselves in its pages.

Hefner founded *Playboy* in 1953 as the first mainstream nudie magazine, modeled after more buttoned-up "gentlemen's magazines" like *GQ* and *Esquire* but including nude centerfolds that the other men's titles wouldn't dare publish. Hefner took a more high-minded line later, claiming that he had founded *Playboy* to champion free speech and sexual liberation, but his initial impetus to publish the nude pictorials was more about protecting his freedom to make a fortune selling magazines, and breasts will always be more marketable than essays by Norman Mailer. His innovation, other than the discovery that beautiful naked women were a winner with the magazine-reading public, was his decision to become a public figure and embody the "*Playboy*" man," thus launching what may have been the first consciously crafted personal brand of the late capitalist era. He divorced his first wife, bought a Mercedes roadster, moved into the first Playboy Mansion in Chicago in 1959, and began cross-promoting the magazine through TV specials and a chain of nightclubs and casinos. In 1974, he moved to the famous

Playboy Mansion West in Holmby Hills, Los Angeles, a massive fourteen-thousand-square-foot compound with the city's only private zoo.

By the time Holly Madison moved into the mansion at the age of twenty-two, Hefner was seventy-five years old. He had entered one of those supposedly rare third acts of American life, having divorced his second wife in 1998 and discovered an enthusiasm for clubbing, fueled by the attention he received from young people in the Hollywood party scene. He began appearing in public often with his seven live-in girlfriends, shilling the gimmick of a geriatric man in pajamas and a captain's hat being fawned over by enough young, gorgeous, interchangeable blondes that they could have formed their own volleyball team. This publicity sparked a surprise rebound for the Playboy brand, with magazine coverage and TV appearances leading to a reality hit with *The Girls Next Door*. By the time the reality show aired, Hef had downsized from his seven girlfriends to only three: Madison, Bridget Marquardt, and Kendra Wilkinson. Maintaining a coterie of such size was cost prohibitive, in part because Hefner's personal finances were so entwined with that of the Playboy Corporation that the company was essentially footing the bill for the women's room, board, and weekly allowances.

I picked up Holly's book because the show had been one of my favorites during my teen years. E! aired reruns of it constantly from 2005 to 2008, and it is something of a classic of the early reality TV genre, a lighthearted and goofy romp following Hefner and his girlfriends in storylines that were almost all about throwing parties, taking trips to Las Vegas, and modeling and shilling for *Playboy* magazine and its associated products. I had rewatched some of *The Girls Next Door* in the years before I read Holly's book, and parts of it were admittedly unsettling from an adult's perspective. The role of "girlfriend" was ambiguous, and the cast members talked so much about how it was their dream to model for *Playboy*—it was impossible to shake the sense that a place in Hefner's harem was a dubious consolation prize. I hated how Holly said that dating Hef made her more aware of her physical "flaws" and how he kissed everyone, even his girlfriends' elderly grandmothers, on the lips. Despite this, and despite knowing Holly's book was considered a tell-all, I was still surprised by all she had to tell. Some of her first descriptions of the mansion, one of the most expensive private residences in Los Angeles, are downright gnarly, as she writes, "At the time, there were nine dogs living in the mansion . . . and the ancient yellow carpeting on the grand staircase was covered in urine stains." Other girlfriends have also described dog shit stuck in the carpet, so it is possible that Holly spared us some details.

She explains how in the late '90s and early '00s, a role as one of the girlfriends was seen as a stepping stone to appearing in the magazine as a Playmate, but the job had devolved over time. At a certain point, Hef secretly decided he wasn't going to let his girlfriends continue to take turns as centerfolds of the month, but he still dangled it as a possibility to keep them beholden to him. The girlfriends were not allowed to date anyone else, had a strict nine p.m. curfew, and had to consult Hef if they wanted to take other jobs or travel, requests he usually denied. They had to take part in weekly mansion events, which included not only buffet dinners, movie nights, and "Fun in the Sun" days but weekly group sex with Hef, Playmates, magazine hopefuls, and other random girls, the details of which are stomach-turning. Holly writes about how despite the grandfatherly image Hef projected on the E! show, he emotionally abused and controlled her, berated her if she changed her appearance or wore red lipstick, and called her names like "bitch" and "cunt." She also describes his nastier proclivities, his "fascination with extremely young women," and, worse, discovering "an old reel stashed away in a drawer full of porn labeled 'Girl and Dog.'"

Even after all these revelations about Hefner, it became apparent that Holly was not going to hold anything back in *Down the Rabbit Hole* when she recounted the story of the escorting service that infiltrated the mansion during her early years there, with the infamous Hollywood madam Michelle Braun employing a long list of Playmates, models, and girlfriends. Holly names names in somewhat unsisterly fashion, telling on the girls who had traded on their proximity to *Playboy* to earn $25,000 paydays doing sex work for millionaires and billionaires around the world. There's a goody-two-shoes tinge to Holly's revelations, despite her insistence that she never judged the women who took on these side jobs, as she contrasts her refusal to participate ("Was she really asking me if I'd consider becoming a hooker!?") with these other women who couldn't resist the "expensive cars, designer handbags, and luxury apartments" that escorting afforded them, in addition to "supporting some pretty nasty drug habits."

Even though Holly held herself apart from these activities, she knows she is destabilizing one of the pillars of the *Playboy* image: the idea that, despite its nudity, it was a classy and tasteful institution that floated above the rest of the sex industry. Hef despised sex workers, attempting to maintain a "no stripper" policy for Playmates (as was the case with escorting, many *Playboy* models and girlfriends had been strippers and simply lied) and even retaining a private investigating service during the years that he owned Playboy nightclubs to ensure that none of the "Bunnies" employed as cocktail servers were earning money from providing sexual services. The key to Hefner's vision of a magazine that would be both explicit and mainstream was in his cultivation of the wholesome Playmate image, a "girl next door" (he harped on this cliché constantly), who was simultaneously stunning, innocent, and available. I guess I had somehow bought into this branding, such that even as a relatively worldly woman in her my thirties I was momentarily shocked that Playmates had been so literally selling sex for money. This strikes me as brainless now. How was having sex with a Turkish billionaire for $25,000 different from having sex with Hefner for a weekly allowance of $1,000, plus room and board, other than that the first was more money for less work?

The realization descended on me in an instant that the line I had imagined separating the entertainment industry and the sex industry did not exist. Despite being the twentieth century's most famous pornographer, Hefner was highly invested in maintaining the hierarchy that cast one of these industries as glamorous and the other as shameful. The stigma that kept his girlfriends and Playmates suspended in a no-man's-land between "legitimate" modeling and sex work allowed him to control them and keep them dependent on him. When I watched *The Girls Next Door* again after reading Holly's book, I was shaken by how much of the bizarre, inappropriate, and even abusive dynamic at the mansion unfolded in view of the television public. To begin with, I had somehow failed to realize in all my years of viewing that the youngest girlfriend, Kendra Wilkinson, was only nineteen when the show began filming—three years older than I was, watching in my childhood bedroom—although they take no measures to hide it, and she celebrates her twentieth birthday in the first season in an episode called "Happy Birthday, Kendra!" Rewatching, I was continually reminded that I am nearly twice the age she was then—and still less than half the age Hef was.

His girlfriends talk blithely on the show about their nine p.m. curfew, and they have to fly to and from Las Vegas in the same day because Hef won't let them spend the night away from him. He does not seem to mind appearing like a controlling father—he often calls himself "Daddy"—although the subject of the women's allowance is mercifully avoided. In later seasons there is a perverse emphasis on them all being one big family, with scenes of the girlfriends piling into Hef's bed in matching pink flannel pajamas, the same ones Holly alleges they were forced to wear for sex. Apparently this wholesomeness (despite the show's nudity and innuendo) was to please Hef, who didn't want to trade in any of the conflict or drama that reality TV has become known for. He wanted Playboy to be depicted as one harmonious community swirling around him, the ringmaster of his own circus, both Willy Wonka and a kid in a candy store. He had final say on what was included in each episode, and after decades courting the spotlight, he was expert at orchestrating his own image. Despite all the red flags blazing, he still comes off as shrewd, fun loving, and beneficent, partly because of how the girlfriends lay it on so thick, describing him as their hero, their savior, the love of their lives. Everyone, in fact, seems to be praising Hef in nearly every scene, like the random aesthetician at a spa who asks, "Is he just as handsome in person?" before waxing Bridget's teenage sister's labia.

This was a man who kept a collection of three thousand scrapbooks, many of them filled with the positive press clippings he employed a staff member just to archive and keep track of. Even more impressive than his ego's ravenous hunger was how eager people were to fill his need, not only E! producers and people on his payroll but journalists, too, who in their natural shabbiness were often so dazzled by the Playboy lifestyle that they were more than willing to slop out breathless plaudits when their deadlines came around. One of the most embarrassing is Wil S. Hylton's 2000 *Rolling Stone* profile, which depicts Hefner playing him like a harp, complaining that other reporters had "come to [him] with a preconceived agenda . . . They end up with a story that's very superficial, without much insight to the man inside." Hylton is more than happy to write whatever Hefner wants him to about "the man inside," casting him as misunderstood and contemplative, a philosopher of American life, who gathers parties to him at his legendary mansion through his personal magnetism, despite longing to be alone. "You're the new Great Gatsby," Hylton told him during one of the weeks he spent not only partying but living at the Playboy Mansion. "Then I frowned," Hylton adds, "because I had no idea what I meant."

I balked at the stunning stupidity of this moment. How could he not get the obvious implications of this sentence, one that he himself had said? Did he not understand the character of Jay Gatsby, one of the most famous in American literature, as the icon of the self-made man, someone for whom achieving the American dream meant alienation from love and meaning, a bisexual socialite who manipulated his male simps even more than he did his women, a disillusioned dreamer who continued throwing great parties even when he was sick of them? (Did he also have no idea that casting yourself as Nick Carraway is the definition of a self-report?) Either Hylton considered these implications to be too on the nose—even for him—or someone fed him this line, which he found himself blurting out at a random moment. I think I know who it could have been.

Hef was even able to assimilate his control freak tendencies into his cult of personality. He wanted to be seen as the consummate editor, curating every detail about his magazine, his house, and the women he surrounded himself with. This is part of what makes the fall of the house of Playboy all the more fascinating, as the things none of us can control—death and the unceasing nature of change—eventually took everything from him, just as it will all of us. By the 2010s, the TV show was over, print media was dying, and Hefner had to begin selling off his assets and tickets to his famous parties, which had once been some of the most exclusive events in Hollywood. The mansion sold in 2016 to an investor who allowed Hefner to live there until his death, which came shortly after, in 2017. The Playboy renaissance of the early 2000s now seems more like a last gasp, a way to shore up the doomed company with flashy investments like a new Playboy Club at the Palms casino in Las Vegas, all designed to make the brand appear ascendant and reinforce Hefner's icon status. Most of these proved as susceptible to the tidal wave of the 2008 financial crisis as the magazine itself.

Reading the headlines when Hefner died, I felt less than

nothing about it. He had receded in my mind to a curiosity of my childhood whom I had rarely thought about since *The Girls Next Door* went off the air, and I was content to keep him that way. Maybe it's the same for you, and I am performing an ironic resurrection act with this essay. That's what I am struggling with as I write this, the conflicting urges to dig him up and let him go. But like Alice down the rabbit hole, Holly's book started me down a path, and I can't turn back. Hefner's life is over, his magazine is finished, his mansion sold, yet I fear we are still living in a wonderland of his creation—and I'm trying to find the escape route.

In 2024, there was a new, unexpected Playboy tell-all, this time from Hefner's widow, Crystal Hefner, which I placed on hold at the library months in advance. Crystal had obediently followed the company line since Hef's death, defending his memory and keeping mum about her life at the mansion. She was still a young woman, but she had lived for seven years as a captive to her late husband, like the wife left in Bluebeard's house after he is killed. She made it clear that with her memoir she would break her silence, refusing to play the loyal wife Hef had hoped for after he died.

Crystal's book is more vulnerable and emotional than Holly's, describing her childhood trauma and how her lower-middle-class upbringing in San Diego led her to long for the glitz and security of the Playboy Mansion. It also provides an insider view of the disintegration of Hefner's life and business as he succumbed to old age, clinging to authority that was quickly slipping through his fingers. By the end of his life, Hefner was

vulnerable to humiliation in ways that he hadn't been in decades. After Bridget, Holly, and Kendra left the mansion, he attempted to replace them with a cast of new girlfriends, but they
lacked the personality and chemistry of the original three and
The Girls Next Door was swiftly canceled. Desperate to keep all
eyes on him, he decided to marry Crystal and, without consulting her, dove into producing a new E! special about their
lavish wedding. Crystal claims the engagement was a pure publicity stunt that she never agreed to, since Hefner never properly
proposed. Hefner was going to earn $800,000 for the special,
while she would get only a $2,500 "talent fee." Seething with
resentment that both a huge life decision and an overwhelming
amount of work were being forced on her, Crystal slipped out
of the mansion secretly during a movie night and broke off the
engagement, forcing Hef to slap stickers that said "Runaway
Bride" on the already-printed promotional wedding issue of
Playboy featuring Crystal on the cover.

Despite the fact that Crystal eventually came back and married him, the damage was done. She made headlines for leaving him and belittled Hef's sexual performance on *The Howard
Stern Show*. And this was only one crack in the facade. Hef was
ordered to give testimony in the rape case against his longtime
friend Bill Cosby about two assaults that had allegedly happened on the grounds of the Playboy Mansion. Holly's book
was published in 2015, the first Playboy exposé Hef had not
been able to squash or cast serious doubt on. On his ninety-
first birthday, the last one he would celebrate, he made one
final request to Crystal. He asked her to be on the board of his
foundation, to help safeguard his legacy. "And I want to remind
you," he told her, "to only say good things about me."

This was the last, impossible request of someone who may have realized that he would shortly lose any ability to stem the tide of allegations against him—that he was in danger of his image transforming from American icon to monster. And when he died, one week before the Harvey Weinstein abuse story became the largest news story in the country, maybe he knew he was getting out just in time. Crystal kept her promise for a while, but even she broke eventually, and the memoir she wrote about Hefner's narcissism and abuse bears an ironic title: *Only Say Good Things*. But this was after the truth had come out, dozens of stories of rape and exploitation, his sixty-year reign of terror made public for the first time. Some who knew him remained loyal. Many more wanted to talk.

The deluge began in 2022 with the A&E series *Secrets of Playboy*, in which dozens of former Playmates, girlfriends, and employees of the Playboy Clubs dating back to the 1960s allege systematic abuse of women on the part of Hefner and the Playboy Corporation. The series is difficult to watch, not only because the allegations are horrific but because they seem to go on and on, making the magazine's notorious casting couch look like innocent fun by comparison. Witnesses and alleged victims on the series claim Hefner violently raped women, drugged them, forced them to participate in group sex, filmed them without their knowledge, and abused underage girls. There appears to have been no end to his depravity, and the show even includes multiple nauseating descriptions of Hefner engaging in bestiality with dogs. Some of the series' claims may carry more weight than others, and each episode is framed with a disclaimer that these are only allegations, and the producers were not formally accusing anyone of any crimes. But if Hefner committed even a fraction of what the show alleges about him, few of us would hesitate to call him a serial predator.

It may be difficult now to imagine how all these beautiful women were drawn into Hefner's inner circle, particularly for my young readers who have not grown up under his shadow. His empire dissolved so quickly after his death that it is hard to imagine how rich, powerful, famous, and revered he was. His estimation of female beauty was once considered so valuable that a woman would give up her freedom to be told he approved of her. There was an irresistible allure to ascending to the echelon of Playmate, like being named Miss America, a concrete symbol of female desirability. In a 2000 *Vanity Fair* profile of Hefner, his girlfriends all talk about having wanted to be a Playmate since they were children, one saying she'd dreamed about it since she was six years old.

And like any charismatic leader, he knew whom to target. As his secretary of five decades told Crystal, "He always chooses the ones with the broken wings." *Secrets of Playboy* is full of women telling the same kinds of life stories: they grew up in poverty or suffered childhood abuse, they were naive and inexperienced, they were shy, they had low self-esteem, they were flattered by Hef's interest in them and easily bullied. And nearly all of them were very, very young. Hefner said in a famous, nauseating quotation that the ideal Playmate was not "the mysterious, difficult woman, the femme fatale," but the "young, healthy, simple girl—the girl next door." Hefner may be more responsible than anyone else for overtly replacing women with girls (his words, not mine) as the apex of female beauty and desirability for the second half of the twentieth century. Fostering his audience's sexual taste for teenagers created cover for his continuing to recruit manipulable women. Barbi Benton, his most famous girl-friend of the '70s, was eighteen when she met him, and his next main girlfriend, Sondra Theodore, was nineteen. He was forty-two and fifty, respectively.

When first reading Holly's book, one word began to ring in my head as she described the kind of loyalty Hef demanded: "cult." Turns out I was not the only one—this connection is hammered so explicitly in *Secrets of Playboy* that one might think Hef was leaning into it. If he wanted to avoid these comparisons, he could at least have declined to purchase the Manson Family's home movies. Anyone who has seen a cult documentary would recognize his methods of control: creating a self-contained compound that isolated the women from the outside world; controlling how they looked, what they ate, and where they could go; delaying payment or meting it out slowly to keep them financially dependent; constantly crossing their personal boundaries and convictions until their sense of iden-tity was broken down. Not only that but he was expert at mak-ing everyone complicit in his misdeeds. Like other cult leaders I've written about, he had female deputies strategically placed to gaslight his victims and deodorize the company's activities, including his own daughter, Christie, who served as Playboy CEO for more than twenty years. And he enlisted Playmates and girlfriends to recruit other women into his bedroom, a role that both Crystal and Sondra say has haunted them.

As we might have expected, Hefner's obsession with recording his life went beyond his giant scrapbook collection. He filmed every one of his famously debaucherous parties, took thousands of drunk naked snapshots of the women he went clubbing with, and secretly made hundreds of sex tapes. (Crystal writes that she personally shredded any of the snapshots she could find, and that Hef destroyed the sex tapes after Pamela Anderson and Tommy Lee's wedding tape was stolen and leaked to the public. One wonders if this was not also because of the potentially illegal nature of these tapes, allegedly filmed mostly without the participants' consent, and possibly even featuring underage girls.) Hefner could use this "mountain of revenge porn," as Holly calls it on *Secrets of Playboy*, to silence anyone who spoke out against him, and this went beyond the models who worked for him to include anyone who ever took an illicit drug or engaged in a sex act at the mansion, a list that might just include many of the most famous people in Hollywood.

The breadth of Hefner's sphere of influence goes some way to explain why there wasn't a comprehensive takedown of Playboy before this—like, for instance, when Hefner was still alive. *Secrets of Playboy* addresses this in the first episode, claiming that Hefner had the LAPD on his payroll and used intimidation and his connections to prevent or bury accusations from whistleblowers. But the reason might be more complicated than that, related to why, despite the extreme nature of these allegations and the corroboration the show provides, it didn't shock the public the same way other takedowns of famous abusers did. No one whom I've mentioned it to, and I regret to say I have mentioned it to many people, had any idea that Hefner was accused of assaulting dogs, which is the one allegation I almost expected to pierce through the noise.

Hefner appears to have inculcated a vast swath of the American public in his cult of personality. Loyal readers of *Playboy* learned at Hefner's feet for decades, believing the image he painted of himself as a hip and progressive bon vivant, and it is even more blatant on *The Girls Next Door* that he was grooming the audience. The show was primarily watched by young women, including myself, and it presents a view of Playboy that is fun, family-friendly, and glamorous, with Hef as the pervy Daddy Warbucks making his girlfriends' dreams come true. Karissa and Kristina Shannon, identical eighteen-year-old twins who became replacement girlfriends in the last season of *The Girls Next Door* along with Crystal, had watched the show as younger teenagers. The twins say on *Secrets of Playboy* that they believed they were being cast for a reality show, not a relationship, and they were shocked when they were expected to have sex with the eighty-one-year-old Hefner.

Hefner amassed so much loyalty that many of the accounts posting about *Secrets of Playboy* online defend him. Comments on social media say that the women should be grateful for the opportunities Hefner afforded them or that "they knew what they were getting into." This is absurd on its face—rape cannot be consented to in advance—but it shows how audiences are gaslighting themselves, trying to shake off their complicity, the sick feeling that these women whose job it was to look like they wanted it did not want it at all. They deny the abuse happened, while at the same time saying, "Well, what did they expect?"

Perhaps this was part of the plan, too. *Secrets of Playboy* includes a chilling clip from an interview with Hefner where he says that if he could have dinner with anyone, living or dead, it would be Jesus Christ. He thinks that Jesus would more than approve of his life, reasoning that, after all, "He forgave the whores." This is the same man who, according to *Secrets of Playboy*, hosted a weekly party called "Pig Night" in the '70s in which he would round up Hollywood sex workers and bring them back to the mansion to be assaulted. And still Hef saw himself as savior and redeemer, the first to create porn with no "whores" in it. Embedded in his image of the classy girls next door who were in his classy sex magazine was a threat. His models were dangled above an abyss that was the word "whore," and it was only his intervention—or his forgiveness—that kept them from falling into it.

This is the power of "whore stigma," as Melissa Gira Grant writes in her invaluable study of sex workers' struggle for legitimacy, *Playing the Whore*. The primary use of this stigma is not only to demean women by calling them whores but to make it such a shameful and dehumanizing insult that it terrifies them into silence. Gira Grant writes, "As long as there are women who are called whores, there will be women who are trained to believe it is next to death to be one or to be mistaken for one." And this is not an irrational fear. Whore stigma creates a category of women whose lives and safety are considered less valuable, for whom rape and other forms of violence should be expected, since, after all, "they knew what they were getting into." "Why do you think your accusations weren't believed?" a host asks Sondra Theodore in the second season of *Secrets of Playboy*. "I think they do believe us," Theodore says. "They just don't care."

In 1985, Miki Garcia, a former Playmate who had been the head of Playmate Promotions, made the most public attempt ever to blow the whistle on abuse at Playboy, testifying before Attorney General Edwin Meese's Commission on Pornography about abuses against Playboy employees. She alleged that women were drugged, raped, and coerced into group sex, and that some suffered with lasting mental health struggles, drug addiction, and even suicide attempts because of their experiences there. This did hurt *Playboy*'s circulation numbers, although they had already started to fall from the height of the magazine's popularity in the 1970s. The commission spooked newsstands, who began to censor explicit magazines or stop selling them altogether. Beyond that, nothing was done to punish Hefner or protect women at his company.

Forty years on, Garcia is still proud of speaking out, even though her resistance was mostly symbolic. "If Hugh Hefner were alive today, he would be in jail," she says on *Secrets of Playboy*, ruing the fact that he dodged the #MeToo wave that finally took down Cosby and others. In reality, the Meese Commission interlude proved how effectively Hefner had backed his opponents into a corner, so that the only authority they could turn to were conservative censors. Meese was one of the most powerful figures in the right-wing Ronald Reagan administration, and the Commission on Pornography would lead to further criminalization of sex work, leaving those in the sex industry more marginalized during the AIDS epidemic. It was exactly the kind of bad PR Hefner lived to spin. Playboy had already sued Meese for infringing on his free speech rights, and it was not difficult afterward for Hefner to cast him as a rogue attorney general using his power to fight "obscenity" rather than corruption or civil rights abuses—because that's exactly what he was.

The most basic lesson of social change is that we will not dismantle power by collaborating with it, and yet we need to learn it again and again. Garcia was compromised from the moment she agreed to speak to Meese, as substantive as her claims were. If she thought more legal action might come from speaking to the attorney general, she did not understand that violence and abuse against women were not the kind of obscenity the Reagan administration was offended by. His presidency was thanks in part to an ascendant Christian right that even then was redefining morality as synonymous with sexual purity. The Meese Commission was not created to shed light on the conditions in the adult industry but to sweep women like the Playmates out of sight. Meese and his allies in the conservative movement may have been willing to use Garcia's testimony to target Hefner and others whom they saw as polluting the minds of the public, but they would never believe that the women abused at Playboy were innocent victims, that they didn't know what they were getting into.

Garcia's testimony was the least of Playboy's worries as it weathered its worst decade, the 1980s. In 1986, it had to close its once iconic chain of Playboy Clubs, capping off what *The New York Times* called "a string of bad luck" that included gaming officials shuttering its London casinos, once the most profitable wing of the Playboy Corporation. In 1982, officials refused Playboy a gaming license for its Atlantic City casino unless it cut ties with Hefner, forcing the company out of the gaming business altogether and paving the way for it to become the Trump(!) Regency in 1989. Nearly every piece of bad luck was precipitated by allegations of fraud, bribery, and self-dealing against higher-ups at Playboy that put them on the wrong side of liquor boards, gaming boards, and the police. Hef may have been drawn to the casino business because the house always wins, but that maxim never holds truer than in dealings with the U.S. government.

A reliance on backroom deals and nepotism formed Hefner's business strategy throughout his entire career. This is one reason he created the Playboy Mansion, a clubhouse where insiders could gather and a place to ingratiate himself to powerful people through his elaborate parties. The models and girlfriends he surrounded himself with were a part of this strategy, too, a perk for men in his inner circle to enjoy. Hef could blame his losses in the '80s on a puritanical culture under Reagan or a vendetta by public officials, but the flaws in his business model were catching up to him. One of the coups in Hefner's lifelong project of fashioning his own image is that he is spoken of as a business icon now, when Playboy was consistently unprofitable, partially because it was difficult to attract investors and advertisers to a pornography company, but also because of his profligate spending and cronyism. Even after grounding the "Bunny Jet" and reducing the Chicago mansion's staff from fifty to twelve (this at a time when Hefner was already living in Los Angeles), the company posted losses of $5 million in 1979.

At the same time, I know Hefner was a business genius, in that he anticipated a switch to a branding economy in which the appearance of wealth is just as important as the real thing. Hefner craved to be taken seriously, with the highbrow writers he put in his magazine, the classy pretensions of his nightclubs, and, once he moved to the West Coast, his efforts to insinuate himself into Hollywood society, hobnobbing with stars he hoped might help him get into the movie business. He was an unremarkable man physically and personally; he had to project his persona onto his possessions, especially the mansion, which became a Gothic extension of himself. This explains his near-exclusive interest in the material things of life, with *Playboy*'s editorial content goading its readers to amass the outward markers of taste and status. At the height of its popularity in the 1960s and early '70s, *Playboy* was seen as a hip urban bible, the thinking man's lad mag, with Hefner as an influential curator of cool whom *Time* magazine called "the boss of taste city" and *Rolling Stone* called "Playboy's philosopher king."

By the 1980s, his serious facade was crumbling. The clubs and casinos were casualties of his incompetence and misman-agement, and Playboy was forced to give up some of its claims to "classiness" when it entered the adult video business in order to make up some of its losses. The new seediness of his image was painful for Hefner, but he also counted on it to protect him. Stories about women and sex are almost always classified as tabloid fodder, cordoned off not only from real news but discussions about broader patterns of exploitation. The more lurid Playboy stories of this time overshadowed reports of Hef-ner's corrupt business practices, ensuring that few connected the dots between his lack of professional scruples and the way he treated the women who worked for him.

This is how many have told the story of Hef's decade of woe: as a noir tale, beginning, as they all do, with a girl. Miss August, 1979. Her name was Dorothy Stratten, and she was the nineteen-year-old blonde who Hefner hoped would be-come Playboy's first legitimate star. She was named Playmate of the Year in 1980 and was just beginning her acting career, hav-ing been handpicked by the A-list director and producer Pe-ter Bogdanovich to star in his new film. Bogdanovich had also handpicked her as his new girlfriend, despite their twenty-one-year age difference. The budding relationship cut off Stratten's estranged husband, Paul Snider, a small-time criminal from her native British Columbia, from the spoils of her ascent to fame, and he killed her and himself on August 14, 1980, just one year after she first appeared in *Playboy*.

As Teresa Carpenter notes in her *Village Voice* article on the murder, "Death of a Playmate," there is a disturbing parallelism between Hefner, Bogdanovich, and Snider. Each, in a sense, wanted credit for "discovering" Stratten, although that distinction ultimately goes to Snider, who met her when she was still a teenager scooping ice cream and allegedly told a friend, "That girl could make me a lot of money." This was what each of the men discovered when he looked at her: dollar signs. Hefner hoped she would elevate him to an actual Hollywood playmaker, and Bogdanovich saw in her a potential muse and box office star. The men had other things in common, too, namely a romantic desire for Stratten that intermingled with the desire to profit off her. Carpenter takes Hefner's word for it that his relationship with Stratten was as a "father figure," since "fucking Hefner [was] a strictly voluntary thing," though she acknowledges that "it never hurts a career." At this point there are many accounts to the contrary, not just about Hefner's coercion in general but Stratten specifically. In *Secrets of Playboy*, a former mansion butler claims to be an eyewitness to Hefner raping Stratten in a hot tub after she rebuffed Hef's advances. This same allegation forms the centerpiece of Bogdanovich's 1984 book, *The Killing of the Unicorn*, which was an attempted takedown of Hefner and his treatment of women.

Bogdanovich held Hefner partially responsible for Stratten's murder, and he wanted to pull back the curtain on Playboy's inner sanctum. As Hillary Johnson phrased it at the time in *Rolling Stone*, the thesis of the book held that "Hefner's sexual theme park was merely another element of a deranged, woman-hating culture that included snuff films and gang rape." The feud with Bogdanovich forms the centerpiece of Johnson's 1986 *Rolling Stone* feature, "Hugh Hefner: Blows Against the Empire," in which she chronicles how "admiration and envy during Hefner's ascendant, golden years [had] given way to general distaste." The article finds Hef in extreme PR mode, fixated on Bogdanovich's assault on "his good name" and fuming that *The Killing of the Unicorn* was as believable as science fiction. When Hefner suffered a stroke in 1985, he blamed it on Bogdanovich and his allegations.

Despite Hef's theatrical response to it, Bogdanovich's book failed to have the impact that he had hoped. Although Hefner's public image would never be the same as it had been—perhaps to be expected after three decades of celebrity—the book did not take him or Playboy down in any legal or business sense. Hef made a full recovery from his stroke and, sensing it was time for reinvention, married Playmate Kimberley Conrad in 1989 and had two more children with her. *The Killing of the Unicorn* was panned by critics, who thought it was tawdry and self-serving. Readers were skeptical that a director with a well-known history of affairs with his young ingenues had a true feminist awakening and thought that if Hefner was a creep, well, then it took one to know one. Bogdanovich was probably the worst messenger for these allegations of sexual abuse, considering that he would go on to marry Dorothy's younger sister when she was only twenty years old after years of apparent grooming, paying for her schooling and modeling classes.

Johnson reported on Hefner's denials with a raised eyebrow—he insisted there was never a casting couch at Playboy, despite his only dating women who had appeared in the magazine for thirty years at that point—but she also seems to see Bogdanovich's points connecting the soft-core pornography published in *Playboy* to "snuff films and gang rape" as far-fetched and hyperbolic, a histrionic slippery slope argument from a resentful, grieving lover. But Bogdanovich was not abstractly theorizing, implying a vague categorical relationship between nude pictorials and extreme abuse of women. He was accusing Hefner of using the glossy appeal of his famous magazine to lure women to be abused and exploited. Forty years later, *Secrets of Playboy* alleges Hefner watched snuff films *and* committed gang rape.

Maybe Hefner just got a break with the timing and source of the Stratten allegations—his stroke, oddly, serving as a stroke of luck—or maybe he performed a public relations sleight of hand, shrouding the allegations against him in a haze of political debate, celebrity ego games, and true crime melodrama. He excelled at pointing out the hypocrisy of his opponents, whether Bogdanovich or the Reagan administration, always finding some way to slither up to the moral high ground and turn the conversation to free speech, sexual liberation, and his beliefs about American progress. He was a symbol peddler, a drama queen with a keen sense of the grandiose narratives that would move the public: the same impulse for mystification that turned him into Mr. Playboy would turn Dorothy Stratten into a Platonic ingenue, pure image, as illusory as a star in the sky.

Stratten was irresistible as media fodder, becoming the subject of two films and countless books and articles in the decade after her death. True crime is a didactic genre that instructs its audience through morality tales about modern life, and its lessons often center on what happens to women who trespass their roles. This is why sex workers have so ambiguous and troublesome a role in many true crime stories. Sex work represents an ironic bastardization of woman's supposed innate capacity to provide love, attention, and comfort. The freedom to profit from sex, a commodity once monopolized by men through patriarchal marriage, makes the sex worker a threat to people attempting to police the bounds of womanhood. She is so threatening, in fact, that a campaign of cultural and political work has gone into vilifying her, with anti-prostitution laws that put sex workers in constant danger of police violence, regimes of gentrification to remove them from their homes and neighborhoods, and popular narratives that portray them as simultaneously tragic and deviant. This is so pervasive that if a sex worker is raped, assaulted, or murdered, her profession is often the only explanation the public, the news media, and the justice system need. True crime stories may mourn the lost honor that led to the loss of the sex worker's life, but they will still relish in the gory details of her demise.

In "Death of a Playmate," Carpenter makes it a point to say, "Snider probably never worked Dorothy as a prostitute. He recognized that she was, as one observer put it, 'class merchandise' that could be groomed to better advantage." Here we see the whore stigma employed in several ways. Dorothy is cast as a naïf taken advantage of by a shady character, but also an abject figure in her own right, whose mere proximity to the sex trade was the gateway to an underworld that would be her undoing. But she was still a good girl, not damaged goods (to build on the merchandise metaphor), uncompromised by full-service prostitution. Snider saw her as an object, a commodity to be sold for profit, which made him a creep and a monster. But Carpenter is also implying that Dorothy ceded her agency when she met him, being "worked" rather than working herself, beginning an inexorable journey to her own murder, which she sleepwalked toward in total passivity.

It sometimes seems like the only function for sex workers in media is to die. There is a long tradition of stories of "fallen women," as with Fantine in *Les Misérables* or Violetta in *La Traviata*, whose short lives are marred by lovelessness, illness, and regret. At the very least we think sex workers owe us their trauma, so that our disgust can be transformed to pity, with victimhood being the only humanity we are willing to grant them. And these fallen women stories are supposed to be redemptive, with their protagonists' deaths as perverse happy endings, an absolution washing their sins away. Maybe that's the submerged, unsayable reason women love crime stories: Dead Girls project a dream of innocence in their perfect victimhood, an innocence that whore stigma strips from living women at the first indiscretion.

It was with this in mind that I began to harbor reservations about the warm reception extended to the 2000s teen stars' recent memoirs. I remember distinctly the vitriol directed at Britney Spears and Jessica Simpson from gossip magazines and late-night TV hosts in the 2000s, and at the time I did not think they deserved sticking up for. I read *Us Weekly* every week of 2007 and felt no guilt about my front-row seat at Spears's public downward spiral. I thought she brought it on herself by being stupid, crazy, promiscuous, and overexposed, for squandering the incredible success that she had perhaps unfairly been given—never thinking that this success may have been the thing that drove her crazy. Reading Spears's memoir, had I just bought tickets to the circus of her downfall all over again?

Stars like Spears were stripped of their privacy at a young age in ways they either did or didn't consent to—through tabloids, paparazzi, sex tapes, reality shows—and now we allow them a redemption arc only if they sell us the last shreds of pain they'd kept hidden. This is also true of the most maligned celebrity of the 2000s, Paris Hilton, who in her 2020 documentary and the memoir that followed dramatically revealed the psychological, sexual, and physical abuse she experienced at the troubled teen boarding schools where she attended much of high school. Hilton's book is one of my favorites of the blonde memoir wave, despite the disdain I once felt for her as an alternative teenager. She will perhaps always be known as the airheaded scion of one of the world's largest hotel chains, the vapid, baby-talking professional party animal, famous only for being famous. But a different Paris emerges in chapters about the cruelty she suffered as a child at these facilities, where she was forced to do intense manual labor, undergo "therapy" where adults and other students berated her and called her names, and spend long stretches naked in solitary confinement. She makes a compelling case that many of the things we know her for are rooted in her childhood trauma, including her famous baby voice, which she says is a result of her chronically tensing the muscles in her neck and shoulders in fear. She writes how when she was finally released from boarding school, she was so malnourished that she was "thin as a blade of grass"—the body type that would make her a sought-after model and sex symbol. It sent actual shivers down my spine to think that the impossibly thin body type that haunted my high school days was a direct result of the horrific abuse of a child.

This tells us all we need to know about the dubious gift beauty can be. Think of the *Playboy* models who, like Dorothy Stratten, were doing little more than existing when the discovery of their beauty thrust them into a new and dangerous world. Surely some of my adolescent resentment toward Spears and Hilton had to do with their being upheld as a standard of female beauty that I could never hope to attain. I know in a way I am reinforcing the cliché image of vain, jealous, catty women, thus the phrase "Don't hate me because I'm beautiful." But of course I'm jealous of beautiful women, in a system where beauty is a currency for women second in value only to actual money. This physical hierarchy holds advantages for the beautiful, but it elevates men like Hefner even more, as the gatekeepers and gurus in whose gaze beauty is decided. They also benefit from how these standards encourage women to hate, envy, and distrust one another, a contempt that often sublimates to whore stigma, with women accusing others who trade on their looks of selling sex. We take it as a consolation that at least we are not so brainless and talentless that we have nothing but our beauty to fall back on. But this is not an actual rejection of the power of beauty and should be seen instead as sour grapes, useful to a patriarchal system, one of whose functions is to separate good women from bad.

This conflict, between women's adherence to the beauty cult and our resentment of the people it champions, produces some of the appeal of the tragic celebrity memoir, as well as spawning the classic think piece genre where a feminist writer reconsiders the sex symbols of their childhood. (I am well aware that this essay and many others I've written could be filed under this category.) A reclamation of these icons of the male gaze for a female audience must overcome women's suspicion of the winners in the game of femininity. To humanize the gorgeous celebrity, the feminist may show how her envied beauty arose in tragedy and led her to ruin. One early example is Gloria Steinem's 1986 biography of Marilyn Monroe, the first *Playboy* Playmate and the blueprint for every blond sex symbol who came after her. Steinem shows the iconic star as traumatized by a childhood of sexual abuse and abandonment, using her beauty and the attention of men in a futile effort to gain the love she lacked in her youth. Steinem's *Ms.* magazine article about Monroe from 1972 was the first step in Monroe's feminist redemption arc, and Steinem describes the overwhelming number of letters she received from women who recognized pieces of themselves in Monroe, either the shared traumas of child sexual abuse and infertility, an overdependence on men for validation and protection, or the cage that beauty can become.

Steinem makes a case for why a feminist biography of Monroe was necessary in light of how her many male biographers mishandled her story. Norman Mailer draws her ire with his 1973 "psychohistory" of Monroe, a document of his infatuation that often tips over into covetous rage. He dismisses Monroe's stories of childhood sexual abuse and sees the lack of interest she showed in sex as an indication that she hated men, a "queen of a castrator." Nevertheless, he describes his failure to ever meet her as "one of the frustrations of his life," because his "secret ambition, after all, had been to steal Marilyn; in all his vanity he thought no one was so well suited to bring out the best in her as himself." In her death, Monroe became a fetish of frustrated desire, a fantasy of the perfect, uncomplicated sex object lingering tauntingly just beyond his reach. The psycho whose history he was writing was his own: his was an account of how male sexuality relates to the sex symbols who had come to dominate popular culture.

This view of Monroe was a common one for the legions of men who loved her from afar. She was the ultimate pinup, which is why Hugh Hefner bought a photograph from the one nude photo shoot she did early in her career for the first issue of *Playboy*, making her—without knowledge, consent, or payment—the first Playmate. Steinem theorizes the appeal of Monroe's persona as that of a "child-woman" who sidesteps the fear and hatred men may harbor for female power by infantilizing herself. Desire for the child-woman could provide a psychoanalytic reading of Hefner's description of the perfect Playmate, "not the mysterious, difficult woman, the femme fatale," but the "young, healthy, simple girl." Hefner carried an undying flame for Monroe, perhaps basing much of his later fixation on large-busted, limpid blondes on her. One-upping frequent *Playboy* writer Mailer in his obsession with a woman who wanted nothing to do with him, he bought the plot next to hers at Westwood cemetery. There they are today, their markers side by side on the same vault, Hefner forcing a creepy unity with her in death that he could never achieve in life.

Steinem was hoping to uncover the real Monroe beneath her baby-talking, sexpot persona, but her portrait resembles another kind of child-woman. Hers is a psychological approach to biography, and she depicts a woman who subconsciously recreated the dynamics of her childhood, trying to seek out some of what was lost. We hear how her desire for parental love led her to become dependent on lovers and producers and acting teachers, how she called the domineering older men she married "Daddy" and "Pa." "She seemed so hungry for the love and approval she had been denied in childhood, particularly from a father," Steinem writes, "that she submerged her own physical pleasure, and offered sex in return for male support and affection." This is Steinem's explanation for why Monroe became such a potent sex symbol, the unending well of her naive longing and need. She fashions an ironic melodrama in which Monroe's manic search for love prevented her from achieving it, as the men she married proved themselves unworthy replacements for an absent father and the many illegal abortions she had, including "butcheries from her early penniless years," led to unbearable pain and barrenness.

This is the problem when we conflate compassion with an attempt at psychological explanation. We do not actually confront the subject in their humanity but rather pin them to a specimen board, their problems diagnosed, a tragedy to be pitied. In Crystal Hefner's memoir she writes how in an interview with the comedian Chelsea Handler to promote *The Girls Next Door*, Handler asked her what her dad thought about her dating Hef and posing nude in *Playboy*. This forced Crystal to explain that her dad died when she was young, to which Handler replied, "Well, there you have it, folks. Daddy issues!" This is an awful moment, made worse by the fact that, as Crystal acknowledges, she *did* have daddy issues, and this question triggered a traumatic flashback to her dad's death when she was twelve, which she was forced to relive while a television audience laughed at her.

The clichés of psychology can be dehumanizing even when

they are appropriate. As useful as trauma can be as a lens to understand our pain and the paths our lives take, it is also a limited one. Too often sex workers and women who sell their sex appeal are treated like trauma zombies, unthinkingly carrying out their self-destruction, led along by pain from childhood. We can see this when the Playmates tell their stories of childhood abuse and poverty on *Secrets of Playboy*. They earn the audience's pity but also its mistrust, as if the demons of their past led them to dangerous situations and compelled them to participate in their revictimization. In the end, we are all products of our experiences, and our life's work is to live out and learn from those circumstances. But we have been in this paradigm too long where every popular narrative is a way to explain individual psychology, with trauma serving as the "reveal" that elucidates the rest of the events of the story.

After I saw *Secrets of Playboy*, I was convinced that the Playboy sex cult, Hefner's predation, and the trauma he caused were what I was writing about. But I couldn't seem to open my laptop and start writing. Instead I researched for six more months, feeling like a guest at the Mad Hefner's tea party, where every time I thought I was getting somewhere I would discover I had bought into some absurdity Hef had planted in my path, so rapt by the spectacle he had made of his life that I was mistaking the real story for the contours of cliché. Hadn't I learned anything by now? What is anything about in America? If it's not about war, it's about work.

Despite Steinem's attempts to humanize Monroe through tragedy, we encounter the star at her most human and endearing in the chapters about her attitude toward work, money, and politics. Steinem describes how early in her career Monroe reacted bitterly to watching the rich flaunt their wealth, remembering "how much twenty-five cents and even nickels meant to the people [she] had known." Through this experience she developed left-wing political ideals, saying of the communists, "They're for the people, aren't they?" In the same chapter where Steinem explores Monroe's lifelong allegiance to the poor, she reveals that "when she got broke enough in those early modeling and acting days, she seems to have exchanged sex for small sums of money." Monroe was happy to admit that she used sex and her body to profit in her career, not only because her sex appeal was the engine of her acting and modeling careers but also through sleeping with producers, gigs as a professional partygoer during her days as a contract starlet, and, noted above, directly taking money for sex. Many of her other biographers puzzled over Monroe's pride of never being a "kept woman" and her refusal to marry for money, but as Steinem explains, "Marilyn supplied sex so that she would be allowed to work, but not so that she wouldn't have to work." To imagine marriage as the best possible outcome of sex work makes sense only in a middle-class schema where economic advantage is gained through leveraged investments, in this case investing sex to get a ring on one's finger.

The middle-class concept of work valorizes so-called knowledge work, a dubious classification coined in the rise of the corporate era to group together high-paying jobs as a tautological argument for why they are high paying. The Wikipedia page lists under the umbrella of knowledge work people in careers as diverse as "ICT professionals, physicians, pharmacists, architects, engineers, scientists, design thinkers, public accountants, lawyers, editors, and academics." The one thing many of these jobs have in common is a concept of labor that correlates the best positions with the least amount of physical exertion. This way of seeing the world will never account for the value one might get out of the repeated activities of daily work, especially for artists. Monroe placed a premium on her personal freedom, as Steinem writes, "because she was sometimes forced to give in, to sell herself partially, she was all the more fearful of being bought totally." Although Steinem sometimes takes a judgmental tone about the "sordid stories" of Monroe's sex work, it is not just sex that she is referring to when she talks about Monroe selling herself. Monroe chafed at being treated as a product by the studio system and developed her own production company as an innovative way to negotiate for better contracts. She is recognizable to me as a working-class artist who wished to keep making art and developing her craft with the fewest obligations possible, particularly to the people who paid her.

All the people I know who have done sex work are artists, and I met nearly all of them working food service. These industries have a natural affinity, both being mostly part-time with no yearly contract, often paying in tips or under the table—perfect for creative people who want as much time for their projects and as little tying them to one place as possible. Growing up as a non-white, working-class, queer, trans, neurodivergent (or all of the above!) artist, you develop certain survival skills that are useful in the service professions. You've had to use your body and your mind, you've had to be physically strong and emotionally tough, you've had to develop a network of other weirdos to lift you up through the discouraging times, and you've had to learn to relate to people and give them what they want. You *make* your money in both the sex and restaurant industries, and often it is handed to you at the end of a shift, concrete evidence of the hours worked. I am not trying to sugarcoat how difficult service work is, whether inside or out of the sex industry—it is often physically exhausting, demeaning, exploitative, abusive, and humiliating. I am only trying to explain why one might still choose it over the ambiguities of a desk job, where what you are being paid to do seems vague, pointless, and ever-changing. I am not the only person I know who left a salaried job at a university to return to their first love of waiting tables.

Steinem is the most famous icon of popular, assimilationist feminism, having risen to prominence in the 1970s through her political organizing with the National Organization for Women and her role founding *Ms.* magazine. I was not expecting the sympathy and nuance in her treatment of Monroe's sex work, considering her involvement in the anti-prostitution and anti-pornography campaigns that would swallow up the feminist movement by 1980. I had always assumed Steinem started out as a rich, prep-schooled nepo daughter, when in fact she grew up in a volatile home with a single mother who struggled with mental illness, just as Monroe's mother did. Perhaps this gave her some sympathy for the limited means poor women have for advancement and how beauty can be traded in the absence of cash. And Steinem was radicalized to the feminist cause by what is still her most famous piece of reporting, the article published as "A Bunny's Tale" in 1963, an undercover exposé of the conditions at the New York City Playboy Club. Despite its breezy tone, the piece is an act of gender and class solidarity, a precursor to Barbara Ehrenreich's 2001 investigation of the struggles of the American service class, *Nickel and Dimed*.

The first Playboy Club was established in 1960 in Chicago to siphon the business accounts of emerging corporate America and to serve as an attraction for horny tourists from the sticks hoping to experience a big-city nightclub. The clubs' main selling point was that they were staffed by beautiful young women wearing the famous Bunny costume, essentially a satin leotard with a bow tie, ears, and a tail. Steinem makes some attempts in "A Bunny's Tale" to distance herself from her subject, as if she wants us to understand that she's better than the women who have to resort to working as Bunnies for real. She tells us preeningly that she was too old to be a Bunny at twenty-six but, we understand, still sexy enough for the role, and she even brags that she scored the highest of all the training Bunnies on the Bunny Quiz.

The piece is nevertheless an important document, and it's a departure from what I envisioned in all the years I had heard about it. I pictured a stereotypically "feminist" takedown of how demeaning it was to wear a skimpy costume, what pigs the customers were, and how evil Playboy was for its objectification of women. Steinem does write about all of these things, but they are not her chief complaints. Instead, she describes the rampant wage theft—Bunnies were forced to give the house a large percentage of their tips and weren't paid for training shifts at all—and the intense requirements for both their physical and emotional labor, which included demands to laugh at comedy shows and "eye-contact" (used as a verb) guests immediately.

There were private detectives planted among customers to be sure that no Bunnies were engaging in sex work with customers but also to check that their costumes were in good order and they "always appear[ed] gay and cheerful." Bunnies were not allowed to date customers but were required to take an STD test, for reasons management refused to explain.

Steinem aimed her takedown at Playboy's fiction that Bunny jobs were lucrative and sought after, with an internal publication boasting that "a Bunny can easily earn twice the amount in a week that a good secretary averages." This is contradicted by a Bunny who asks Steinem, "If you can type, what the hell do you want to be a Bunny for?" Once women were lured to the club by promises of high wages, they were told that they were now part of the "Playboy family," an initiation that came along with obligations that they show their loyalty and give their all to the organization. Reading this, I had a creepy flashback to how Hefner insisted Playboy was a family on *The Girls Next Door*. The word "family" serves the same purpose in both instances: to blur the boundaries of professional and personal relationships to get people to do more work than they are being paid for. I can say from experience that the bosses at my restaurant jobs were always telling me the staff was a family. The food service industry tries to convince employees that they are not toiling at a low-paying job but a part of some special club, which is why management often rewards extra work with alcohol and pizza parties, rather than money. This ploy exploits real love that exists among staffers, with whom getting through a busy shift can feel like surviving a battle in the trenches. But even if I can see my restaurant coworkers as brothers and sisters, I've never actually felt authentic parental love from managers or owners.

When Steinem noted the "Bunny Mother" and "Bunny Father" who led the staff at the Playboy Club, I wrote in my notes, "Don't bunny mothers eat their young?"

The talk of family was only one way that Playboy attempted to obscure how crappy the Bunnies' job really was. A hiring ad claimed the role was suffused with the "glamorous and exciting aura of show business," where "the Playboy Club is the stage—the Bunnies are the stars." It made the Bunnies sound more like performers than cocktail servers, which was how Playboy justified the scrutiny it paid to the workers' grooming, costumes, expressions, movements, and banter with customers. "You know what we are?" a Bunny tells Steinem indignantly, as if she's just realized it. "We're waitresses!"

Although "A Bunny's Tale" is remembered now as a Playboy hit piece, it is more powerful as an examination of the lives of restaurant workers, puncturing the mystique of the Bunnies' iconic image to reveal them as girls schlepping drinks just like the ones at any cocktail bar. Steinem mentions to another Bunny that perhaps they ought to have a union, an idea that is only now gaining steam in most parts of the restaurant industry, despite the food service being one of the largest and most exploitative employers of the working class. The industry relies on an itinerant workforce, with workers going in and out of the industry and switching jobs often, preferring to leave a bad job rather than fight for better treatment. Food service can also serve as a stepping stone, with some hoping glamorized jobs in restaurants will lead to higher-paying opportunities in either sex work or entertainment, like with the Bunnies who became *Playboy* models. Holly Madison writes in her memoir about being a Hooters Girl when she became Hef's girlfriend, which was when the connection between the three industries struck me. Waiting tables combines physical labor—delivering food, clearing tables, managing restaurant stock, cleaning—with emotional labor and performance, a mini act you put on at each table to try to exude as much personality and care as you can to convince customers to be generous with you.

Gira Grant writes about the terrible arguments non–sex workers will often use for decriminalization when they are trying to be helpful: that if their activities were legal, sex workers could be taxed, STD tested, and registered. As Gira Grant points out, these workers already pay taxes, get tested for their own self-interest, and are registered and surveilled by police. The idea that the best argument for decriminalization is regulation and not safety betrays a disastrous lack of insight from actual sex workers. When I read this, I thought of a labor quandary I was involved in at my last service job, in a fine-dining restaurant where there was a service charge that added 20 percent to the final tab in lieu of tip. There were bold letters on the menu that proclaimed it a "NO TIPPING establishment," despite that not being strictly true, since we were allowed to collect tips, and I often entered a busy shift praying for at least some of them. Customers loved this system, since it had the appearance of a progressive move to provide servers with an automatic gratuity. In reality, the service charge went to supply a nebulous "high hourly wage," one that I believe was much lower than I would have gotten if I were making tips. We were constantly doing battle with management to get them to at least communicate to customers that they had the option to pay us more.

It's not that servers love the American ritual of restaurant tipping, where everyone is expected to give 20 percent more than the stated price on their bill. We know as well as anyone that it is an arcane system with an ugly past that has allowed restaurants to take on as little responsibility for their employees as possible, with many states allowing them to pay servers around two dollars an hour, displacing all the onus for providing their wages onto the customer. But usually no one asks the workers if a service charge and "fair wages" would be any better. It is so similar to labor issues Gira Grant describes in the sex industry, where the public and the powers that be collude to decide what would be best for sex workers without ever consulting them, even when working toward goals like decriminalization. As she writes, sex work does not have to be "good work" to be considered work, and it does not have to be empowering for sex workers' demands to be legitimate. Workers do not have to wait for a perfect world to ask for living wages and dignity in whatever industry we find ourselves in.

It was a shock when I discovered Steinem's writings on Monroe that pop culture feminism went all the way back to the '70s. I had associated it with millennial essayists writing paeans to Britney Spears, the Marilyn Monroe of our generation, one of which I published in my first book. It is part of the postmodern tradition for women writers to use female celebrities as avatars to explore our conflicted relationship to femininity, both acting out Oedipal hit jobs on the forces that have shaped us and showing love to the parts of ourselves that are irrevocably shaped by ideology.

I will never deny that this approach to feminism is inert and muddled compared to actual political organizing. When the women's liberation movement began in the 1960s, feminists were perfect in their strident opposition to the forces that authored their oppression, wearing work shirts and jeans in defiance of gendered norms, going everywhere in pairs as a way to reject the idea of a movement celebrity. Steinem's ode to Monroe shows that even by 1972 the center had softened. The push to root out patriarchy quickly became conflated with a generalized interest in the lives of women, which is still the source of most conflict around the definition of the word "feminism." Pop culture feminism allows us to have our cake and eat it, too, to continue feeding our fascination with the lives of the women the oppressive overculture conditioned us to find the most interesting, namely those with beauty and privilege. This is why I sometimes hesitate to call myself a feminist writer, despite the word "patriarchy" being on practically every line of both of my books. I can rail against postfeminism all day, but my sensibility was forged by it to such a pathological extent that even as I tell people to focus more on the lives of real women and less on celebrities, I cannot stop spewing words about Paris Hilton, *Sex and the City*, and the Bling Ring. I am a part of the problem. But I am hoping that my writing can perform a kind of exorcism: in looking at Hefner from every angle, I may finally be able to get Playboy out of my system.

Early feminists took on *Playboy* directly. The most infamous confrontation was between Hugh Hefner and the feminist writers Susan Brownmiller and Sally Kempton on *The Dick Cavett Show* in 1970. Despite Cavett making constant undercutting quips and Hefner insisting that he had done more to advocate for legal abortion than almost anyone, the feminists win the day, getting Hefner on his heels when he slips and calls them "girls." Brownmiller and Kempton land many immortal lines, including Brownmiller's famous gauntlet-throwing moment: "Hugh Hefner is my enemy." I encourage you to look up the clip. It is beyond entertaining to watch the women eviscerate him, objecting to how Hefner depicts "an image of women at an arrested development" and asking him why he's not willing to come onstage with a cottontail attached to his ass. This was a time when the women's liberation movement was full of energy, and feminism was drawing popular support that few other radical movements have in this country. Watching this victory for Kempton and Brownmiller, it is painful knowing how Hefner would bamboozle feminists in the decades to come. As Ellen Willis illustrated in 1984 in her indispensable Second Wave postmortem "Radical Feminism or Feminist Radicalism," even on that night in 1970, feminism was fracturing in ways that would soon render the movement unrecognizable to many of those who had started it.

Willis writes that radical feminism had its roots in leftist organizing, with "those of us who first defined radical feminism [taking] for granted that 'radical' implied antiracist, anticapitalist, and anti-imperialist." By 1975, radical feminism had ceded almost all ground to cultural feminism, a reformist movement rooted in mainstream, center-left politics; in self-improvement; and with an emphasis on policing male violence and sexuality. This Willis refers to as *Ms.*-ism, showing the significance of Steinem, who would soon become the high priestess of cultural feminism. She was camera ready and glamorous, beloved by the mainstream media and the Democratic Party. Radical feminists tried to discredit her in 1975 by publicizing the fact that she had worked full-time for the CIA for more than ten years, attending and surveilling international youth festivals. She was defiant about the experience, saying that what she called "the Agency" was "liberal, nonviolent and honorable." She chose to ignore all the ignominy the Agency was involved with during her tenure there, including the assassination of the Congolese prime minister and independence leader Patrice Lumumba. But Steinem's connection to the most notorious organization in the American government did nothing to dim her shine, proving that the feminist movement was by then populated with women who did not necessarily see it as a node of a worldwide struggle for liberation.

This is where I return to the Hefner-feminist confrontation on *The Dick Cavett Show* with more hesitation. In 1979, Hefner would become Brownmiller's enemy in a more literal sense, when she founded Women Against Pornography, a lobbying group that would become an active participant in the Meese hearings. This group swept up many mammoths of the women's movement, including Steinem, Andrea Dworkin, Bella Abzug, and Adrienne Rich in a misguided, reactionary, and unfortunate preoccupation with porn and prostitution. Their crusade revealed an obsession with images, as the feminists put forth an almost postmodern argument that if women were never shown being brutalized or demeaned, it would no longer happen—showing no concern for to the fate of the women who participated in creating these images once they had succeeded in outlawing them and not much for the economic forces or personal motives that might cause the women to participate in the sex industry in the first place. Their political actions were often catastrophic for actual sex workers, as with their campaign to clean up Times Square, where they conspired with Mayor Ed Koch and the theater industry to close the pornographic theaters, sex shops, and peep shows the district had once been known for. As we know, this campaign of urban revitalization did not succeed in eliminating the pornography industry, which was at the time benefiting from the gold rush that followed the invention of the VCR. Instead it rendered sex workers in New York more marginal, isolated, and invisible, in addition to being a major step in the gentrification of Manhattan, a transformation that would be a boon to the tourist and finance industries and a disaster for Black and Hispanic communities and the poor.

Feminists' anti-porn campaigns could sometimes transform into marauding shame brigades, as with Dworkin's 1978 anti-porn march through San Francisco where activists harassed strippers and sex workers. The movement had become a referendum not on male domination but on what they saw as bad women, who collaborated with the enemy and jeopardized the feminists' vision of their own liberation, which was inescapably middle class and white. The term "TERF," an acronym for "trans-exclusionary radical feminist," used to bother me, since I thought transphobic bigots should not be associated with any liberation movement and especially not with feminism, considering that they reserve their most virulent hatred for trans women. I have to acknowledge now that TERFs are the modern-day debris in the dustbin of the Second Wave. Many of the reactionaries leading the movement by the 1980s were virulently anti-trans, believing that trans women misunderstood what it meant to be a "real woman," thinking it was all about wearing women's clothes. They were once again busy being offended by images of women rather than the conditions of their actual lives.

As jarring as it is to confront this feminist right turn, it was the outcome of flaws in women's liberation that existed from its beginnings. As Willis writes, early radical feminists, mostly coming from white, middle-class backgrounds, tried to sidestep notions of race and class to imagine women as a totalizing political class, with men's oppression of women being not only separate from those struggles but the original class struggle. This philosophy sprang from a wild idealism, a belief that one day all women around the world would rise up with one voice and overthrow their oppressors, motivated only by solidarity and sisterhood. Early movement actions like consciousness-raising groups where women discussed their lives, based on Maoist and Black radical practices, were not intended to be therapeutic but to direct the movement through identifying patterns in women's experiences. All too often, though, these experiences were abstracted into beliefs that aligned with essentialist views of sex: Women were nurturing, nonhierarchical, communal, and gentle. Men were violent, competitive, and hungry for power. This simplified view of womanhood alienated those who did not conform to it, and the movement fractured early on into numerous opposing groups even in its most militant wing. It is not difficult to see how these fissures, helped along by a new conservative strain in national politics, would result in a movement that closed the political horseshoe. Feminism gave way to morality crusades about pornography and, as it was known then, "transsexualism," with those who had once been left-wing radicals finding themselves entrenched with their former political enemies on the Christian right.

Despite the dream they espoused of unifying women all over the world under one feminist banner, the failure of the Second Wave of feminism was in their refusal to actually imagine themselves in community with all women. This is certainly the critique that Black feminists continue to have of the white feminist establishment, that white women expect them to fall in line and are bemused when they have their own perspectives, leaders, and demands. From a dream of sisterhood, feminism replicated a hierarchy that exactly reproduced the American status quo of class division and racial caste.

Steinem writes in the afterword to "A Bunny's Tale" about the consequences she suffered from writing the piece, including losing out on reporting assignments simply for having written about being a Bunny. She also notes the harassment Hefner continued to target her with for decades, including both a baseless and expensive libel suit and the repeated printing of her Bunny photo in *Playboy*, often alongside a blooper mistakenly published by a wire service where her breast has fallen out of her dress at a formal event. What she is describing here is the fallout of whore stigma, the abuse she became vulnerable to by even the barest proximity to the sex industry. But she does not appear to have taken the right lesson from this. In a way, she seems to find it unfair that she was the target of sexism when she was doing her respectable, middle-class job of journalist— it's not like she was a real Bunny! The main problem addressed by feminism should not be that educated, powerful women are subject to men's disrespect, a disrespect that denies them opportunities to be taken seriously and advance professionally. The problem is that even in this supposedly feminist paradigm it is considered acceptable to treat certain women with disrespect, violence even, when it is those vulnerable people that any movement for liberation must stand behind. The problem is, as Gira Grant writes, that "we permit some violence against women . . . in order to protect the social and sexual value of other women." Here we see a glimpse of the solidarity that could have grown from "A Bunny's Tale" and from Steinem's stated realization that "all women are Bunnies."

If Steinem's feminism started with a labor exposé, *The Jungle* in heels and cottontail, by the '90s hers was the feminism of Take Your Daughter to Work Day, a simplistic plan to advance the cause of women by initiating them early in the American cult of work. Sex workers have always represented class slippage, as in the days when "courtesan" was roughly interchangeable with "socialite," and they are seen by many as cheating the system by charging for something that should be free. This means that whore stigma is as much about labor as feminine virtue, with the threat that sex workers pose being, as Gira Grant quotes from Kathi Weeks, that they "call into question the supposedly indisputable benefits of work." Thus a woman terrified of being called a whore will insist, like Paris Hilton does, that she is "a working beast." Hilton's memoir pulls on my heartstrings so expertly that I can overlook that much of it is cringey declarations of her business acumen, as she casts the activities of her party girl days as developing multiple revenue streams and shills the NFTs she made with "fierce women artists." What a perfect patriarchal double bind, that one of the few paths women can take to avoid being demeaned for their sexuality—other than dying tragically—is to glorify the heights of capitalism. It is not enough to be a worker busting your ass to make coin on your shift. You must be a mogul with multiple revenue streams. What a hollow consolation prize, to get revenge on those in power by working frantically to become just like them. Not to mention that this route to respectability makes solidarity impossible—aren't we told that it's lonely at the top? Moguls don't have peers, only competitors.

Crystal Hefner does a little of Hilton's professional posturing in her book, describing the rental properties, crypto portfolio, and brand partnerships she got on her way to becoming "a savvy businesswoman." This she contrasted with her public image, writing of rude interviewers, "They thought I was sex crazed or a sex worker or sexually deviant in some mysterious way." I think of Holly Madison's horror in *Down the Rabbit Hole* that someone thought she was a "hooker." Or one of Hef's former girlfriends, who said on *Secrets of Playboy*, "It wasn't prostitution. I was working for a company." It's not that I don't understand the reason for these denials or think they should not be allowed to make them. But it is a little sad watching them contort their stories to avoid admitting the obvious, a truth they know everyone already sees: of course they were sex workers.

An *LA Times* article from February 2022 describes the "vicious feud" that resulted from *Secrets of Playboy*, with former Playmates and Bunnies lashing out at those who had chosen to tell their stories of abuse. "These are 85-year-old women running around with their bunny ears on," one interviewee said, "and I'm bursting their bubble." There is also the beef that has raged between Holly and a few of the other girlfriends since the days when Hefner had seven of them, which was reignited by dueling interviews on *Secrets of Playboy*. Hefner's orbit was like a snake pit, where the women, far from the happy sister-wives he wanted them to portray, were constantly pitted against one another, creating such an atmosphere of suspicion that Crystal says she didn't have a female friend the entire ten years she lived in the mansion.

Whore stigma is the author of so much discord among women. It is the insecurity that causes us to police one another, wielding the same threat that is held against us, that any misstep and we risk tumbling down into the realm of bad women. And who benefits? Hugh Hefner could hardly have had better luck with the trajectory of the feminist movement. He was able to accurately portray his feminist enemies as scolds who had revealed their own hypocrisy and authoritarianism, more worried about dirty pictures than any real female empowerment. He successfully rewrote his legacy as a business titan, a crusader for free speech, against racism, for free love and women's liberation—*he* was the real feminist! No wonder the women who once knew him are so bitterly angry at one another now. Who is there left to be angry at? Hef's dead. It's over. He won.

Hugh Marston Hefner was born in Chicago in 1926, the oldest son of straitlaced Methodists whom he described as cold and conservative. He was a nerdy kid fascinated by movies and comic strips, and he would often recount the origin of his narcissistic wound, being turned down by his crush when he asked her to the high school hayride. He received a bachelor's degree in psychology and then married in 1949, having two children with his first wife before divorcing her in 1959. He founded *Playboy* magazine in 1953, which developed a reputation for the quality, progressive literature it published as well as its nude centerfolds. He started the Playboy Clubs in 1960, inspired by a bar he and *Playboy* staff would visit after work called (I'm serious) the Gaslight Club.

Through the success of the magazine, Hefner cultivated his own celebrity, hosting the TV programs *Playboy's Penthouse* and *Playboy After Dark* in the 1960s. He became notorious for the elaborate parties he hosted at his Hollywood mansion, surrounded by *Playboy* models and celebrities. Throughout his career he was targeted by the U.S. government and anti-pornography groups for purveying obscenity, experiences that turned him into an advocate for free speech and an end to puritanical views of sex. He was known for his progressive stances on integration and civil rights and is credited with launching the careers of Alex Haley and Dick Gregory. He had two more children with his second wife in the early 1990s. *Playboy* remained relevant for decades, and the '90s stars Pamela Anderson, Anna Nicole Smith, and Jenny McCarthy all got their start in the magazine. Hefner was a pop culture icon into old age, with a successful reality show on E! in the 2000s. He was married three times in total, leaving the thirty-one-year-old Crystal Hefner a widow when he died in 2017, at the age of ninety-one.

In the earliest days of the magazine, he started publishing installments of the Playboy Philosophy, a sprawling manifesto that would eventually reach eighteen chapters and, paginated for a modern-day word processor, 277 single-spaced pages. In it, he lays out his entire theory of a healthy society, focusing particularly on the importance of civil liberties and an end to the reign of Christian sexual morality. The Playboy Philosophy becomes more arcane over its pages, in the weeds of law and history, with sections titled "Sex in Early Judaism," "Medieval Sex," and "Sex and the Church Courts" and three separate chapters on sodomy. At its core is a libertarian treatise on the importance of legal pornography to American freedom, forming a kind of perv's wing of the Chicago school. When his wife Crystal claimed in her book that he had been addicted to prescription speed during the years he was writing it, the Playboy Philosophy started to make a lot more sense.

It is not that the Playboy Philosophy is unreasonable. Indeed, it takes pains to appeal to common sense, old-fashioned values, and the United States's grandiose vision of itself. Most of us would agree with the broad strokes of Hefner's interpretation of history, that conservative religious notions of morality served to subordinate women, place arbitrary limits on natural human sexuality, and make a mockery of the separation of church and state. But if we must congratulate Hefner for advocating a sexual openness that was once unheard of, we must also admit that these ideas were in service to something larger. While I wouldn't exactly classify any of it as philosophy, much of the Playboy Philosophy would more accurately be called marketing, arguing not only for Hefner's vision of Western civilization but for why *Playboy* magazine was the force making this vision a reality. The first installment spends pages detailing *Playboy*'s "considerable influence on society," quoting from article after article about the magazine *in* the magazine. The Playboy Philosophy is like a religious scripture, the Book of Hef, as he drilled into his readers that they were part of a vanguard of hip and important men who were freethinking and fun, the absolute center of American discourse. I will never deny that Hefner was prescient in his approach to creating a product, intuiting the value of pitching something not for a general audience but for a select demographic. "He can be a sharp-minded young business executive, a worker in the arts, a university professor, an architect or engineer . . . ," the Playboy Philosophy writes of the magazine's ideal reader. "He must be . . . a man of taste, a man sensitive to pleasure, a man who . . . can live life to the hilt. This is the sort of man we mean when we use the word *playboy*."

This was the real point, to consolidate his audience around an ideology in which *Playboy* magazine was a secular bible of American values. His philosophy is an overt celebration of capitalist excess, with Hefner chiding his audience, "To some of us capitalism is almost a dirty word. It shouldn't be. It's time Americans stopped being embarrassed and almost ashamed of their form of government and their economy." Hefner rues how the spread of socialist sentiment during the Great Depression created an obsession with the "Common Man," a trend he blames for spreading anti-intellectualism and discouraging progress, in addition to popularizing what he sees as an unfair resentment toward the rich. He believes there must instead be a celebration of the "Uncommon Man," the embodiment of the American dream who, using his inborn gifts of daring, intelligence, and ambition, can rise to the height of American industry and politics.

It isn't Nietzsche, but in expressing his dream of the United

States as a meritocratic utopia, he approaches the philosophy, or even theology, that the superrich in this country still subscribe to. He sees sex as a domain where the capitalist can exercise the freedom money affords him, unhampered by the country's outmoded loyalty to Puritan religion, which was fixated not only on inhibiting sexuality but pushing the moral values of charity, equality, and humility, all of which were nuisances for an Uncommon Man wishing to enjoy all life has to offer. The Playboy Philosophy's focus on sexual taboos and prohibitions is part of a larger mission to break the ties binding America to an old social order and holding it back from fulfilling its true destiny as a secular holy land of free market capitalism.

Hefner aims in his philosophy to promote a new strain in the culture, to turn it from the nihilistic youth movements of the 1950s and form an "Upbeat Generation," who "awakened America's natural optimism, rebel spirit and belief in the importance of the individual." These were men in their twenties and thirties who were taking on roles of authority in business and government and, in Hefner's view, moving America quickly into the future. This section almost reads like a Silicon Valley puff piece from 2010, describing the optimistic twentysomethings undaunted by the financial collapse who were refashioning the American way of life in sunny California. This is important to understand about *Playboy*, too: it was the result of a new communication technology, the ability to cheaply print color photography in magazines, being used—as they always are—to distribute pornography. If it wasn't Hefner, it would have been someone else, something he was keenly aware of. But like a tech CEO faking his way to a billion-dollar valuation on hype and smoke, Hef knew it was not your innovation but your philosophy, the ideals embodied in your brand, that distinguished the Uncommon Man.

In all of this, one identifies an (almost) unnamed enemy enforcing the old moral order in the United States, one that was always in the frontlines of charges for social reform and temperance, conspiring to hold men back from the heights that they aspire to by insisting they think of the collective good: women. In one installment he makes promises for the topics readers would be treated to in upcoming issues of the magazine:

> a vivisection of Momism and the Womanization of America, charting the manner in which one of the sexes has successfully wrested control of our culture from the other; a review of the effect Womanization has had on our manners and morals, on business, advertising, books, newspapers, television, movies and magazines.

Excuse me, *what*-ism?

Momism was the invention of the legendary crank Philip Wylie, a pulp writer and social critic who became a bestselling author with his 1942 essay collection, *Generation of Vipers*, and who is now best known for being, as the *LA Review of Books* put it, "the man who hated moms." He wrote about Momism and "Womanization" for *Playboy* several times, whining that women had remade society in the midcentury not through positions of power in politics or industry but through sanctimonious guilt-tripping and consumerist avarice. He resented the cult of American motherhood that in his view had made women lazy, self-indulgent harridans who expected their husbands to provide everything for them. It is an age-old tactic of anti-feminists to blame women for their own oppression, and the situations he ascribes to women's greed and degeneracy were really a product of the benevolent sexism that narrowed women's roles to wife and mother in the postwar years. This is obviously incel shit, like modern manosphere commentators describing gendered expectations in dating as women living life on "easy mode." (Wylie expresses such raw misogyny that you might assume his mother was the scum of the earth. Your conclusion would be unfounded, however. He grew up without a mother.) His arguments are mostly ad hominem, like when he complains of mothers eating bonbons and drinking six cocktails a day, or how they know "nothing about medicine, art, science, religion, law, sanitation, civics, hygiene, psychology, morals, history, geography, poetry, literature, or any other topic." But his real objection to moms becomes clear in his tirade about their fervor for "organizations." "Organizations, she has happily discovered, are intimidating to all men . . . ," he writes. "They frighten politicians to sniveling servility and they terrify pastors; they bother bank presidents and they pulverize school boards."

Wylie's real problem was not with the easy life he believed stay-at-home moms enjoyed but with the political power they wielded when they worked together. This power threatened even Uncommon Men because of the very moral authority that a patriarchal society had conceded to mothers, making the role the apotheosis of respectability for women. Admittedly this collective power is not an inherent good. White mothers have been leaders in most of the far-right moral crusades of the last hundred years, standing in angry opposition to civil rights, gay rights, and now trans rights. But stay-at-home mothers and mothers in general, whether they wish to acknowledge it or not, are marginalized by our views of womanhood and the family, responsible for huge amounts of unpaid work that they are gaslit into thinking is not work at all. In *Playing the Whore*, Gira Grant notes that sex workers once had allies in these mothers, as in an early activist group called "Whores, Housewives, and Others." In 1982, the English Collective of Prostitutes occupied a church, supported by Women Against Rape and Black Women for Wages for Housework. All wore black masks, so no one could distinguish the sex workers from the housewives who protested in solidarity with them. As Gira Grant writes, "Had this image of feminism found its way to me before any of those now iconic shots of that more ubiquitous icon of seventies feminism, Gloria Steinem . . . I could have paired Steinem's with another: a feminism both of and for the streets."

This is a stark comparison: the anonymous protesters in black masks, the beautiful celebrity feminist standing alone. In a way it is the triumph of the Playboy Philosophy, the ascendancy of the brand economy that would turn individuals into entrepreneurs of themselves. Hilton talks idealistically about the power of social media in allowing women to "own their own image," so they can profit off the sale of beauty instead of men like Hefner. But this is not just about posting pictures but about the fact that image has become the only commodity in the global financial system. (It makes sense that Hilton is so gung ho about cryptocurrency and NFTs, which surreally abstract the idea of a commodity, being little more than names that are bought and traded.) A brand is not a product but an engine to sell other stuff, something Hefner understood from the beginning. He writes about the readers who "began purchasing Playboy products in considerable quantities: everything from cuff links, ties, sport shirts, tuxedoes and bar accessories . . . all with the Playboy Rabbit as the principal design and principal motivation for the purchase." The Playboy Philosophy exists in part to encourage this spending orgy, promoting hedonism as a sacred American value. After all, he claimed, "the acquisition of property—and in the 1960s property may mean a handsome bachelor pad, elaborate hi-fi rig and the latest sports car—is the cornerstone of our American economic system."

Now in the 2020s, I fear we are living in Hefner's America, where marketing and consumption are the main tools of collective meaning making. Hilton speaks with desperate tones in her book about the pains she took to protect her reputation and therefore her brand, a motivation that led her to keep quiet about her experiences of childhood abuse until she was in her mid-thirties. "My brand was more than my business," she writes; "it was my identity, my strength, my self-respect, my independence, my whole life." What a desolate situation, when the persona representing both your business ventures and yourself is conflated and inflated to such an extent that to lose it would be to lose your life. Tell me, how is this assault on our identities, turning them into commodities to be sold, not infinitely more degrading than a sex worker temporarily "selling her body"?

When I was researching this piece, the rap mogul Diddy began to receive his long-awaited reckoning, with an avalanche of accusations of sexual and physical abuse, human trafficking, and assault that even exceed the accusations against Hefner in *Secrets of Playboy*. It struck me, amid all the criminal allegations, that exploitation had been a cornerstone of how Diddy operated his record label, Bad Boy Records. He hoarded the rights to his artists' work for decades, so that the family of his most legendary collaborator, the Notorious B.I.G., was denied the profits from his music until 2023. It reminded me of how Hefner wielded the rights to photographs shot for *Playboy*, making anyone who even tested to be in the magazine sign a release that would make the images his property in perpetuity. He had no compunction about using them without the subjects' knowledge, as we see with Steinem's Bunny photograph. In 2011, Playboy TV was taken over by the world's largest pornography company, MindGeek (at the time it was known ominously as Manwin), and it acquired the rights to distribute Playboy's massive catalog of videos and photographs. These images are now plastered all over pornographic websites, much to the embarrassment of many former *Playboy* models, hundreds of whom posed for the magazine long before the internet existed. It is the sexual aspect of this situation that catches our attention and pulls at our heartstrings, the idea that these women were transformed into porn performers when they never imagined their pictures going beyond the magazine. Obviously sexual exploitation and violence are horrific, and there is no doubt that they are tools of gendered domination in the patriarchal order. But in Hefner and Diddy we might see a broader pattern, one that allowed them to be celebrated as business geniuses until they were revealed as sexual predators.

Why do we speak positively about a person creating a business "empire," when empire is the most brutal political innovation of all time, an organized force of conquest raping, enslaving, stealing, and murdering to extend the faceless power of a state across the globe? This is a connection #MeToo did not make explicit enough. It's easy to cast the revelation of a successful man's history of preying on women as a case of Dr. Jekyll and Mr. Hyde, a dark secret marring his otherwise impressive accomplishments. We don't want to acknowledge that this violence goes hand in hand with a system of predation that is not only legal but encouraged under our economic system. We cannot eradicate it by removing bad actors, those who are easy to peg as narcissists and sociopaths, but only by acknowledging that exploitation is the point of our economic system, a free market that requires winners and losers, common men and Uncommon Men.

The titans of the branding economy do not just own their own images; they own other people. This is why financial companies have been buying up the rights to the music of legends like Bob Dylan and Bruce Springsteen, not to profit from the plays on their songs in the short term but to manage a portfolio of brands in the long term. A brand is a piece of marketing not only intended to appeal to the public but to these brokers who invest in them and distribute them, giving those at the top of the food chain immense power to direct culture and politics. It's no wonder Hilton described her brand in such stark terms, as her identity, her strength. Think about it: yes, she runs a successful personal brand. But how does it generate money? By partnering with other brands and corporations. And what does she use to promote it? Instagram. TikTok. YouTube. They are the big bosses, and they own all our asses.

Many times when I was writing this piece, I lost heart. I wondered if there was a point in having sympathy for the Playmates. Was I only indulging my secret postfeminist sympathies, childishly playing with the blond Barbies of the Y2K imagination? Were they the women whose plight was the most important to focus on in this desperate age? Surely there were other sex workers who more deserved my attention, especially since many *Playboy* models stubbornly refused solidarity with other women in the sex industry. These were the same questions I asked when I would get deep in my feelings about a new celebrity memoir. My heart sank when I read in Hilton's memoir about the judge who sentenced her to jail in 2007 for breaking the terms of her parole after a DUI. She spent her entire thirteen days in prison in solitary confinement, having constant PTSD flashbacks to her time in detention as a teenager. I stung with sympathy for Hilton as she described how this traumatic experience was laughed at on late-night shows and internet forums. But it also made me think about the women who were in this jail with her. How many of them had childhood trauma? How many of them had been incarcerated as teenagers? How triggering was this experience for them, when they did not have fame, privilege, or money and were going to be there longer than thirteen days?

Children of the Y2K era are nostalgia monsters, partly because the internet has archived so much of our childhoods, with the movies, TV shows, and icons of our past preserved in amber. Our lives have also been segmented by seismic changes, both the transformation of our world through tech and the looming collapse of both our ecological and economic systems. The past is a comforting place, a soft-focused and unchanging world, where objects were solid, narratives were continuous, effect followed cause. That's probably why nostalgia for the 1990s will continue to be a dominant strain in popular culture, rendered as a prelapsarian dreamworld that we imagine (incorrectly) to be before the internet, before global warming, before the war on terror. The present feels uncanny and procedurally generated; the grainy, analog '90s feel so *real*.

This is the work of nostalgia, to segment the past from the present, so we can continue to fail to learn from it. Paris Hilton and the *Playboy* Playmates stand in for the awful regressive culture of my childhood, where the spectrum of women represented in popular media was thinner, younger, richer, and more vapid than it ever had been before. My nostalgia allows me to feel an ironic affection for these absurd pop phenomena, to have fun with them in the same way I did then, when I didn't know any better. I can also humanize the women who sold this image to me, understanding them as exploited girls who were victims of the same machine. But this does not account for my anger, how I wish things could have been different, the constraints I still experience from the pop culture that shaped me. Why can't I just let it go? I experience a kind of Freudian repression, where ambiguous memories of my past continue to recur, and I have no choice but to sublimate them into ironic affection. It is how many of us feel about our parents. We are angry about things they did and allowed to happen, but at the same time we are conflicted because we love them and they did their best. Instead of working to make peace with this complex reality, we force ourselves to look back fondly on the worst parts of our childhood (as with people who say, "My parents spanked me, and I turned out just fine!"), thus carrying those mistakes of the past forward with us into the future.

We must acknowledge nostalgia as a key emotional tool to maintain the status quo, a drive keeping us loyal to the past instead of the future. It tells us we are right to be dissatisfied with the present, but that the past is the refuge from our current troubles, rather than the source of them. And in distracting us from our inner dissonance, our anger, our confusion, our guilt, it leaves us open to mass manipulation. Celebrity memoirs are always praised for being comprehensive, candid, and raw, but they are still extensions of stars' personal brands, tender parts of themselves that they have been made to sell. Even this "humanization" is a product and a way to reinforce their status as Uncommon Women, not the "whores" they were branded as but savvy, intelligent, soulful. We are still avoiding the real issue, the broader dehumanizing system that says that some people are worth more than others, and all of us are merchandise to be bought and sold.

Am I giving Hefner what he wanted, making him seem important and larger than life? He was a famously nostalgic person, and the Playboy Philosophy celebrates the folk heroes of his childhood, from Horatio Alger to Charlie Chaplin to Charles Lindbergh. He projected himself into this same role, wanting to be, as his widow Crystal writes, "a giant of American history: respected, admired, and heroic." Maybe he hoped that if his star grew bright enough, his indiscretions would be forgotten in the glaze of nostalgia. And perhaps he got his wish—at least for now. I think about the women today who wear Playboy-branded clothing or, even more dramatically, get the Playboy bunny tattooed on them. Holly talks about how she and other girlfriends and Playmates would get bunny tattoos, describing them as "brands" in the literal sense of the word. This has always disturbed me. At first, I thought about how a rabbit is a prey animal, a sickening reminder of Playboy's former predator in chief. Now I also think of the original meaning of "brand," as a mark of ownership. I return to the passage from the Playboy Philosophy where Hefner lists the Playboy "cuff links, ties, and sports shirts" readers would buy as a way of declaring their loyalty to Hefner, counting themselves as members of his movement. Hef knew that when they bought a piece of Playboy, he bought a piece of them. When we think of what he did to the women he branded as his own, not only controlling their images but their bodies and every minute of their lives, do we want to bear his mark, to identify ourselves as citizens of his empire? I know I am on shaky ground criticizing people for the lighthearted kitsch they are attached to from their childhood. I'm the one reading Britney Spears's memoir instead of real books, and I've spent five years organizing images from Y2K magazines on Pinterest in the name of writing this book. As I've said before, I'm part of the problem, which might just mean a part of history. But *Playboy* is not a magazine anymore. It is only a symbol. Hef's stroke of genius. An icon so compelling that we still chase it down a hole where nostalgia turns everything upside down, so that patriarchy is progressive and indoctrination is freedom, merging finally with the hole in the wall of a vault at Westside cemetery where Hef lies next to Marilyn Monroe, having gotten everything he wanted. It's only a little rabbit, but somehow it started everything.

OTHER SOURCES

INTRODUCTION

When I say "cult experts," I am mostly referring to interviews with Steven Hassan on the *Mormon Stories* podcast.

Much of the background on the Puritans here came from Stacy Schiff's history of the Salem Witch Trials, *The Witches*.

For more on persuasive design, in addition to terrific writing on topics including hippie communes, the socialist demand for leisure, and duration and attention in art, read *How to Do Nothing* by Jenny Odell.

In earlier drafts of this introduction I shoehorned in Dwight McDonald's unified theory of cultural production, "Masscult and Midcult." Maybe I'll get it into the next book.

Silvia Federici's 2020 book *Beyond the Periphery of the Skin: Rethinking, Remaking, Reclaiming the Body in Contemporary Capitalism* was useful here and throughout on the economics of twenty-first-century womanhood.

THE ENUMERATED WOMAN

The Australian sociologist Deborah Lupton is probably the world's leading theorist of self-tracking, and her work was of great use to me in researching this piece. A few other academic sources I consulted:

> Yesheen Yang's essay "Saving the Quantified Self: How We Come to Know Ourselves Now" from *Boom: A Journal of California*, 2014.
> Marissa Doshi's "Barbies, Goddesses, and Entrepreneurs: Discourses of Gendered Digital Embodiment in Women's Health Apps," from *Women's Studies in Communication*, 2018.
> Chris Till's "Exercise as Labour: Quantified Self and the Transformation of Exercise into Labour" from *Societies*, 2014.

In addition to *You Are Not a Gadget*, Jaron Lanier's *Who Owns the Future?* assisted me here and throughout to understand the tech business model and endgame.

Sabrina Strings's *Fearing the Black Body: On the Racial Origins of Fatphobia* got me thinking about how eugenicist our "optimized" images of health and fitness are.

FOUNDERING

Vanity Fair seems to have a big, juicy feature on a tech corporate scandal every month. Their journalism has been invaluable to me as I wrote this book and a source of hours of entertainment.

Some of the most thorough coverage of the FTX scandal can be found at the Coffeezilla YouTube channel.

Sarah Nicole Prickett's incredibly awkward 2012 interview with Aaron Sorkin for the *Globe and Mail*, "How to get under Aaron Sorkin's skin (and also, how to high-five properly)," was one of the few Sorkin takedowns available . . . until now.

Also relevant to the ideas here: "The Rise of Neo-Feudalism" by Katherine V. W. Stone and Robert Kuttner from *The American Prospect*.

LEAN IN/BEND OVER

Tressie McMillan Cottom and Sarah Jaffe have both written about "trickle-down feminism" in *Dissent*.

As will become clear, my copy of *The Essential Ellen Willis* was my most-treasured resource and inspiration as I wrote this book. (Okay, I have two copies.)

I had originally wanted to reference Janet Malcolm's 2006 essay "The Art of Testifying," on why Supreme Court hearings are an insulting, unnecessary farce in this essay.

STARDATE

The two volumes of Edward Gross and Mark A. Altman's *The Fifty Year Mission: A Complete, Uncensored Oral History of Star*

Trek provided much of the background information on *Star Trek* included here.

A majority of the behind-the-scenes tidbits about *Sex and the City* come from Jennifer Keishin Armstrong's book *Sex and the City and Us*.

A few favorite academic articles about *Star Trek*:

> "Popular Imagination and Identity Politics: Reading the Future in *Star Trek: Next Generation*" Brian L. Ott and Eric Aoki from *Western Journal of Communication*, 2001.
>
> "*Star Trek*, Global Capitalism, and Immaterial Labour" by Dan Hassler-Forest from *Science Fiction Film and Technology*, 2016.
>
> "Space and the Single Girl: *Star Trek*, Aesthetics, and 1960s Femininity" by Patricia Vettel-Becker from *Frontiers: A Journal of Women's Studies*, 2014.
>
> "The Persistence of Difference: Postfeminism, Popular Discourse, and Heterosexuality in *Star Trek: The Next Generation*" by Lee E. Heller in *Science Fiction Studies*, 1997.

I actually like *The Age of Innocence*, for the record.

The most succinct Third Wave Feminist manifesto is "Becoming the Third Wave" by Rebecca Walker from 1992.

"Ernest Mandel and the Economics of Late Capitalism" by Marcel Van Der Linden in *Jacobin*, in addition to *Jacobin*'s other coverage on the long waves of capitalism, greatly aided my understanding of Mandel's work.

REAL TIME

Sadly, the eight-million view video of the flooded island is now listed as private. There are others who have replicated the experiment, however.

Dan Olson's video "Minecraft, Sandboxes, and Colonialism" was how I found the book *Video Games and the Global South*. His videos in general are indispensable on video games, Web 3.0, and the vast scale of modern scams.

Alexander Avila has a great video essay on *The Sims* and social constructivism, "Did *The Sims* Make You Gay?"

TEEN PEOPLE

Some of the first research I did for this book was reading Amanda Mackenzie Stuart's *The Empress of Fashion: A Life of Diana Vreeland*, about the legendary *Vogue* editor, as well as Vreeland's book *D.V.* Vreeland barely appears in the final manuscript, but we can consider her a patron saint.

Hazel Cills not only investigated the history of Trauma-Rama for *Jezebel*, she also wrote a great piece for the same site on the teen era that came next, "The Rise and Fall of the Pop Star Purity Ring."

Atoosa Rubinstein made a comeback in 2021 with a confessional email newsletter designed to appeal to her former *CosmoGirl* readers. Heather Schwedel profiled her at the time in *Slate*, under the headline "A Teen Magazine Icon Is Shattering Her Legend, One Jaw-Dropping Confession at a Time. Why?"

In her essay "This Is Not my Beautiful House," former *Lucky* editor Kim France paints a picture of the surreal perks given to editors-in-chief during the magazine industry's final boom time.

THE RABBIT HOLE

As of this writing, all the episodes of *The Girls Next Door* are available on Amazon's Freevee platform.

My original lede for this essay involved Irving Wallace's 1961 biography *The Twenty-Seventh Wife*, about the Latter-Day Saint prophet Brigham Young's wife Anne Eliza Young. I was going to tie the nineteenth century moral outrage over Asian harems and Mormon polygamy to the feminist response to Hefner's cortège of seven girlfriends. I quickly realized that I had written three thousand words about the failings of nineteenth century feminists before I even got to Hefner, so I had to cut it.

The Beauty Myth by Naomi Wolf and *Fearing the Black Body* by Sabrina Strings both helped me to think about the weapon that beauty standards can be.

Lois Romano's 1983 profile of Christie Hefner in *The Washington Post*, "Christie Hefner, Daughter of the Revolution," is a fascinating read.

For more on Gloria Steinem's work with the CIA, read "When the Student Movement Was a CIA Front" by Aryeh Neier in *The American Prospect*.

ACKNOWLEDGMENTS

I will always be grateful to my agent, Monika Woods, for supporting me, enabling me, and believing in me. Thank you to Jessica Williams, the coolest, smartest, and most patient editor there is. Thanks also to Peter Kispert, Eliza Rosenberry, Julia Elliott, Ploy Siripant, Liate Stehlik, Benjamin Steinberg, Peter Hubbard, Jennifer Eck, Michelle Meredith, Nancy Tan, Chloe Foster, Allison Carney, and the rest of the team at Mariner/William Morrow. The care you've taken with my work means everything to me.

Thanks to all of my beautiful friends who have been literal lifesavers in this crazy string of years. I have to shout out my beloved Memfriends, especially Caki Wilkinson, Marcus Wicker, Emily Skaja, Karyna McGlynn, Brent Nobles, Mark Mayer, Ashley Colley, and Katie Fredlund. Thank you to my Twin Cities crew: Emily Jones, Brett Defries, Kat Lamp, Marek Poliks, Deirdre Lamp, Katie Kelly, Ryan White, Karen Parkman, Connor White, Emma Törzs, Sally Franson, and Claire Comstock Gay. Thank you to Virginia Zech, Ed Skoog, Andrew Martin, and Laura Kolbe. Thank you to Handley Woodall and my B-Club buddies. I love you all!

Thank you to all my colleagues and students at the University of Memphis. Thanks also to Rebecca Cochran and Anna Heinzerling.

I will never be able to give adequate thanks to my family, whom I love more than anything. My gratitude always to Tim Stuart, Fred Stuart, Willo Stuart, Anderson Stuart, Mike Stuart, Dan Whelan (honorary), Peg Hornsby, Jeff Hornsby, Brigid Hornsby, Michael Hornsby, and Gino Hornsby. Mary Bolin, Bob Bolin, Charlie Bolin, Tom Bolin: I don't know how I got so lucky to be born with you as my family.

This book is dedicated to my true love, Dan Hornsby—there is no chance I would have finished it without you.

ABOUT THE AUTHOR

ALICE BOLIN is the author of *Dead Girls: Essays on Surviving an American Obsession*, a *New York Times* Notable Book. She has been nominated for Anthony and Edgar Awards. Her nonfiction appears in *The New York Times Book Review*, *New York* magazine, *Los Angeles Review of Books*, and *The Paris Review Daily*. She lives in Minneapolis.

ABOUT

MARINER BOOKS

MARINER BOOKS traces its beginnings to 1832 when William Ticknor cofounded the Old Corner Bookstore in Boston, from which he would run the legendary firm Ticknor and Fields, publisher of Ralph Waldo Emerson, Harriet Beecher Stowe, Nathaniel Hawthorne, and Henry David Thoreau. Following Ticknor's death, Henry Oscar Houghton acquired Ticknor and Fields and, in 1880, formed Houghton Mifflin, which later merged with venerable Harcourt Publishing to form Houghton Mifflin Harcourt. HarperCollins purchased HMH's trade publishing business in 2021 and reestablished their storied lists and editorial team under the name Mariner Books.

Uniting the legacies of Houghton Mifflin, Harcourt Brace, and Ticknor and Fields, Mariner Books continues one of the great traditions in American bookselling. Our imprints have introduced an incomparable roster of enduring classics, including Hawthorne's *The Scarlet Letter,* Thoreau's *Walden,* Willa Cather's *O Pioneers!,* Virginia Woolf's *To the Lighthouse,* W.E.B. Du Bois's *Black Reconstruction,* J.R.R. Tolkien's *The Lord of the Rings,* Carson McCullers's *The Heart Is a Lonely Hunter,* Ann Petry's *The Narrows,* George Orwell's *Animal Farm* and *Nineteen Eighty-Four,* Rachel Carson's *Silent Spring,* Margaret Walker's *Jubilee,* Italo Calvino's *Invisible Cities,* Alice Walker's *The Color Purple,* Margaret Atwood's *The Handmaid's Tale,* Tim O'Brien's *The Things They Carried,* Philip Roth's *The Plot Against America,* Jhumpa Lahiri's *Interpreter of Maladies,* and many others. Today Mariner Books remains proudly committed to the craft of fine publishing established nearly two centuries ago at the Old Corner Bookstore.